RAISING HOPE

4 PATHS TO COURAGEOUS LIVING FOR BLACK YOUTH

Anne E. Streaty Wimberly
and Sarah Frances Farmer

Raising Hope: 4 Paths to Courageous Living for Black Youth

The General Board of Higher Education and Ministry leads and serves The United Methodist Church in the recruitment, preparation, nurture, education, and support of Christian leaders—lay and clergy—for the work of making disciples of Jesus Christ for the transformation of the world. The General Board of Higher Education and Ministry of The United Methodist Church serves as an advocate for the intellectual life of the church. The Board's mission embodies the Wesleyan tradition of commitment to the education of laypersons and ordained persons by providing access to higher education for all persons.

Wesley's Foundery Books is named for the abandoned foundery that early followers of John Wesley transformed into a church, which became the cradle of London's Methodist movement.

Raising Hope: 4 Paths to Courageous Living for Black Youth

Copyright 2017 by Wesley's Foundery Books

Wesley's Foundery Books is an imprint of the General Board of Higher Education and Ministry, The United Methodist Church. All rights reserved.

Unless noted otherwise, scripture quotations are from the *New Revised Standard Version of the Bible*, copyright 1989, Division of Christian Education of the National Council of Churches of Christ in the United States of America. Used by permission. All rights reserved.

Scripture quotations marked (NIV) are taken from the Holy Bible, New International Version®, NIV®. Copyright © 1973, 1978, 1984, 2011 by Biblica, Inc.™ Used by permission of Zondervan. All rights reserved worldwide. www.zondervan.com. The "NIV" and "New International Version" are trademarks registered in the United States Patent and Trademark Office by Biblica, Inc.™

All web addresses were correct and operational at the time of publication.

ISBN 978-0-938162-34-6

17 18 19 20 21 22 23 24 25 26—10 9 8 7 6 5 4 3 2 1

Manufactured in the United States of America

HIGHER EDUCATION & MINISTRY
General Board of Higher Education and Ministry
THE UNITED METHODIST CHURCH

This book is dedicated to youth and leaders
of the Youth Hope-Builders Academy (YHBA),
whose lives tell the story of courageous hope.

CONTENTS

ACKNOWLEDGMENTS

The imperative need for hope and courage that comes from God and informs courageous living along the sojourn of life is not a new message in the Black community. It is one that has been passed by adults to the young in each successive generation from the beginning of our presence in this country. In our process of writing this resource on raising hope, we have been reminded of those who modeled and communicated meanings of hope-bearing and courageous living to us and of many who affirmed that this message must not be delayed for young people in the current era. Celebration and gratitude are due Anne's parents, the late Rev. Robert H. Streaty Sr. and Mrs. Valeska Streaty, leaders at Second Methodist Church, now New Hope United Methodist Church, and other mentors in Anderson, Indiana, who during her childhood and adolescence surely modeled courageous living in ways that highlighted its requirement and made it concrete in their views of life's possibilities and actions that brought a promising future into view. The same tribute and thanks are extended to Ms. Roslyn Poole, Sarah Farmer's mother, who from her childhood forward remained an inimitable bridge to opportunities. The leaders in Upward Bound and Chester Eastside Ministries, especially the Rev. Bernice Warren, Bunty Barus, Elizabeth Dunlap, Michael Robinson, and Wanda Moore, who conveyed the importance of peacemaking for adolescents, were surely agents of hope in Sarah's life.

Numerous pages could be filled with names and narratives of individuals who have informed our preparation of this resource. Among them are the leaders and youth participants of the Youth Hope-Builders Academy (YHBA) of Interdenominational Theological Center (ITC) from 2002 forward, whose roles in summer retreats and congregational activities provided both impetus and inspiration for our writing. We gained from them a surety of not simply the need but ways of providing pathways for courageous living for Black youth. Insights, encouragement, and gentle nudges toward further reflection along the way have come from manuscript readers and reviewers, including Minister Pamela Perkins, Dr. Casina Washington, Dr. Richelle White, Dr. Indonesia Wilson, Mrs.

Pamela Jones, Ms. Byanka Tucker, Dr. Robert H. Hughes, Mrs. Nwaka Hughes, and Dr. Edward Wimberly. Further support for the ideas and formation of the manuscript were set forth in the May 4, 2016 lecture entitled "The Courage to Hope: Empowering Adolescent Joy Amidst the Challenges of Life" that we were invited to present at the Yale Youth Ministry Institute, a project of the Yale Center for Faith & Culture Adolescent Faith and Flourishing Program, New Haven, Connecticut.

Throughout the preparation process, our husbands, Dr. Edward Wimberly and the Rev. Ronnie Farmer, have been unwavering in their love, counsel, encouragement, and moral support. Most particularly, Sarah's husband and children allowed time to steal away in order for writing to go forth. For these family members who are dear to both of us, we are grateful.

FOREWORD

This book, *Raising Hope: Four Paths to Courageous Living for Black Youth*, written by Anne E. Streaty Wimberly and Sarah Frances Farmer, is a much-needed corrective to the negative assessment of today's youth and the hopelessness that accompanies such an assessment. Wimberly and Farmer offer a positive view of the aspirations and potential of today's youth, which challenges the too-often-heard narrative of disrespect, lack of motivation, immorality, and destructive behavior used to characterize our youth.

Wimberly and Farmer are not wild-eyed optimists whose conclusions are divorced from reality. In fact, their assessment is based on years of working with, listening to, and encouraging young people, and the good they have seen in the youth they have mentored.

These authors and researchers are familiar with the challenges young people face today and how hard it is for them to negotiate the treacherous twists and turns that confront them. However, they have come to know that the greatest asset that young people can have is the strength and courage that come from hope, that amazing belief in the possible despite the challenges. Anne and Sarah have experienced that hope in their own lives and in the lives of the youth they have been privileged to work with and see grow. That is why they are committed to "raising hope."

This book, however, is more than a story of the promise of today's youth and the value of hope. Even as the book challenges youth to believe in themselves and their potential, especially those who are African American and have the battle of racism to fight, it also challenges adults, especially churchgoing adults, to get involved in the lives of youth. Those dual challenges provide the framework for the book's discussions of the paths that will allow hope to be nurtured, strengthened, and sustained so that a new generation of youth can reach their potential.

Perhaps the authors say it best when they write, "This book is about ways to move youth in the direction of embracing hope and entering into hope in action, recognizing that it will demand courage on the part of young people and the leaders who dare to be agents of hope." It is my prayer that those who read this important text will become members of an ever-increasing cadre of adults and youth who will be guilty of raising up and sustaining hope.

Edward L. Wheeler
February 2017

PREFACE

This book is about hope. We were compelled to write it because of the goodness we see in young people, the opportunities we want for them, and the opportunities we know they want for themselves. The youth we encounter remind us that they seek a bright and meaningful future; but we and they know all too well that even amidst life's possibilities, the forward journey is not without challenge. They are looking for and need pathways that point toward, and prepare them to move resolutely and courageously into, a future of hope. They are also looking for agents of hope to care for them and guide them along the way. The church must be on the front lines of this endeavor, hearing the stories of youth, standing for and with them in times of crisis and need, setting an agenda that raises hope when it wanes, and assuring them that God has a plan and a future of hope for them. How may we begin? For us, the starting point is naming and celebrating the goodness we see.

We rejoice when we receive invitations to high school graduations and find ourselves in an auditorium filled with others who have reached that pivotal marker in their life journeys. Added joy follows with the news of those who are college bound, and in the words of some, "I'll be the first in my family to go to school beyond high school." We celebrate when a high school football player's mom tells of her son's leading the family prayer time and carrying with him a card that includes the words of Jeremiah 29:11, "For surely I know the plans I have for you, says the Lord, plans for your welfare and not for harm, to give you a future with hope." Our delight soars because of youth we know who choose to be part of their congregation's mission trips in order to make life better for struggling families within and beyond the United States; others who, while in high school, mentor elementary and middle school youth; a group of teens who form a "Stop the Violence, Turn Up the Peace" brigade intent on furthering communal transformation through conversations with peers, police, and other adults to foster harmony and justice; and still another group who embark on a video project called "The Courage to Live: Moving from Conflict to Peace."

Do these youth represent only the few? The answer is an unequivocal

"No!" There are numbers beyond them who, on a daily basis, reveal in their attitudes and actions the meaning of courageous living, which is seen in their unmistakably hopeful outlook on life and tenacity of being in life—in spite of obstacles—and spelled out in the words of a teen, "I'm not gonna let nobody stop me! I'm gonna be somebody!" Actually, our forthright response to this assertion is: "You are already somebody!"

Again, we must not be blind to the very real challenges young people face. The next step is to acknowledge that the stories of young people are myriad and reflect their experiences in families, schools, communities, and larger society. They live in an era of technological explosion, web-based interconnectedness, political and interracial upheaval, an uneven spread of educational and economic opportunities, and frankly, an undeniable picture of difficult and life-taking challenges. The forceful message, "Black Lives Matter!" has made public a movement, which began with seeds planted by the 2012 death of Trayvon Martin in Florida, followed by seeds that sprang up after the 2014 shooting of Michael Brown by white police officers in Ferguson, Missouri. This cry became more emboldened following the deaths of unarmed Black citizens in New York, Maryland, New Jersey, Oklahoma, Wisconsin, Ohio, California, Louisiana, Texas, and Arizona, and the 2015 massacre of nine Bible study and prayer meeting participants at Emanuel African Methodist Episcopal Church in Charleston, South Carolina. It is further heightened by what appears as an era of increasing interracial tensions, racial segregation, and continuing racial disparities, in addition to intra-ethnic group violence and the insistence that justice must prevail and hope will triumph.

We confess our dismay that the need for affirmation of the value of and rightful respect for Black lives exists in the twenty-first century in ways that remind us of past journeys of Black youth, including our own. Indeed, just as the promise of Black youth propelled us to write this book, so also painful experiences in the sojourn of today's youth and remembering our own pushed us forward in our writing. The text provided space for us to reflect on the powerful interventions that gave way to hope in our lives and that must happen for young people today. Thus, as we reflect on our own years as teenagers, we have found ourselves revisiting the concerns of the present in light of particular past events.

Anne's story. Anne's adolescence proceeded during the dawning of the Civil Rights Era. During those years, attention on police brutality surfaced due to the death of ten Black males at the hands of police officers in New York in a four-month period in 1951.[1] Emmett Till, a fourteen-year-old visitor from Chicago to Mississippi, was brutally murdered and his body dumped in the Tallahatchie River in 1955. The 1954 Supreme Court ruling in the *Brown v. Board of Education* case prohibited school segregation following decades of separate and unequal schooling for Black children. It became the boiling point for white resistance, including the need for federal troops to oversee the desegregation of the high school in Little Rock, Arkansas, in 1957.

Rosa Parks refused to give up her seat to a white passenger on a bus in Montgomery, Alabama in 1955, followed by the acceptance of Martin Luther King Jr. as president of the Montgomery Improvement Association. He became the leader of the Montgomery boycott and the subsequent nonviolent movement for justice, which spurred police-sanctioned violence and involved harassing, beating, bombing homes, and killing Black people who pressed for equal rights and justice. While there was no cry of "Black Lives Matter!" at that time, leaders in the National Association for the Advancement of Colored People (NAACP), the Alabama Christian Movement for Human Rights (ACMHR), the Congress of Racial Equality (CORE), the Southern Christian Leadership Conference (SCLC), and church leaders formed a network of nonviolent protesters who carried out boycotts, sit-ins, and, later, freedom rides while singing "We Shall Overcome."

During this era, Anne's local, predominantly white public high school in Indiana provided education without offering institutional support. She recalls not being afforded the services of the school guidance counselors or being included as part of college tours. The general course of study was the only available option with a firm "not for you" when her parents and she requested college preparatory studies. Going to the

---

1   A thorough overview of police violence alongside the larger issue of racial injustice and the battle for justice in New York City appears in: Martha Biondi, *To Stand and Fight: The Struggle for Civil Rights in Postwar New York City* (Cambridge: Harvard University Press, 2003).

movies meant being seated in the segregated section of the balcony. Outside of school, family resources were meager. Healthcare was non-existent. But where prejudice prevailed, life's prospects seemed blocked, and scant economic means held sway, the family and faith community together served as affirming and empowering agents of hope, engendering trust in God's for-us-ness and the ability of young people to both survive and thrive. Really, they were God "with skin on" for others her age and for Anne. They insisted on naming young people's gifts, creating places to develop them, and encouraging them along the way, giving them courage to act on the mantra they taught: "Keep on keeping on no matter what!" In that protected environment, young Blacks heard the words "You are somebody!" and were instructed to "never, ever forget it!" They also gave this related message: "Remember where you came from and, in remembering, give back to community."

Across the years, teaching young people, youth ministry, and writing have continued to be Anne's ways of fulfilling a promise to God and those who nurtured her to share with others what was so richly given to her. But it is more than that. It is her response to God's calling to serve the youngest among us so that they too will flourish, live out God's promise for their lives, and pass it on.

Sarah's story. Sarah's years of adolescence came several decades after the Civil Rights Movement, in the 1990s during the New Economy era, a time that marks the onset of the Internet age. During those years, the unemployment rate decreased, and the United States experienced economic expansion. However, a racial divide sparked welfare reform based largely on racialized opinions that pointed to pathology as a cause of Black people's participation in the Aid to Families with Dependent Children (AFDC) program.[2] At the same time, the 1991 Civil Rights Act reiterated the principles of the 1964 Civil Rights Act as a means of ruling

---

2   See: Jeffrey Frankie and Peter R. Orszog, "Retrospective on American Economic Policy in the 1990s, *"Brookings Report* (Friday, November 2, 2001), www.brookings.edu /research/retrospective-on-american-economic-policy-in-the-1990s/; and Robert C. Lieberman, "Race and the Limits of Solidarity: American Welfare State Development and Comparative Perspective," pp. 23–46 in: Sanford F. Schram, Joe Soss, and Richard C. Fording, eds., *Race and the Politics of Welfare Reform* (Ann Arbor, MI: The University of Michigan Press, 2003).

against employment discrimination based on color, race, gender, and religious creed. The ruling sparked nearly 24,000 civil rights employment cases in US District courts by 1997. In 1991, Rodney King was beaten by white officers of the Los Angeles Police Department. The 1998 Report of the Human Rights Watch (HRW) details the persistence of police brutality cases in fourteen large cities across the United States from late 1995 through early 1998.[3]

Black Americans became involved in Pan-African justice in 1991. Under the leadership of Randall Robinson, TransAfrica protested the forcible return of Haitian refugees to their country as a result of US policy; and earlier actions of this organization led to the end of apartheid in South Africa, which finally occurred in 1994, with the election of Nelson Mandela as president.[4] In 1997, President Bill Clinton gave a public apology to the survivors of what became known as the Tuskegee syphilis experiment. The US Public Health Service (PHS) was guilty of egregious medical racism over a forty-year period (1932–1972). The experiment exploited hundreds of Black men, who were unknowing participants; and resulted in denied care, lies about treatment, death for many, pain and suffering for all, plus ongoing stigmatization and poor health management for them and their family members.[5]

Amidst all that was happening in this decade, Sarah remembers her first experience in a public high school in Pennsylvania in 1995. That day, she walked to school with her peers. The bars on the windows and the guards outside the building immediately caught her attention, as did the scarce academic resources once she was inside. As soon as she entered, she saw the stark contrasts in the facility's maintenance and aesthetic features compared to the Catholic junior high school she

---

3   Human Rights Watch, *Shielded from Justice: Police Brutality and Accountability in the United States* (New York: Human Rights Watch, June 1998).

4   The role of TransAfrica is presented in Nan Cho, "TransAfrica Forum (1977–)," www .blackpast.org/aah/transafrica-1977.

5   A full examination of the experiment is presented in Susan M. Reverby, *Examining Tuskegee: The Infamous Syphilis Study and Its Legacy,* John Hope Franklin Series in African American History and Culture (Chapel Hill, NC: The University of North Carolina Press, 2013).

recently attended. The economic disparities of the community served by the high school were also striking.

Sarah stood in line with other students gathered for the routine "check in." As she walked through a metal detector to get her backpack searched and receive a "pat down" with the metal detector wand by a male attendant, she thought, "Wow! Are we that bad that we have to go through this everyday?" The prevailing narrative that surrounded the school was super-predatory, and it made her afraid. It also created an environment of suspicion. By a *super-predatory narrative*, she means the situation sparked in her a story that inner-city youth are immoral and capable of violence.[6] But at the time, she lacked the critical tools to analyze the underlying assumptions that informed her thoughts and shaped the identity of the school.

In Sarah's life, however, agents of hope introduced her to pathways of courageous living. People who served as community gatekeepers funneled a host of neighborhood resources including a community center to sustain and guide her way forward. They offered tutoring and homework assistance to neighborhood youth, provided worship services, and made space available for youth to experience the arts through dance, drama, instrumental music, and visual arts. Other resources flowed through church youth group leaders who created space to connect with like-minded youth. These agents of hope fought against the climate of fear and injustice that seemed to paralyze courageous living in her community. Instead, they invigorated courageous living by laying out a pathway of hope. These experiences of her own adolescence evoked in Sarah the desire to do the same in the lives of young people today.

Our links with other leaders and the journey ahead. We are not alone in our desire for the lives of Black youth to survive and thrive. Neither are we alone in the awareness that it takes agents of hope to help pave pathways for young people to see hope and claim it, knowing that it will take courage—the audacity to keep going in spite of

---

6   I make reference to the dysfunctional view of inner-city schools in Sarah Farmer, "Criminality of Black Youth in Inner-city Schools: 'Moral Panic,' Moral Imagination, and Moral Formation," *Race, Ethnicity and Education* 13, no. 3 (September 2010): 367–81.

tough times—to live out that hope in everyday life. We have seen and worked beside many whose ministries are testaments to God's call to make possible young people's courageous living. Of particular note are past and present leaders in the Youth Hope-Builders Academy (YHBA), a Lilly Endowment, Incorporated funded outreach theological program for high school youth of Interdenominational Theological Center (ITC) in Atlanta, Georgia. The stories of youth and leaders in this book bear witness to the critical role these agents of hope play in engaging youth in pathways that inform courageous living. In telling the stories and describing their meaning and uses in ministries with youth, our desire is to widen the circle of engagement. In this effort, we have continued to be driven by our deeply felt belief that hope and living courageously are not luxuries. They are a matter of life and death. Indeed, young people want to reach out for pathways to life and ways to live that can, in fact, lead to the kind of joy that the world cannot give or take away. But it takes more. There is a continued need for ever-increasing numbers of agents of hope to be there for Black youth, to stand with them, and to serve as their guides.

A CALL FOR PATHWAYS TO COURAGEOUS LIVING

Brave is seeing hope through the hurt, being able to look through the tragedies and being able to see hope anyhow. Such hope will give you the courage in painful times to keep living for Christ.

—Vashti M. McKenzie[1]

For in hope we were saved. Now hope that is seen is not hope. For who hopes for what is seen? But if we hope for what we do not see, we wait for it with patience.

— Romans 8:24–25

[A CENTERING STORY[2]]

A rousing discussion arose in the group of teens who gathered for a summer program for high school youth called the Youth Hope-Builders Academy (YHBA).[3] The conversation followed a time of journaling in response to the questions: "How would you say adults view young people

---

1 Vashti M. McKenzie, "But Some of Us Are Brave," *The African American Pulpit* 4, no. 3 (Summer 2001): 56–59 (59).

2 We begin with a centering story in this introduction and at the beginning of each of the chapters to focus attention on the thoughts and actions of young people and youth ministry leaders who provide a focus for the material that follows. Stories lift up the actual voices of people and provide live illustrations; they guide reflection on the content of each chapter.

3 The Youth Hope-Builders Academy (YHBA) is a theological program for high school youth at the Interdenominational Theological Center (ITC) in Atlanta, Georgia, that received funding from the Lilly Endowment, Incorporated.

today?" Does what they think matter?" When the leader opened the floor, one teen rose and said,

> I've got a lot to say. Many people try to talk about all of us young people, saying that we are a lost generation and that we are not going to do anything with our lives, especially as young African Americans. I don't know about anybody else here; but I know that I have heard so many people make negative and pessimistic comments in reference to our generation like: "Kids today don't have respect for anybody. They're hung up on their music, their cell phones, and social media." Well, I wholeheartedly disagree with these types of comments. Sure, those things are important to us. Yeah! There's no way I could do without it. But there's more that's happening than that! It's tough out there in the world these days. There's lots of haters. If you don't do a certain thing, join up with a certain group, or even dress a certain way, you're dissed—left out. Lots of bullying is going on. The pressure's on all the time. Adults today don't get it. They don't understand all that. It's a different world out there.
>
> Let me just add one more thing. A lot of times, the adults in the church give us a hard time too. That's why a lot of kids don't bother going to church. But I do. And I believe—no, I know—we were handpicked and chosen by God to be born. Isn't that what it says in 1 Peter 2:9?[4] If God took out the time to choose us, don't you think that God chose the best and wants the best for us?

Another teen followed with these words:

> I agree that some adults have negative things to say, but not everybody talks down to us. I personally have received words of encouragement, saying "We know you can make it! You've just gotta have the will!" Does it matter what they say? Of course it does! But, when they say it, you kind of say to yourself: What does that mean? Well, what comes to me is that it's up to me. I've got to believe deep inside me that I'm going somewhere positive in life no matter what anyone says or does. But I still say that I want to know somebody's behind me, that somebody believes in me and is there for me when things get rough. You know what I mean? It has to be more than words. I don't want to feel like I'm just hanging out there alone.

---

4   The teen's reference is to 1 Peter 2:9: "But you are a chosen race, a royal priesthood, a holy nation, God's own people, in order that you may proclaim the mighty acts of him who called you out of darkness into his marvelous light."

Then came a loud voice:

> You're right! I wrote down, and I have to say, that I know life
> alone is a daily struggle. I have to be honest! There's a strug-
> gle all the time against temptation, competition, bullying, rac-
> ism, school, work, the economy, and even in the spirit realm.
> Things happen that are not good. Let's face it! There's a strug-
> gle to stay alive! Adults don't have it easy either. Sometimes
> there are more bills than money, and all that's left is to trust
> God. Hey, just look around you. Where some of us live, you see
> nothing but concrete; or if there's grass, it's high-rising grass,
> plus there's closed down shops. There's no familiar face next
> door, and we don't know what's in store tomorrow. There is a
> struggle spelled with capital letters: STRUGGLE! And there isn't a
> lot of hope that things will change. That's the truth!

A quick response from still another teen came, "Well, I just want to
say that no matter what or how much we have or don't have, we've
got to have, in fact, faith and hope stored in our hearts." Almost simultaneously, several youth shouted, "But adults have got to show us the way.
None of us can go through life by ourselves!" "We as youth need adults
for us and not against us!" "We need to be loved and told that we are
loved." "Well, we have something to offer too. We need adults to listen to
us and give us a chance to show what we know. Everybody has to be
for one another. We all have to know that we can make it!"

IT'S A DIFFERENT WORLD

The voices of young people today are windows to the real stuff of their
lives. In fact, when we as adults listen carefully, we become privy to their
"biographies of the soul" that reveal their thoughts, deep emotions, life
predicaments, and profound insights, given with daring forthrightness.[5]

---

5   James Hillman makes reference to "the biography of the soul." It is pertinent here
     because what is meant by this metaphor differs from what he refers to as a "case
     history." A case history provides factual details of events that are to lead us to analysis,
     diagnosis, and a treatment plan. However, "the biography of the soul" or "soul history"
     speaks of a vital, inner experience of a real feeling self. It is more than just a story.
     It is, as Hillman states, rife with "inner images and feelings" or "soul-stuff." What he is
     getting at is an understanding of an alternate genre of story, a narrative that reveals
     what is happening at the core or soul of one's being. A discussion of the meaning of
     "the biography of the soul" is found in James Hillman, *Healing Fiction* (Barrytown, NY:
     Station Hill Press, 1983), 24–49.

As such, the soul stories of young people are essential and powerful means of stirring within us, or in fact, pressing us as adults to grasp what is deeply important in their journey called life. We may frame it in the question raised by psychologist James Hillman, "What does the soul want?"[6] His answer is that the soul's goal is healing or to achieve the aim of "maturity, completion, wholeness, actualization."[7] It is yearning for community, a place of belonging, purpose, and meaning.[8] But here, we want to place the deep longings of young people, namely teens, in terms of hope. By *hope*, we are referring to a positive disposition, attitude, or frame of mind about their existence in the world. For Christians, hope is also a generating force enlivened by faith that becomes translated in behavior—hope in actions that mirror the life of Jesus Christ. These views of hope extend to young people's thinking about who they are—their sense of themselves as valued creations of God, as capable human beings with gifts and talents that hold promise for their hope-bearing contributions to the communities and world in which they live.

Hope, as described in this book, correlates with relationships with adults who see Black youth as valuable people and who commit to be present with them. These relationships foster an environment where youth can speak freely, raise questions, receive help in making sense of suffering, make hope-bearing decisions on their unfolding stories, and act with courage on those decisions. The qualities of lives characterized by hope cannot be formed and maintained without extended networks of caregivers—a village—on whom young people can rely for support and guidance.

The requirement of hope for young people, and support from caring, nurturing others, hold particular salience for Black youth.[9] This is particularly the case since there is great anxiety among them about their present and future lives. Frankly, the question many are asking each day is, "Will I

---

6   Ibid., chap. 3, "What Does the Soul Want?" 85–129.

7   Ibid., 105.

8   Ibid., 107–8.

9   Our identification of Black people refers to persons whose ethnic cultural identity is African American, diasporic African or of African heritage. From this viewpoint, African American, African, and Black people are used interchangeably.

live to see tomorrow?" More than ever before, Black youth need people with more life experience than they have to act as mirrors of hope that can lead them to say, "I see now what's possible." Mirroring functions as a mimetic moral process wherein youth embrace and act on behaviors they identify as their own.[10] There is a critical need for hope agents—wise models and behaviors of living with hope. But, in addition, young people must have programs, opportunities, and experiences that can carve out pathways that will help them sort out what is going on in their lives and provide direction from a Christian faith perspective—even in a consumer culture where a theological frame seems to be an anathema. Indeed, we note in our work with young people and research outcomes that young people's involvement in faith-based story sharing, arts and athletic endeavors, and community service are deterrents to self-destructive behaviors and help to build and sustain hope and hopeful thinking.[11] So, how shall we proceed? Here at the outset, we will call attention to the historic Black Church story that must not be forgotten but whose emphasis must be reclaimed. We will also highlight an unfolding story of changing times.

AN UNFOLDING JOURNEY OF YOUTH MINISTRY

An important legacy of the Black Church has been this institution's role as a stable spiritual refuge, primary relational community, and hope-building guide for the young amid the challenging realities of their everyday lives. The Black Church has a long history of sponsorship within and beyond religious programs and a host of other activities for uplifting Black youth. From the turn of the twentieth century to recent years, the

---

10 Reference to the importance of adult modeling of love, care, and respect as part of a process of mimetic moral work appears in: Anne Streaty Wimberly, "Give Me Mentors: Pedagogies of Spiritual Acompaniment," in *How Youth Ministry Can Change Theological Education—If We Let It*, eds. Kenda Creasy Dean and Christy Lang Hearlson, (Grand Rapids: William B. Eerdmans, 2016), 79–99 (86).

11 A thorough review of studies and outcomes of a national study that documents the role of religion and youths' faith-based involvement in promoting high self-esteem, more positive attitudes about life, and altering and promoting avoidance of risky behaviors such as substance abuse, risky sexual behavior, suicidal ideation, and suicide appears in Jill W. Sinka, Ram A. Cnaan, Richard W. Gelles, "Adolescent Risk Behaviors and Religion: Findings from a National Study," *Journal of Adolescence* 30, no. 2 (April 2007): 231–49, http://repository.upenn.edu/spp_paper/54.

historic efforts of the Black Church to identify and respond to the struggles and promise of youth is chronicled in reports of studies undertaken by W. E. B. Du Bois;[12] Benjamin E. Mays and Joseph Nicholson;[13] E. Franklin Frazier;[14] Carter G. Woodson;[15] C. Eric Lincoln and Lawrence Mamiya;[16] Andrew Billingsley;[17] and most recently by Anne Streaty Wimberly, Sandra L. Barnes, and Karma D. Johnson.[18] In their commentary on the notable communal role of the church over time, Lincoln and Mamiya state:

> Perhaps one of the most important functions that black churches performed for young people was to provide a place where they could meet older adults, men and women, who could serve as role models for them. . . . Studies have shown that black pastors and laity have been important role models for black youth.[19]

Our personal stories echo this sentiment. As we indicated in the preface, our journey in writing this resource has brought memories of the necessary and important role of adults in our lives. Most particularly, we recall family members and other adults who unhesitatingly responded as we navigated our journeys as African Americans into and through childhood and adolescence. Despite the tough realities of life, we heard the words: "Anne, you are a valuable creation of God. God's got a plan for your life, and you must never forget it!" "Sarah, just as Paul said to Timothy, 'Stir up the gift God has given to you, and don't

12   W. E. B. Du Bois, *The Negro Church* (Walnut Creek, CA: Altimira Press, [1903] 2003).

13   Benjamin E. Mays and Joseph W. Nicholson, *The Negro's Church* (New York: Institute of Social and Religious Research, 1933).

14   E. Franklin Frazier, *The Negro Church in America* (New York: Schocken Books, 1964).

15   Carter G. Woodson, The History of the Negro Church (Washington, DC: The Associated Publishers, [1921] 1945; Carter G. Woodson, *The Mis-Education of the Negro* (New York: Tribeca Books, 1969).

16   C. Eric Lincoln and Lawrence H. Mamiya, *The Black Church in the African American Experience* (Durham, NC: Duke University Press, 1990).

17   Andrew Billingsley, *Climbing Jacob's Ladder: The Enduring Legacy of African-American Families* (New York: A Touchstone Book, 1992); and Andrew Billingsley, *Mighty Like a River: The Black Church and Social Reform* (New York: Oxford University Press, 1999).

18   Anne E. Streaty Wimberly, Sandra L. Barnes, and Karma D. Johnson, *Youth Ministry in the Black Church: Centered in Hope* (Valley Forge, PA: Judson Press, 2013; Sandra L. Barnes and Anne Streaty Wimberly, *Empowering Black Youth of Promise: Education and Socialization in the Village-minded Black Church* (New York: Routledge, 2016).

19   Lincoln and Mamiya, *The Black Church in the African American Experience*, 312–13.

be afraid!'" These reassuring reminders of our value and the promise of life had a remarkable way of overriding obstacles we confronted. But it was not simply the words spoken to us that made a difference.

In the church of Anne's youth, an annual ritual during a designated Sunday worship was the naming of gifts of all the youth whose twelfth birthday occurred during the year. As we stood in front of the congregation, the oldest members of the church described the gifts they observed. The oldest members, parents, and pastor then laid hands on the youth as the pastor prayed for a future of hope. The church leaders then identified areas in the life of the church where the youths' gifts could be nurtured. Because of the gift of music and teaching, Anne was tapped as pianist for the children's choir and to play a hymn for the congregation to sing one Sunday each month, as well as to be a periodic apprentice in the adult Sunday school class with responsibility for reading scripture and commenting on its meaning.

Sarah vividly remembers opportunities her mom found for her involvement in arts and the importance of daily prayer and maintaining a relationship with God. As her parent, Sarah's mom was the bridge to experiences provided by other adults, such as the leaders in an Upward Bound program whose guidance aroused Sarah's vision and courage for her journey forward.

For both of us, pathways of hope created and guided by Christian leaders moved us toward God's plan for our lives and brought us where we are now in ministry with young people. It is not just our personal stories that come to mind. The book entitled *Keep It Real: Working with Today's Black Youth* begins with the story of a multigenerational forum on youth and family issues in Decatur, Georgia, during which a thirteen-year-old youth told of wounding attitudes and treatment of Black students in and beyond school.

A grandmother responded to the youth with words of assurance, guidance, and affirmation:

> In her sharing, this community sage told part of her own story of maltreatment not simply in our society where racist ideologies prevail but also in the home of her childhood where, as a stepchild, she was not affirmed and was on the receiving end of abusive language. Her final words to the

young teen were these: "You are a precious child of God. You are beautiful. I love you, and I want you to know God loves you too. Don't you let nobody turn you around."[20]

Many Black churches have continued to carry forward the historic role of the Black faith community in the lives of youth through creative efforts and programs of promise.[21] As noted in the book, *Keep It Real*,[22] and in programs detailed in *Youth Ministry in the Black Church*,[23] youth ministry leaders have sought to stimulate young people's consciousness of themselves as fearfully and wonderfully made (Ps. 139:14) and of God's plans for a future with hope for them (Jer. 29:11).[24] In these programs, the voices and experiences of young people are placed at the center in ways that evoke their awareness and action on their possibilities and that claim the biblical promise of joy that comes in the morning (Ps. 30:5b). Hope does emerge when teens are engaged in intentional and creative pathways wherein they envision and claim their valued selves and a positive future for their lives. We affirm the statement of Lopez and his associates that "Hope can flow from one person to another's life, thereby influencing how the latter person sees the world and pursues goals."[25]

There have been pivotal times along the way when crossroads have appeared in the church's ministry with youth. At these times, the prophetic voices of leaders have literally shouted that more is needed;

---

20 Anne E. Streaty Wimberly, ed., *Keep It Real: Working with Today's Black Youth* (Nashville: Abingdon Press, 2005), xi–xii.

21 An entire chapter on programs of promise appear in Anne E. Streaty Wimberly, Sandra L. Barnes, and Karma D. Johnson, *Youth Ministry in the Black Church*, 149–176.

22 Anne E. Streaty Wimberly, *Keep It Real: Working with Today's Black Youth*.

23 Anne E. Streaty Wimberly, Sandra L. Barnes, and Karma D. Johnson, *Youth Ministry in the Black Church*.

24 Teens in the Youth Hope-Builders Academy learn, for example, about black teens who made Civil Rights history (see http://family.go.com/printout/parenting/pkg-teen/article-767165-black-teens-who-made-civil-rights-history-t/), and biblical role models including, for example: seventeen-year-old David (1 Sam. 17); the little girl who was a helper of Israel (2 Kgs. 5); the three young men Shadrach, Meshach and Abednego in the fiery furnace (Dan. 3); young Daniel (Dan. 1); Esther—from orphan girl Hadassah to Queen (the book of Esther); the boy with the fish and loaves (John 6).

25 Shane Lopez, Sage Rose, Cecil Robinson, Susana C. Marques, and Jose Pais-Ribeiro, "Measuring and Promoting Hope in Schoolchildren," in *Handbook of Positive Psychology in Schools*, Richard Gilman, E. Scott Huebner, and Michael J. Furlong, eds. (New York: Routledge, 2000), 47.

crises have abounded and demanded immediate attention. Particularly at the beginning of the Civil Rights Era of the late 1950s and early 60s, Martin Luther King Jr. preached about the deep concerns, weariness, and disillusionment of young people regarding the realities of life.[26] He observed young people who had become unsure about their faith in God and whether or not they could rightly rely on the future.[27] Because of this reality, King portrayed youth as "knocking at the door of midnight" in search of the dawn made possible through their receiving the "bread of hope."[28] Yet he also observed churches that were not providing this "bread," and called on them to address issues of irrelevancy and meet the challenges of the time.[29]

In the waning decades of the twentieth century, Lincoln and Mamiya issued a similar warning of the church's deep struggle with relevance in the wake of new and ongoing social problems and a recognized need for spiritual and moral nurture. They indicated that a major deterrent to dealing with the needs of youth is the propensity of many contemporary churches to direct attention and programmatic efforts toward adults.[30] The results of their study reveal a clear need for attention to youth, not simply in areas of spiritual uplift, but in education and socialization of youth, especially given the continuing struggle they confront with racial identity and an affirming sense of self.[31] In many instances, the past struggle for relevance has become a very real, present concern. The difficulty of congregations in keeping up with changing and challenging times has negatively affected the way they reach and relate to youth, especially those in the teen years. The point in the essay, "Give Me Mentors," must be taken to heart. Even in cases where congregations have sought to "provide young people with caring,

---

26 See Martin Luther King Jr., "Draft of Chapter VIII, 'The Death of Evil Upon the Seashore,'" July 1962–March 1963, pp. 494–504, in Clayborne Carson, et al., eds., *The Papers of Martin Luther King, Jr., Volume VI: Advocate of the Social Gospel, September 1948–March 1963* (Berkeley, CA: University of California Press, 2007), 501.

27 Ibid., 498.

28 Ibid., 502.

29 Ibid., 494, 499.

30 Lincoln and Mamiya, *The Black Church in the African American Experience*, 316.

31 Ibid., 317.

Christian-centered, and faith-forming mentoring relationships . . . many of these well-meaning programs—fearful of 'turning off' teenagers—have inadvertently re-cast them as consumers of experiences rather than as critical thinkers who are actively engaged in constructing their life worlds."[32] The question rightly emerges: what, then, must congregations yet do to build and maintain youth ministries in this present age?

SEEING CHALLENGE, ENVISIONING POSSIBILITY

It is important to note that Black youth are not a monolithic group. Differences exist in terms of geographic region, neighborhood, socioeconomics, and family makeup, as well as educational attainment levels and employment status of heads of households. However, there is a common link across these differences, which is found in "their experience in the United States and . . . the continuing legacy of oppression and discrimination that affects their daily lives."[33] They share a common awareness of racial identity and the Black self that develops contextually and is uniquely challenged in wider society where they confront racism, discrimination, and, in the case of a disproportionate number, difficult urban conditions, poverty, and a host of related circumstances.[34]

Facing Realities of Being Black

The unique experience of being Black in America is a precipitating factor in stress, anxiety, and grief in Black people in general and youth in particular.[35] This reality creates urgency for response, as expressed in the anguished voices of adults. As one said, "The situation today is urgent. We've got to figure out a way to turn things around if our young people—if we—are to have a future." These adults hear the cries of

---

32   Anne Streaty Wimberly, "Give Me Mentors: Pedagogies of Spiritual Accompaniment," 83.

33   American Psychological Association (APA) Task Force on Resilience and Strength in Black Children and Adolescents, "Resilience and Strength in Black Children and Adolescents: A Vision for Optimal Development," (Washington, DC: American Psychological Association, 2008), 17–18, http://www.apa.org/pi/cyf/resilience.html.

34   Ibid., 32.

35   Anna Laurie and Robert A. Neimeyer, "African Americans in Bereavement: Grief as Function of Ethnicity," Omega 57, no.2 (2008): 173–93 (175).

young people: "Help us! Too many of us are dying!" Together with youth, there is widespread hunger for hope in an era of great anger and distress over, for example: killings of Black youth by law enforcement, rising incidences of Black-on-Black crime, detention centers built adjacent to schools, disproportionate numbers of young people in detention centers and prisons, high rates of unemployment, poor housing conditions, disproportionate incidence of depression among adolescents, rising adolescent suicide rates, and family instability.[36]

Although there is evidence of resilience and high self-esteem, particularly of Black girls—even in tough circumstances[37]—a troubling pessimism exists in far too many youth, as indicated in study results appearing in the *Journal of Health and Social Behavior,* which reveals that half of Black young people between the ages of twelve and twenty-five believe they would not live beyond age thirty-five.[38] The findings of another study that included poor Black youngsters ages five to thirteen

---

36 See: Cathy J. Cohen, *Democracy Remixed: Black Youth and the Future of American Politics* (New York: Oxford University Press, 2010), 2; Orlando Patterson, ed., with Ethan Fosse, *The Cultural Matrix: Understanding Black Youth* (Cambridge, MA: Harvard University Press, Reprint edition, 2016), 1–2; African American Policy Forum and Columbia Law School's Center for Intersectionality and School Policy Studies, *Black Girls Matter: Pushed Out, Overpoliced and Underprotected: A Report,* 2015, AAPF_BlackGirlsMatter-Report.pdf, 19–23, www.atlanticphilanthropies.org/app/uploads/2015/09/BlackGirls Matter_Report.pdf; American Civil Liberties Union, "Talking Points: The School-To-Prison -Pipeline," www.aclu.org/files/assets/stpp_talkingpoints_pdf, 1–4; Howard University Center for Urban Progress for the Lutheran Hour Ministries, *Faith-Based Organizations and African American Youth Development: A Report* (Washington, DC: The Howard University Center for Urban Progress, 2003), 6; Walter W. Shervington, "We Can No Longer Ignore the Rising Rate of African-American Suicide," President's Column, *Journal of the National Medical Association* 92, no. 4 (February 2000): 53–54; and Kimya N. Dennis, "The Complexities of Black Youth Suicide," Scholars Strategy Network, Cambridge, Massachusetts, www.scholarsstrategynetwork.org/brief/complexities-black -youth-suicide, accessed September 2015. An example of juvenile detention centers being constructed close to schools is the Coosa Valley Youth Services, Juvenile Detention Center in Anniston, Alabama, which is located 1 minute (0.3 miles) from the Black Middle School with majority Black students.

37 Studies show that the collective orientation in Black culture in which Black girls are raised contributes to the results showing their higher self-esteem levels than all other racial ethnic groups and Black boys. See American Psychological Association, "Resilience in African American Children and Adolescents," 46.

38 Tara D. Warner and Raymond R. Swisher, "Adolescent Survival Expectations: Variations by Race, Ethnicity, and Nativity," *Journal of Health and Social Behavior* (American Sociological Association, 2015): 1–17, doi: 10.1177/0022146515611773O, http://www .asanet.org/journals/JHSB/DEC15JHSBFeature.pdf.

uncovered their awareness of a classist bias in society that limits chances for the poor. They shared thoughts that their background, poverty, and appearance were insurmountable barriers. It was as though their background was "an intractable 'scarlet letter' that would close doors to job possibilities."[39] Historical and cultural sociologist Orlando Patterson makes the further claim that Black youth are "trapped in a seemingly intractable socioeconomic crisis, yet are among the most vibrant creators of popular culture in the nation and the world."[40]

In spite of talent, accomplishment, and contributions to church and community, studies document a continuing pattern of distorted portrayals of Black adults and youth, particularly Black men and boys in mass media. In addition, there is underrepresentation of Black persons with positive life development, association of Black men with criminality and idleness, limited representation of inspiring characters with a broad and varied array of qualities beyond those in sports and music, predominant focus on intractable problems, and absence of stories that trace the history of ongoing anti-Black bias.[41] Tech culture and the impact of the media also contribute to troublesome realities and thwarted hope in ways that differ from previous generations. Youth are troubled by media that set the tone for beauty in ways that sexualize young girls and negate the beauty of their Black color and hair.[42] And, even though

---

39 Susan Weinger, "Children Living in Poverty: Their Perception of Career Opportunities," Social Work Faculty Publications, Paper 5 (Western Michigan University, 1998), 324–25, http://scholarworks.wmich.edu/socialwork_pubs/5.

40 Orlando Patterson, ed., with Ethan Fosse, The Cultural Matrix: Understanding Black Youth (Cambridge, MA: Harvard University Press, Reprint edition, 2016), 1.

41 A report of these data are found in Topos Partnership, with consultants Janet Dewart Bell and Eleni Delimpaltadaki Janis, "Social Science Literature Review: Media Representations and Impact on the Lives of Black Men and Boys," The Opportunity Agenda, A Project of Tide Center (October 2011): 13–14, https://opportunityagenda .org/literature_review_media_representations_and_impact.pdf. Find additional data in A. C. Martin, "Television Media as a Potential Negative Factor in the Racial Identity Developmental of African American Youth," Academic Psychiatry 32, no.4 (July–Aug. 2008): 338–42, PubMed:18695037, doi:10.1176/appi.ap.32.4.338.

42 See Adrienne Trier-Bieniek, ed., The Beyonce Effect: Essays on Sexuality, Race and Feminism (Jefferson, NC: McFarland & Company, Inc., 2016), 127–28; Race and Technology, "'Whitewashing' in Mass Media: Exploring Colorism and the Damaging Effects of Beauty Hierarchies," Race and Technology: Exploring Race and Community in the Digital World (December 10, 2014), www.raceandtechnology.wordpress

they fully participate in the world of social media, they are nonetheless aware of the downside that is revealed in this form of communication.

An insightful article by Marilyn Price-Mitchell draws on the responses of teens to the question, "How has online social networking influenced your relationship with friends and family?" Based on the input of the teens, she identifies ten disadvantages: (1) deficiency in emotional connectedness; (2) ease in permission to be hurtful; (3) decline in face-to-face communication skills; (4) tendency not to express one's true feelings; (5) threats to ability to be considerate, thoughtful, and sympathetic; (6) difficulty in feeling connected in face-to-face communication; (7) tendency toward laziness shown in messaging or blogging rather than going to the message receiver or tweeting someone elsewhere in the same house; (8) a slanted or less-than-authentic self-image by conveying pictures and stories that are not wholly true or real; (9) lessened closeness among family members; and (10) becoming easily distracted or almost oblivious to all else that is happening around the self.[43] Yet, in spite of the disparaging outcomes of participation in social networking, there is no rush to abandon this form of communication. Consequently, hope-building pathways and the strategies to carry them out must be bold enough to engage young people in experiences with and beyond social media that counter the disadvantageous effects of social networking and offer alternative and relevant pursuits.

Envisioning Responses

There is desperate need for pathways to hope and courageous living in the lives of Black youth. They want to tell their stories and need caring others who will be present with them and hear them, recognizing that sharing their personal narratives and having access to the stories of others who've come through the storms of life "are essential to their identity, sense of self, and hope. Story sharing is a way of comprehending,

---

.com/2014/12/10/whitewashing-in-mass-media-exploring-colorism-and-the
-damaging-effects-of-beauty-hierarchies/.

43   The list here is paraphrased. The actual list appears in Marilyn Price-Mitchell, PhD, "Disadvantages of Social Networking: Surprising Insights from Teens," www.rootsofaction
.com/disadvantages-of-social-networking/.

analyzing, and dealing with life."[44] Hope happens when youth are invited into telling, assessing, and envisioning the positive unfolding of their stories and are placed in touch with lives of Black predecessors and stories in scripture that provide models and inspiration for living amid the mayhem of daily living. In addition to story sharing, Anna Laurie and Robert Neimeyer remind us that artistic expression is an established way of communicating life's stories as well as expressing and ameliorating grief.[45] In terms of physical activities and experiences, art is a particularly powerful means of focusing on conflict resolution among youth, both individually and in groups.

Black youth experience multi-levels of violence from self-inflicted damage (intrapersonal violence), harm occurring in close relationships (interpersonal violence), harm brought about by aggressive behavior in communities or neighborhoods (communal violence), and assaults on their being and self-esteem from various forms of discrimination and racism (systematic violence). Hope blossoms when young people are engaged in experiences through which they develop coping skills to deal with resulting hurt, frustration, grief, and anger. Conflict resolution approaches are resilience-building and hope-bearing means whereby youth critically evaluate situations, discover ways to respond, and cope in helpful ways.[46]

Young people need positive connections in their everyday lives. They want to know that they belong, are valued and regarded as contributors to community, and are afforded opportunities to make a difference in the world they inhabit. Hope for meaning in life can happen as they are enabled to engage in behaviors that benefit others. Positive connections happen as young people are exposed to places, people, and activities that give them ideas for future vocation, engage them in life and academic skills-building, and set before them the need

---

44 See Robert E. Birt, ed., *The Quest for Community and Identity: Critical Essays in African Social Philosophy* (Lanham: Roman & Littlefield, 2002), 66–67.

45 Anna Laurie and Robert A. Neimeyer, "African Americans in Bereavement: Grief as a Function of Ethnicity," *Omega* 57, no. 2 (2008): 173–93 (187).

46 See American Psychological Association Task Force on Resilience and Strength in Black Children and Youth, "Resilience and Strength in Black Children and Youth," 45–46.

and opportunities for community service that enhance self-affirmation while attending to the well-being of others.[47] The intent is to heighten Black youths' awareness and embrace of a positive sense of self and their gifts and to provide opportunities for gift development and vocational fulfillment. Like Lopez and his associates, a hope-bearing response assumes that young people will choose and take the risk of entering into activities and environments where they feel respected and not demeaned.[48] Moreover, they build on the assumption that pathways are useless without approaches and guides who give attention to their sense and promotion of "we-ness" or of themselves as part of a welcoming and sharing community.[49] Recognition is also given to young people's desire and need for opportunities that promote their agency or their ability to ponder, assess, and act on decisions about their lives that result in their assertion, "I can do this!" or, "I will not give up."[50]

The important point we are raising in this book is that—in light of all that bombards youth in today's fast-paced, tech-saturated, violence-ridden, struggling existence—their cry is for raising the flag of hope and doing so in a way that gives them the courage to live through and even in spite of it all. Responding to this cry must become the responsibility of church leaders and other adults, by forging pathways and strategies that affirm the claim of the youth in the opening, centering story that they are "handpicked and chosen by God to be born" and are, therefore, worthy of hope-filled lives.

This view of Black youth counters the often-heard view of them as being "at risk." But the American Psychological Association Task Force on Resilience and Strength in Black Children and Adolescents adroitly reframes this understanding with the statement that the goal is for healthy, optimally functioning Black children and youth who become so because they have been "placed 'at promise' as opposed to 'at risk.' They are at promise to become contributing members of

---

47   Ibid., 51.

48   Lopez, et.al., "Measuring and Promoting Hope in Schoolchildren," 46.

49   Ibid., 44.

50   Ibid., 38

families, schools, communities, and the broader society. In this way they will emerge as agents for meaningful and sustainable positive change."

AN INVITATION TO ENGAGE YOUNG PEOPLE IN RAISING HOPE

This book is about ways to move youth in the direction of embracing hope and entering into hope in action, recognizing that it will demand courage on the part of young people and the leaders who dare to be agents of hope. It all begins with the voices of the youth and leaders getting in touch with the self's story, calling, and commitment. Thus, this book is also an invitation to you, the reader, to enter into a process of recalling stories told by young people in your environment, inviting stories, and getting in touch with your own story of adolescence. It is about your envisioning, not simply what might be done, but what you will do to raise hope in this era when, for many, hope has become elusive. We want to make clear that this is not about the attainment of hope infused with courage, as though somehow hope is a *product* or prize to be claimed or won. No! What we are after is young people's ongoing soul-deep embrace of hope and ways of living courageously based on a tenacious faith in God and our standing with them amidst life's adversities.

The upcoming chapters are intended to guide the remembering and envisioning process. We will draw on the experiences of youth, our ministries with youth over the years, and our experiences in team leadership with others in the Youth Hope-Builders Academy (YHBA), a program for high school youth begun in 2002. The program's summer retreats and congregation-based ministries focus on promoting Black youth's formation of a valued ethnic-cultural and Christian identity, their theological understanding and practices of the Christian lifestyle and leadership, and their movement toward hope-building Christian vocation according to their gifts and interests.

The youth in the program typically come from congregations across the denominational spectrum and from churches of various sizes. They represent all socioeconomic levels and a variety of family structures with two parents, blended families, single parents, foster caregivers, grand-parents and other kin-headed households, and other cross-generational arrangements. Over the years, youth have come with their own unique "biography of the soul." These stories provide glimpses of the everyday stories of both promise and pain of youth beyond the academy. As we have heard their stories, we are reminded that fulfilling the calling of ministry with youth to raise hope requires us to be mindful of young peo-ple who never attend church, those who are recruited by and join gangs as a means of establishing a place of belonging, youth in detention cen-ters and prisons, and teens whose hopes are dashed by their brutal enslavement in the sex trafficking industry. These are young people who may rightly be called *hidden figures* and who must be found and given attention. In fact, we point to them here because, though seeming to be hidden, they exist and they matter. They are part of the realities of the times in which we now live, and they must not be forgotten.

The promising news from these kinds of endeavors is that we hear and see, over and over again, evidence of young people's remarkable accomplishments in a variety of vocations, freely given service to church and community, and positive influence through artistic and sports en-deavors. This outcome is seen, for example, in Youth Hope-Builders Academy (YHBA) graduates who are teachers, lawyers, entrepreneurs, social workers, pastors, visual and performing artists, and others in com-munications, culinary arts, medicine, global missions, and a variety of other vocations including the vocation of family life.

PATHWAYS TO COURAGEOUS LIVING: SETTING THE DIRECTION

This book is organized in two parts. Part 1 centers on "Envisioning Coura-geous Hope and Courageous Living." Its three chapters present a vision of the nature of courageous hope that is needed in young people, the role of church leaders and other adults in promoting and nurturing cou-rageous hope, and reasons for mandatory action. Chapter 1 is entitled "A Hope-Building Agenda." It explores hope as an essential human qual-ity and a divine promise which must receive pivotal attention in the lives of youth. We make the claim that attention to hope has remained a vital historical agenda in the lives of Black people; and this agenda centers on belief in God's faithfulness and both a vision and ability to survive and thrive amidst difficult life circumstances. At the same time, the chapter describes the portent of hopelessness fraught by tough and seeming insurmountable life experiences and makes clear that current disparaging circumstances that bring about various levels of thwarted hope in youth must not be denied. In response, the hope and future for Black youth lies in attentiveness to a ministry goal of guiding youth in ways that contribute to every aspect of their well-being and their flourishing: relationally, physically, psychologically, economically, vocationally, and spiritually.

Chapter 2 details what is involved in "Forming Courageous Hope and Enacting Courageous Living." The chapter presents the idea that, because of challenging circumstances faced by youth, there is need for more than hope. The hope of youth must be infused with courage to overcome fear, decide what is best to do, discern why it is best, and to act forthrightly despite difficult circumstances. The chapter describes the nature of courageous hope that allowed Black forebears to keep on keeping on through life's toughness, in ways that provide mirrors for young people's well-being and flourishing. It goes on to describe courageous hope as a choice, an empowering attitude, a faith-filled posture in life's wilderness, and an ongoing creative sojourn. We do not dodge the reality that there are challenges to forming courageous hope and that, in the midst of the complexities of life, a young person may see a fatalistic picture over one of hope and courage. But our position is that the role of leaders is to be agents of hope who find ways to inspire, instill, and support hope infused with courage in young people. The chapter ends with a suggestion for inviting youth into story sharing about courageous hope, followed by a sample guideline for raising courageous hope through story.

Entitled "Being and Becoming Agents of Courageous Hope," chapter 3 centers on the role of youth ministry leaders and other adults in establishing the settings and developing plans to engage youth in pedagogies that nurture their formation of hope and courageous living. We make the claim that in order for these leaders to become agents of hope, they must be prepared and willing to give soul-deep response to the realities of young people's lives. Response means that leaders arrive at a disruptive awareness or mindfulness of the realities faced by youth, which disturbs them to the point of inexorable response and courageous commitment to act with and on behalf of youth. It becomes a matter of action, emerging from the very soul or heart of the leader and directed toward the affirmation and assurance of the ongoing living soul or breath of life given to young people by God, in defiance of all that would call this into question. The chapter also makes the claim that ministry carried out by agents of hope evolves from their own practical spirituality of courageous hope, shown in their calling to youth ministry that values youth and relies on God's guidance with an ongoing connectedness with God.

Part 2 emphasizes "Entering Pathways to Courageous Living." It begins with chapter 4, entitled "Steps Toward Pathways to Courageous Living." This chapter presents a brief review of four pedagogical pathways—also referred to as programmatic thrusts—that are directed to youth's formation of courageous hope. Attention is given to a *narrative pathway*, a *creative pathway*, a *peacemaking pathway*, and a *pathway of exposure*. The chapter also describes the key strategies of *invitation*, *presence*, and *guidance* to be carried out by agents of hope in the four pathways. This summary is followed by the presentation of four pedagogical pathways to young people's courageous living.

The narrative pathway appears in chapter 5, entitled, "Sharing the Soul's Story: A Narrative Pathway." This chapter presents story sharing as an act of receiving and offering "biographies of the soul." We place emphasis on the obligatory nature of young people's story sharing, given the tendency for them to be both unseen and unheard in a variety of ways in church and the wider community. We make the claim that story and story sharing have hope-building power and can evoke in young people new insights needed for assessing prevailing circumstances, making hope-bearing choices, and taking courage-filled actions in the forward journey of life. The pivotal role of agents of hope lies in inviting, being present with, and guiding young people in story sharing in ways that connect with God's story and the lives of Christian faith exemplars for guides for courageous living. The essential role of leaders in posing questions to facilitate youths' inquiry, evaluation, and decision-making is also lifted up.

A second pathway is artistic in nature. This programmatic thrust appears in chapter 6, "Artistic Expression: A Creative Pathway." It is considered a powerful tool for activating hope and a critical resource for youth in contexts of adversity, providing a cathartic space where youth can name their pain through poetry, music production, or visual arts. Artistic expression makes possible truth-telling in ways that are impossible through spoken language. But art pedagogy also moves from the practice of *creative truth-telling* to *expressions of resistance* against adversity and *envisioning bridges to hope*. We put forward the essential role of agents of hope in terms of the strategic uses of invitation that creates space to interpret through art activities the everyday stories they are living, an in-person presence as a means of bearing witness to the stories of youth and helping them through times when they question the veracity of hope and courage, and guidance that takes place through creating artistic spaces wherein youth can arrive at and express a vision of possibility for their lives and ways to act on it. The chapter ends by proposing a continuum of art-making.

Chapter 7, "Transforming Conflict: A Peacemaking Pathway," is a necessary response to intrapersonal, interpersonal, communal, and systemic violence in the lives of youth and the culture of violence that pervades our wider society. The guiding assumption of the chapter is that violence is a learned response to conflict that can be disrupted with conflict resolution skills. The chapter further highlights the significance of adolescents' awareness of their own internal as well as external triggers to violence by and against them; their capacity to build resilient attitudes and behaviors; and the transforming impact of learning how to love, respect, and accept the humanity of others. These pivotal aspects of forming courageous hope that becomes activated in courageous living comprise the center of a pedagogical approach that invites youth into defining violence; understanding violence as a multilevel occurrence; and engaging in conflict transformation practices of resilience-building, human connectedness, and shalom. The content, then, literally becomes a path by which youth come to understand and learn new and hope-bearing responses to conflict. The chapter describes the role of agents of hope as inviting young people into conflict-prevention, conflict-intervention, and reconciliation practices; being present as creators of spaces of openness, story sharing, problem-solving, and healing. They are guides who tend to young people's peacemaking with self, God, others, and the world.

Chapter 8 centers on young people's engagement in a "Quest for Awareness: A Pathway of Exposure." This fourth programmatic thrust emphasizes the necessity of Black youth's exposure to a multidimensional SPACE (spiritual, political, academic, cultural, and educational) of enrichment experiences that can foster youth's positive identity and purpose in life and empower their sense of self-agency in acting on that purpose. In contexts of adversity, it becomes difficult for youth to see and access connections to hope-filled activities that have the potential for building capital in these zones of SPACE. As a pathway to courageous living, intentionally planned experiences of exposure learning occur in diverse ways: life- and skills-based experiences that contribute to academic success; worship, discipleship and other spiritual enrichment that provide a spiritual foundation youth need to thrive amidst adversity and move toward Christian vocation according to their gifts and talents; Black history and intercultural immersion that nurture their identity; intergenerational connections of importance in envisioning their lives forward and experiencing the meaning of God's family; and civic involvement through which they internalize their role in service, justice, peacemaking, and repair of the world. The chapter presents the essential role of agents of hope in terms of their invitation to and accompaniment of youth in structured enrichment opportunities: being mentoring, supportive, and encouraging presences; and guiding young people in conversations and actions that affirm, challenge, advise, and give direction for life decisions and vocational aspirations.

In every programmatic thrust, the underlying view is that there is an eternal hopefulness on which Christian faith stands and pathways through which this hopefulness is activated. The intent of these pathways to courageous living is to evoke new or renewed awareness of hopefulness and ways to activate it in everyday life. These pathways also build on Black people's historical belief in God's promises, the faithful nearness and activity of God, and God's empowerment of youth and all of us to embrace and activate the courage to hope that makes possible a vision of life's possibilities and the ability to act on it.[51]

Each of the four chapters includes a set of three implementation strategies. Called *relational strategies*, these approaches center on:

(1) *Invitation*. This regards the invitation of youth to participate in activities that offer something beneficial for their consideration and that receives their contributions of ideas, insights, and proposals for action.

(2) *Presence*. This strategy appends invitation and is a mandatory response to the yearning of youth for acceptance. It is expressed through welcome, a sense of the leader's co-journeying alongside youth in ways that open conversation that is mutually active, and allows for tough questions to be asked and answers to be probed.

(3) *Guidance*. In connection with invitation and presence, guidance entails leaders' ensuring an environment that inspires and facilitates young people's decision-making skills. These relational strategies are critical distinguishing marks in the implementation of each one of the pathways because of their emphasis on the leaders' valuing them, the "biographies of the soul" they bring, and addressing the soul's hope of making hope-bearing decisions on their unfolding stories, and acting with courage on those decisions.

---

51   An example of a Black pedagogy of hope is proposed that uses a historical biographical method that engages the role of the adult griot/guide as a key agent of hope who tells the stories of forebears, engages participants first as listeners, then in conversation that is to evoke mirroring through artistic expression. The pedagogical model is found in Anne E. Streaty Wimberly, "A Black Christian Pedagogy of Hope: Religious Education in Black Perspective," in James Michael Lee, ed., *Forging a Better Religious Education in the Third Millennium* (Birmingham, AL: Religious Education Press, 2000), 158–77.

[PART 1]

ENVISIONING COURAGEOUS HOPE AND COURAGEOUS LIVING

A HOPE-BUILDING AGENDA

If you lose hope, somehow you lose that vitality that keeps life moving, you lose the courage to be, that quality that helps you go on in spite of all.

— Martin Luther King Jr.[1]

For surely I know the plans I have for you, says the LORD, plans for your welfare and not for harm, to give you a future with hope.

—Jeremiah 29:11

[A CENTERING STORY]

It was time to meet with prospective hope-builders who would make up the group for a summer residential program. They had already written an essay that gave highlights of their lives and a statement of their interest in becoming a hope-builder. Moreover, a pivotal part of their writing, as well as the conversation with us and other program leaders, was their point of view on hope. Very quickly, the dialogue centered on meanings of hope. Frankly, it appeared that they both needed and were anxious to talk about hope. They had written a lot about it, and they said even more, which at times included taking back their essays in order to read and comment on what appeared there. Our role as listeners was to receive what they had to say. Because we were intent on

---

1   Martin Luther King Jr., "A Christmas Sermon on Peace," in *A Testament of Hope: The Essential Writings and Speeches of Martin Luther King Jr.*, ed. James M. Washington (Copyright by Coretta Scott King, Executrix of the Estate of Martin Luther King Jr., 1986. New York: HarperSanFrancisco, a division of HarperCollins Publishers, 1991), 257.

hearing their thoughts, we did not interject our ideas. Rather, at various times, as noted in the conversation, we simply raised questions such as: "Would you say more about what you mean?" or "Is there more that you would like to add?" Their thoughtfulness and candor were striking and can help us center on the needs this book addresses.

Often these conversations began with a brief statement such as the following: "When I think of the definition of hope, I think of the phrase 'to believe and wish for something with all your heart, body, and soul.'" When asked, what does "with all your heart, body, and soul mean?" the teen replied, "It's like everything in me—my whole self— is wanting or hanging on for something to happen, like wanting to make the football team, which I did." Others gave much attention to the great need for hope that is epitomized in their words: "Hope is needed worldwide. Everybody needs hope. It is needed from the president of the US to the mayor in the cities. It is needed in homes, on the streets, on the battlefield, and most of all in the church." Another remarked, "There are so many troubles in the world today, most that we don't even see on the news. In the world today, I would say a lot of people need hope to live day by day. People are hoping that maybe this month nobody will get sick, and they'll be able to pay the light bill; or, hopefully, our house won't get foreclosed; or, hopefully, they'll get a job they just interviewed for."

The view of hope of most of the young people was intensely personal. It emerged in the poignant statement of one teen, "It seems that hope doesn't happen without a struggle. I'm struggling, and I have questions about hope." When asked, "Would you say more about what you mean?" the reply was, "I would like to think that hope is a belief that whatever may be going on, there is no doubt that it can be worked out. But, sometimes, it's not easy to hope, like when you want somebody you love to live and then they die."

One youth stated the following, "My definition of hope is personal. It is a desire for a better future for the community and that I can make a difference. I have already learned that there will be challenges to achieve it. Being in a predominantly White school isn't easy. I'm being bullied every day. There are stereotypical views of Black students; that

I'm not capable and not supposed to accomplish anything. But I am capable. I am doing well, and I am determined to keep doing it." Another youth remarked, "Hope is the belief that things will get better. I experience hope every night before I go to sleep. It is hope that I will wake up, because you never know when your last day is, and I hope that it isn't mine." Still another said, "Hope is knowing you are able to do something others say you cannot. It is a feeling of power in your darkest hour." The words of another: "There is a big challenge to hope for youth today. The challenge is having something to believe in. The world today doesn't exactly have too many things a youth can have hope in or cling onto in hard times. I need hope. Hope is needed in the world. What do we do to get it?"

For several youth, the conversation shifted from challenges associated with hope to the source of hope and their role as hope-builders, as noted in the statements:

> There was a time in my life when my hope went down the drain. Life was hard. But one day, a mentor gave me a video that spoke to my situation. Each time I watched it, new hope slowly started to form inside me. When I see people around me who might have trouble with their own hope, I help them to the best of my ability. . . . Hope is knowing that God will make a way and that I will do my part. I say *my part* because I need to have hope in me. It gets hard to keep hope in my getting through school and into my future because I have messed up in so many places. I'm getting my hope back, though, through my music and other people who remind me of the motto, "Keep the faith and pray." For me, that means God's got a plan to use me in some way that benefits others. I need to pray that God will help me do the right thing.

Still another said, "Hope comes when you or anybody is down and someone helps you up and shows you there is something worth fighting for. It's like when someone tells you it's no use, and you're persistent in your dream. Hope works when you work with it." In response to the question: "What do you mean by that?" the teen said:

> There was a chance that I would miss out on a school trip if I couldn't get the finances for it. My friend told me to just give up on it. But I was hoping somehow that it would happen. I was determined to go and started asking my friends' families if I could wash their cars. They let me do it, and some of

> them even gave me extra money. I got enough to make the trip. I had to put a little of my own energy in the hope I had. That's what I mean by "hope works when you work with it."

Two other youth shared the following:

> Hope is knowing there is always something or someone that will help. In my mind, that translates to faith—faith that, no matter what, God will be there helping you along, even through the deepest waters. Sometimes things happen that make me struggle and grow a little tense. These are times that test my hope. But that's where prayer comes in. For me, God, prayer to God, and hope go together.

> Hope is believing in something when you can't see or feel it, but you know it is there. I personally experienced hope in my life when I accepted Jesus Christ as my Lord and Savior. I couldn't see him, but I knew he was present and speaking to my heart. I also think about hope in regard to my future. It's not a clear picture yet. It's like seeing one part of the puzzle but knowing God sees the whole picture and has plans for my future of hope.

HOPE AS AN ESSENTIAL HUMAN QUALITY

The centering story holds powerful messages for youth ministry leaders, other church leaders, and adults with whom young people relate. The voices of these youth reveal deeply held convictions about hope and their need for it. In fact, their statements reflect a yearning for the kind of hope in their lives that we described in the introduction. They seek a positive disposition, attitude, or frame of mind about their existence in the world. Several of them point to hope as a generating force, enlivened by faith, which moves to hope in action through making a contribution in the world.

At the same time, youth in the centering story question the presence and meaning of hope amidst the struggles of life; they want to know or sometimes even discover on their own what to do when hope seems in short demand. We glean from these young people an obvious openness and desire to share their thoughts with caring listeners and guides. Conversations point to activities—through writing, journaling, audio-taping, open sharing, or other means—wherein they enter into "self-talk," that opens the way for them to assess their thoughts and beliefs and either imagine or concretely determine how to move forward with hope.[2]

In what follows, we will explore hope as an essential human quality and give attention to its importance in the lives of youth. With its various dimensions, our intent is to point to what constitutes human flourishing and joy amidst struggle in the lives of Black youth.

Human Beings Are Born to Hope

At this point, we want to accentuate our basic, undergirding premise that human beings are born to hope—to have expectations or to anticipate and wait for a desired good that brings satisfaction and joy. Hope is not an inert but an active feature of human existence. This innate human quality requires attention and must be nourished! Moreover, we want to make the case that the church and its leaders can and must be agents of hope by both envisioning and implementing pathways that contribute to and nurture young people's hopefulness to the end that they become hope-builders in today's and tomorrow's church and world.

Erik Erickson says hope is "the earliest and the most indispensable virtue inherent in the state of being alive."[3] An unspoken form of hope, that reflects a waiting posture, is revealed in an infant's reach and cry for the touch of a caring other to fulfill the need for nourishment.[4] Anticipatory hope is implied in a youngster's plea, "When are we going to see Grandma?" It is concrete evidence of a high school senior's attitude and conviction about an open and possible future when she says, "My hope

---

2   See Shane J. Lopez, Sage Rose, Cecil Robinson, Susana C. Marques, and Jose Pais-Ribeiro, "Measuring and Promoting Hope in Schoolchildren," in *Handbook of Positive Psychology in Schools*, eds. Richard Gilman, Scott Huebner, and Michael J. Furlong (New York: Routledge, 2000), 45.

3   Erik H. Erikson, "Human Strength and the Cycle of Generations," *Insight and Responsibility* (New York: W.W. Norton, 1964), 118.

4   Donald Capps draws attention to multivalent properties of hope that include *waiting* for the presence or appearance of something external to actually appear; *anticipation* of satisfying one's longing for the presence of a desired object; *pining* or recalling a missed object and desiring the satisfaction that object could provide; and *hoping* that involves one's believing that a desired object is not simply available but will satisfy one's desire. See Donald Capps, *Agents of Hope: A Pastoral Psychology* (Minneapolis: Fortress, 1995), 33–37.

is to be the first in my family to go to college." For one of the teens in this chapter's centering story, it is evidence of an identified future of promise, that "God's got a plan to use me in some way that benefits others." It is the expression of inner strength heard in the voice of the youth in the centering story that "hope is knowing you are able to do something others say you cannot." Hope can be heard in expectant voices of persons in search of a job, a mate, or a home, and in the anguished tone of those who are longing for a way out of or around tragedy and loss.[5] Voices of resistance claim hope when they carry signs and proclaim: "Black lives matter!"

Hope in a Divine Promise

Consider this gospel hymn, "Hope's Anthem": "My hope is in You, God. / I am steadfast, I will not be moved / I'm anchored, never shaken / All my hope is in You,"[6] or in the gospel song, "Though the storms keep on raging in my life . . . / my soul has been anchored in the Lord."[7] These illustrate divine promise of a new existence.[8] Hope is further captured in the words of an old Black woman, who, in spite of personal loss and ill-health, says: "I feel like if we were all in a ditch and I happened to crawl out, I'd want to reach back and get somebody, if not but one, and pull him out, too. Let's all come out, if possible."[9]

---

5 Capps identifies hope as an "attitudinal disposition" or "the implicit conviction or tacit belief that the future is an open one, and that it holds possibility for us." He also indicates that hope is an inherent strength. It is that sustaining element in life in the face of wounded confidence and impaired trust (ibid., 28).

6 The song, "Hope's Anthem," is written by William Matthews and Christa Black Gifford, Bethel Music Publishing (ASCAP)/Christajoy Music (BMI), 2010, https://bethelmusic .com/chords-and-lyrics/hopes-anthem-hopes-anthem/.

7 The song, "My Soul Has Been Anchored in the Lord," was written by Douglas Miller. The lyrics appear on https://www.lyriczz.com/lyrics/douglas-miller/21104-my-soul -has-been-anchored.

8 Moltmann emphasizes hope as a divine promise that "originates from God's creative possibilities." Hope emerges from the "God of hope," whose promises are eschatological or coming and not yet as well as already present, that is understood as realized eschatology. See Jürgen Moltmann, ed., The Experiment Hope, trans. M. Douglas Meeks (Philadelphia: Fortress Press, 1975), 49–51.

9 These were the 1982 words of Anita Stroud recorded in Emily Herring Wilson, with foreword by Maya Angelou, Hope and Dignity: Older Black Women of the South (Philadelphia: Temple University Press, 1983), 55.

Indeed, these examples of hope demonstrate the view of noted Black theologian Howard Thurman, that in the hope-activating life of God, one envisions one's "ability to put oneself in the life of another and to look out upon the world through the other's eyes—to enter into the feeling and thinking and reacting of another, even as one remains oneself."[10] Theologians Jürgen Moltmann and Howard Thurman express similar views, that amid the realities of life there must be faith that God is involved in our lives, and that our highest hopes, yearnings, imaginings, and joy have their source in God and witness to God's Spirit in us, allowing us to recognize God's presence in the lives of others.[11]

But there must also be a community of hope within which the life of God and God as the Source of hope are lived, shared, and nurtured. The way people view, internalize, and act on hope does not happen in a vacuum. Historical, cultural, contextual responses to life in general and tough events in particular frame understandings and the necessity of hope. People form communal attitudes and behavioral perspectives on hope. They act to maintain a hopeful disposition rather than a despairing one. Their views and actions are then passed on to successive groups that can exercise power in ways that resemble those of the past. In fact, the historic Black Christian community lived and carried out a Black Christian hope agenda that is worthy of remembering as it relates to the formation and nurture of Black youth today. Yet what is also instructive is what has taken place over time that mandates a new hope agenda for the sake of Black youth.

THE UNFOLDING BLACK HOPE AGENDA

Historically, hope has been the energizing core of the sojourn of Black people in the United States. A deep and abiding hope for God's liberating action was carried out in clandestine worship, where the language

---

10   Howard Thurman, *Deep Is the Hunger: Meditations for Apostles of Sensitiveness* (Richmond, IN; Friends United Press, 1951; New York: Harper & Row, 1964), 165–66. Citations refer to the Harper & Row edition.

11   See Howard Thurman, *Deep Is the Hunger,* 163–66; Jürgen Moltmann, *The Experiment Hope,* 182–83.

and symbols of communal hope emerged in ritual dances, music, prayers, sermons, and testimonies. Communally expressed hope was based on a biblical faith, through which Black people imagined their exodus into a "promised land." This means of proclaiming hope expressed their resistance to humiliation, torture, and death; and was a method, to use Howard Thurman's words, "to try to achieve a sense of self in a total environment that threatened the self."[12]

The toughness of life during the period of enslavement was followed by the realities of oppression in the Reconstruction years and thereafter. Yet the Black church, family, neighborhood, and voluntary associations persisted—as well as a common core of communal norms—as dominant mediating structures between the private lives of Black people and the oppressive structures of wider society.[13] These mega-structures created a sense of home for Black people, nurtured belief in God's faithfulness, and helped forge people's courage to hope, as demonstrated in a decisive insistence to keep on keeping on, as in the old song's words: "I shall go, I will go to see what the end would be."[14] A signal role of the church was to ensure that young people survived and thrived as hope-filled and hope-giving Christians, despite life's difficult circumstances.

This legacy of the hope agenda, begun during the era of slavery, followed Black people into the mid-twentieth century. While a vision of a beloved community fueled an era of hope, it also became the central theme of a freedom movement directed toward peace, justice, and safety of all God's people. However, the assassination of the movement's leader, Dr. Martin Luther King Jr., brought forth the exceedingly thorny question: "What is there to hope for?" Although the efforts of the Civil Rights and Great Society Movements that followed resulted in

---

12 Howard Thurman, *The Luminous Darkness: A Personal Interpretation of the Anatomy of Segregation and the Ground of Hope* (New York: Harper & Row, 1965), 5.

13 The concept of mediating structures is set forth by Peter L. Berger, *Facing Up to Modernity: Excursions in Society, Politics, and Religion* (New York: Basic Books, 1977), 130–41.

14 Melva Costen emphasizes that worship, in particular, continued to provide both environment and opportunity for Black people to raise hope in the face of adversity. See Melva Wilson Costen, *African American Christian Worship* (Nashville: Abingdon, 1993), 78.

perceptible strides toward accomplishment for many Black people,[15] many others experienced little or no advancement. Their plight was one of failed life chances and abject poverty resulting in a horrifying sense of meaninglessness, lovelessness, and hopelessness.[16] Moreover, in their 1990 book, *The Black Church in the African American Experience*, Lincoln and Mamiya highlight the tenuous hold of Black churches, particularly on urban youth and young adults.[17] A pattern of social disconnection, particularly among many youth in urban and center city areas, began to extend beyond the church and, in some important respects, coincided with the disconnection of churches from them, making community resources inaccessible.

Much has already been said about real and tough circumstances of Black youth. The youth in the centering story gave a personal face to young people's struggles with hope. In fact, one of the teens confessed that "sometimes, it's not easy to hope, like when you want somebody you love to live, and then they die." Because of these realities, we must not evade consideration of the hopelessness experienced by Black youth, how it develops, and what to do about it. The portent of hopelessness happens when the vision, expectation of, and search for any of the characteristics of hope are thwarted, repeatedly interrupted, or denied. When young people are hopeless, they literally experience themselves as being stuck.

---

15   A discussion on the movement from hope to hopelessness in the Black community appears in Anne E. Streaty Wimberly, "A Black Christian Pedagogy of Hope: Religious Education in Black Perspective," in *Religious Education in the Third Millennium*, ed. James Michael Lee (Birmingham, AL: Religious Education Press, 2000), 155–58.

16   Statistics show that the income of Black families grew during the 1990s so that 56 percent of these families had an annual income of $35,000 or more compared to 36 percent in 1969. However, this growth was reversed during the recession beginning shortly before the end of the first decade of the new century. The percentage of households with an annual income of $35,000 or more decreased to 51 percent in 2014. Of greater alarm was the percentage of Black households making $15,000 below poverty line, (from 19 percent in 2000 to 24 percent in 2010). These statistics are set forth in "African American Income," BlackDemographics.com, http://blackdemographics.com/households/African-america-income/. Commentary about the resulting meaninglessness, lovelessness, and hopelessness is found in Michael I. N. Dash, Stephen C. Rasor, and Jonathan Jackson, *Hidden Wholeness: An African American Spirituality for Individuals and Communities* (Cleveland: United Church Press, 1977), 55.

17   See C. Eric Lincoln and Lawrence H. Mamiya, *The Black Church in the African American Experience* (Durham: Duke University Press, 1990), 382–83.

In some cases, over time, hope becomes suppressed—goes under-cover—and seems inaccessible. The loss of control over life's vicissitudes tears away at any hope for change. The futility of the inaccessibility of hope erupts in anger and rage; turned inward toward self, resulting in depression, substance abuse, risky sexual behavior; or it results in aggressive and violent behavior turned outward toward others. As noted mental health leaders, Alvin Poussaint and Carolyn Adkinson reminded us several decades ago, endangered hope can emerge in aggressive behavior, "the attacking of those like oneself (other blacks) whom one hates as much as oneself. Or aggression can be directed toward those who generate anger and rage."[18] Most often, these responses develop over time. Like a cancer, they oppose the innate inclination of humans toward hoping. They intervene like weeds and choke hope out of one's life. In many instances, there is a sort of "slippery slope," or movement in stages, from hopefulness to a denial of the hope that still lies deep within them.

This slippery slope happens to young people in stages. The first stage may be called *hope questioning*. In this stage, youth may simply say, "I've got questions about hope." Or they may ask the pointed question, "What is the use of hoping?" A single critical situation, such as having to drop out of school or losing a friend, may trigger that question. Sometimes a question about God answering prayers, followed by "Right now, I don't see it," emerges. This stage is really a time of lament that, if acknowledged with help, support, and direction from caring others, hope can be restored.

A second stage is *hope regression*. Here optimism about the future gradually diminishes, because of a series of difficult life events or unresolved circumstances, as in the case of a teen who was being bullied and experiencing racial profiling. His grades and interest in school began to slip, and later he learned of his parent's impending divorce. Like this teen, other young people's hope gradually fades as few or no solutions appear to be forthcoming to meet unfolding and

18   Alvin Poussaint and Carolyn Atkinson, "Black Youth and Motivation," in *Black Psychology*, ed. Reginald L. Jones (New York: Harper & Row, 1972), 118.

seemingly insurmountable challenges. This goes beyond the question, "What is the use of hoping?" Young people begin to believe that things are going from bad to worse and the possibility of a turnaround seems unlikely. Yet, in this circumstance, a resurgence of hope in young people becomes possible when adults are available to hear their stories of trauma, serve as mentoring guides who engage them in envisioning, and pose a range of approaches to "weather the storms of life," followed by choices of responses and follow-up on those the youth choose to act upon.

A third stage is called *hope denial*. In this stage, young people are literally "stopped in their tracks." All pathways to hope appear to be cut off, or they are overwhelmed by sudden or unrelenting clusters of stressors. For example, these challenges may include some of those already mentioned in addition to tremendous loss, such as the death of loved ones or friends, being the victim of crime and violence, mental or physical abuse, serious or debilitating illness of self or revered others. They don't experience hope for changes or outcomes in their life situations or life chances. The consequence of this prolonged series of negative experiences is a sense of foreclosure of hope. They are at a point of denying the existence of hope and at risk for problematic outcomes, such as substance abuse, depression, suicide, or aggressive behaviors toward self or others.

But remember our assertion that young people—as all people—are born to hope. So hope never simply disappears. It isn't necessarily the case that young people are unaware of hope or are wholly lacking in hope or even that they have hope in one instant and suddenly don't have it. When speaking with teens about behavior that is hurtful to others or themselves, what inevitably emerges is their own deeply felt desire or hope for attention to and reversal of their experiences of woundedness or life's catastrophes. Recall the youth in the centering stories who told of being bullied at the predominantly white high school and of confronting stereotypical views about the ability of a Black person to achieve. This youth's response was, "I am capable. I am doing well, and I am determined to keep doing it." In short, our position here is that hopelessness need not be the last word. Hope releases us from succumbing to "an internal catastrophe."[19] However, a new hope agenda must be set in place that addresses today's youth.

HOPE AND A FUTURE FOR BLACK YOUTH

Psychologists and educational leaders, including teachers, counselors, social workers, and administrators, have engaged in research resulting in the formulation of a hope theory that elucidates understandings of hope, hopeful thinking, impediments to hoping that lead to hopelessness, and pathways to hope. Hope theory posits that there are "high-hope people," who maintain positive feelings even in the face of impediments, and who can learn from experiences with bad outcomes.[20] This research has also uncovered connections among levels of hope in young people. The importance of this research lies in what it suggests for our understanding of the presence of hope versus its denial among Black youth. Of particular interest are findings that hope is positively related to views of the self and the future, satisfaction with life and well-being, physical health, academic achievement, and athletic achievement.[21]

Research findings indicate that youth with higher hopeful thinking have positive self-esteem and views of their self-worth. They also believe they have the ability or competence to move positively through life.[22] Evidence also suggests that hope is related to life satisfaction, health, and well-being.[23] On this basis, young people who have high levels of hope tend to be proactive with self-care and make healthy choices that promise positive outcomes and hope for the future.[24]

---

19   Jürgen Moltmann, ed., *The Experiment Hope*, trans. and foreword M. Douglas Meeks (Philadelphia: Fortress Press, 1975), 186.

20   C. Richard Snyder, "Hypothesis: There Is Hope," in *Handbook of Hope: Theory, Measures, and Applications*, C. Richard Snyder (New York: Academic Press, 2000), 14.

21   Shane J. Lopez, Sage Rose, Cecil Robinson, Susana C. Marques, and Jose Pais-Ribeiro, "Measuring and Promoting Hope in Schoolchildren," in *Handbook of Positive Psychology in Schools*, eds. Richard Gilman, E. Scott Huebner, and Michael J. Furlong (New York: Routledge, 2009), 39–42.

22   Ibid., 39.

23   Ibid.

24   Ibid., 40.

Conversely, youth may imagine a positive life direction for themselves, but hope becomes stifled by limited access to health-sustaining resources, which may be compounded by circumstances and experiences that thwart positive life chances. In her book, *Black Youth, Delinquency, and Juvenile Justice,* Janice Joseph also makes the point that thwarted hope of young people contributes to their negative behaviors. Thus, youth who lack a sense of hope are more at risk for drug and alcohol use, gang involvement, teen parenthood, crime, and delinquency, including Black-on-Black violence and early death.[25] These outcomes are the most devastating response to pain and the sense of hopelessness.[26]

With regard to school, research shows a connection between hopeful thinking, motivation, and academic achievement. Youth's embrace of hopeful thinking fosters eager investment and good academic outcomes. However, this thinking becomes obstructed by intimidating and inadequate educational environments, where they are treated by teachers as inadequate, sense that they are expected to fail, have low parental support, and find themselves in a school-to-prison pipeline, which is informed by expulsions and referrals to law enforcement in school, followed by mistreatment by law enforcement outside school. This results in youth's frustration and anger, which builds within them.[27] Moreover, research results indicate that interpersonal struggles between young people and adults or peers within or outside school, including their observations of or actual experiences of conflict and violence, have the effect of cutting short hopeful thinking.[28] Yet there is also evidence that young people's hopefulness, resilience, and ability to thrive are promoted and nurtured through support given to them by an extended network of caregivers; their active involvement and responsibility-taking in

---

25 Janice Joseph, *Black Youth, Delinquency, and Juvenile Justice* (Westport, CT: Praeger, 1995), 168–69.

26 Ibid, 169.

27 Lopez et.al. point especially to the correlation between low hope experience and high anxiety as well as diminished competence in envisioning and using adaptive coping strategies. See "Measuring and Promoting Hope in Schoolchildren," 40.

28 Ibid., 42.

community life including the church; their embrace of spiritual beliefs, guiding values, and sense of a higher purpose; exposure to affirmative cultural values and traditions; opportunities to express and contribute the gifts of self to others and institutions; and formation of skills and problem-solving that help them cope with life's struggles.[29] The important point here is that in youth ministry we must keep at the forefront the importance of hope in the lives of young people and the need to confront thwarted hope where we see it. This may mean, as theologian Jacquelyn Grant declares, that leaders must repudiate the notion that there is "something wrong with Black youth. . . . Black youth are often merely victims of their circumstances. In other words, something is really wrong with the larger society, and that something is manifested in the particular experiences of young people."[30] Placing both at the center provides impetus for the direction of ministry with them. Making it happen also requires that we have an overall view of the nature of hope-filled living that we desire for young people.

THE MULTIDIMENSIONAL NATURE OF HOPE-FILLED LIVING

The goal of ministry with Black youth is the development of hope infused with courage that becomes reflected in courageous living and their ability and will to move tenaciously forward in life that brings both pain and promise. We know that attaining this goal is not a simple matter. Attention must be given to all that makes for their well-being and contributes to their flourishing. Miroslav Volf points to the nature of well-being or flourishing in three ways: a life that goes well (circumstantial dimension), a life that feels well (affective dimension), and a life that

---

29   American Psychological Association (APA) Task Force on Resilience and Strength in Black Children and Adolescents, "Resilience in African American Children and Adolescents: A Vision for Optimal Development" (Washington, DC: American Psychological Association, 2008), 25, 44, 52–54.

30   Jacquelyn Grant, "A Theological Framework," in *Working with Black Youth: Opportunities for Christian Ministry*, eds. Charles R. Foster and Grant S. Shockley (Nashville: Abingdon, 1989), 71.

is lived well (agential dimension).[31] Here, we draw attention to the multidimensional and interrelated nature of optimal subjective experiences of well-being that nurture and reflect hope.[32] From this perspective, hope and the courage to act on it hinges on young people's well-being.[33] In what follows, we propose six interrelated dimensions: relational well-being, physical well-being, psychological well-being, economic and vocational well-being, spiritual well-being, and intellectual and creative well-being.

1. Relational Well-Being

Subjective experiences of relational well-being refer to young people's participation in interdependent living environments that include peer, family, religious, and local and wider social networks that affirm personal value and belonging as human beings. They are treated as

---

31 Miroslav Volf, "The Crown of the Good Life: An Hypothesis," in *Joy and Human Flourishing: Essays on Theology, Culture, and the Good Life*, eds. Miroslav Volf and Justin E. Crisp (Minneapolis: Fortress Press, 2015), 127–36.

32 Reference to the nature and significance of subjective experiences appears in Martin E. P. Seligman and Mihaly Csikszentmihalyi, "Positive Psychology: An Introduction," *American Psychologist* (January 2000): 1–14 (8). Donaldson and his colleagues highlight elements that contribute to quality of life and prevent pathologies in Stewart I. Donaldson, Maren Dollwet, and Meghana A. Rao, "Happiness, Excellence, and Optimal Human Functioning Revisited: Examining the Peer-reviewed Literature Linked to Positive Psychology," *The Journal of Positive Psychology: Dedicated to Furthering Research and Promoting Good Practice* 10, no. 3 (Routledge): 185–95, doi:10.1080/17439760.2014.943801, http://dx.doi.org/10.1080/17439760.2014.943801. The dimensions being presented also appear in literature in terms of well-being and do not focus directly on hope in the lives of Black adolescents. The dimensions appearing here reflect the multidimensional and interrelated character of well-being described in pastoral care literature, principally by Howard Clinebell. See Howard Clinebell, *Anchoring Your Well-Being: A Guide for Congregational Leaders* (Nashville: Upper Room, 1997). The dimensions are also framed in Anne E. Streaty Wimberly, "Congregational Care in the Lives of Black Older Adults," in *Aging, Spirituality, and Religion,* Vol. 2, eds. Melvin A. Kimble and Susan H. McFadden, (Minneapolis: Fortress Press, 2003), 105–6. It must be added that several dimensions (e.g., identity, emotional, social, cognitive, and physical development) appear as developmental domains in the report of the American Psychological Association (APA) Task Force on Resilience and Strength in Black Children and Adolescents, "Resilience in African American Children and Adolescents: A Vision for Optimal Development" (Washington, DC: American Psychological Association, 2008), 25.

33 See Anthony Ong, "A Life Worth Living: The Science of Human Flourishing," in Department of Human Development, Outreach & Extension (Cornell University), 1–2, http://human.cornell.edu/hd/outreach-extension/upload/ong.pdf.

persons whose dignity and worth is equal to that of others, and they exhibit the same toward others. This conduct extends to their receiving respect, nonhumiliation, and nondiscriminatory attitudes or actions from others and showing the same for others. Within this kind of relational environment, young people experience themselves as living for and toward others in ways that exhibit concern and compassion for others. They are assured of receiving justice and seek the same for others; they know they have a right to voice their political views and prepare for political participation as citizens.[34]

From an ethnic-cultural perspective, subjective experiences of relational well-being extend to young people's connections to their ancestry, including forebears who mirror values and behaviors needed for moving through the tough realities of life's journey. Moreover, young people are immersed in life-sustaining culturally relevant resources in community, such as programs and activities that affirm who they are as Black persons and respond to their interests and needs.[35]

2. Physical Well-Being

Subjective experiences of physical well-being center on life, bodily health, and bodily integrity.[36] The emphasis on life refers to young people being able to remain alive for the full length of normal existence and not dying prematurely. The experience of bodily health is their ability to function physically, be sufficiently nourished, have adequate shelter and to have necessary, affordable resources that can contribute to these outcomes. Physical well-being extends to young people's bodily integrity, reflected in being safe and out of harm's way. It is their experience of security against violence perpetrated against or observed by

---

34 These relational qualities draw on those set forth in M. C. Nussbaum, *Women and Human Development: The Capabilities Approach* (Cambridge: Cambridge University Press, 2000), and summarized in Sabina Alkire, "Dimensions of Human Development," *World Development* 30, no. 2 (2002): 188, https://www.unicef.org/socialpolicy/files/Dimensions_of_Human_Development.pdf.

35 These characteristics build on perspectives presented in Anthony Ong, "A Life Worth Living," 105.

36 This understanding of physical well-being draws on perspectives presented in Sabina Alkire, "Dimensions of Human Development," 188.

them. Moreover, this form of well-being takes on an active stance in actions that reflect their insistent optimism that their lives matter.[37]

3. Psychological Well-Being

Subjective experiences of psychological well-being are reflected in personal wholeness of mind as well as acceptance and value of young people's identities by self and others. This aspect of well-being extends to inner peace and a positive self-view, and includes others who affirm their ethnic-cultural appearance, color, physique, body size, language, and cultural artifacts in a culture that sets forward a bias that repudiates Black ethnic norms. Moreover, this form of well-being is seen in young people's capacity and opportunity to deal with harsh realities of life in life-affirming, life-giving ways, in contrast to self-negating or destructive behavior toward self or others. Psychological well-being extends to young people's experiences of developing as human beings in ways that utilize their knowledge and potential, and improve their lives. It is having a sense of purpose and their own agency to choose, evaluate, and make use of opportunities to act on life-affirming values.[38]

Psychological well-being is connected to relational well-being through young people's experiences of positive attachment to things and persons beyond themselves. It is noted in young people's capability "to love those who love and care for [them], to grieve their absence; to experience longing, gratitude, and justified anger; not to have one's emotional development blighted by overwhelming fear and anxiety, or by traumatic events of abuse or neglect."[39] At the same time, these experiences depend on their receiving listening ears and guidance from caring others and models that mirror the positive self and human connections.[40]

---

37   See Anthony Ong, "A Life Worth Living," 105.

38   This latter emphasis on purpose, agency, choice, and opportunities is found in Carol D. Ryff and Corey Lee M. Keyes, "The Structure of Psychological Well-Being Revisited," *Journal of Personality and Social Psychology* 69, no. 4 (1995): 720, 723–724, http://www.midus.wisc.edu/findings/pdfs/830.pdf.

39   Sabina Alkire, "Dimensions of Human Development," 188.

40   Ibid., Anthony Ong, "A Life Worth Living," 105.

4. Economic and Vocational Well-Being

Subjective experiences of economic and vocational well-being occur through young people's access to and attainment of economic, educational, and occupational resources needed to sustain life and care for self and others for whom they are responsible materially. It is "having the right to seek employment on an equal basis with others and to work as a human being."[41] Moreover, this facet of well-being extends to opportunities for life accomplishment that says, "God gave me intelligence, gifts and talents that I'm supposed to be able to develop and use, that somebody is supposed to help me develop, and that should lead to and go beyond economic and material sufficiency.[42]

5. Spiritual Well-Being

Our description of young people's subjective experience of spiritual well-being builds on what Christian Smith describes as beliefs, attitudes, commitments, and behaviors resulting from constructive practices that provide moral order, learned competencies, and social organizational ties.[43] Based on Smith's focus on moral order, we propose here that spiritual well-being is noted in young people's choices and embrace of personal virtues and self-regulating behaviors that are grounded in long-standing religious traditions and narratives; that evolve from spiritual experiences, such as prayer, or personal experiences of conversion, healing, or divine guidance; and that are patterned after adult and peer group role models of constructive life practices.[44] Spiritual well-being may be further described in terms of learned

---

41 Sabina Alkire, "Dimensions of Human Development," 188.

42 Anthony Ong, "A Life Worth Living," 105–106.

43 The description of spiritual well-being that begins in this section draws on Christian Smith's assertion that religion may influence the lives of adolescents in positive ways through the provision of moral order, learned competencies, and social and organizational ties. His systematic presentation of these religious effects among adolescents appears in Christian Smith, "Theorizing Religious Effects among American Adolescents," *Journal for the Scientific Study of Religion* 42, no. 1 (2003): 17–30, http://csrs.nd.edu/assets/50016/theorizing_religious_effects_among_american _adolesents.pdf.

44 See Christian Smith, "Theorizing Religious Effects Among American Adolescents," 20–22.

competencies that also improve life chances. Learned competencies include young people's experience of leadership skills they have observed, learned, and have opportunity to practice in the faith community and that are transferable in the home, school, community, and workplace. The experience of learned competencies connects with psychological well-being in the emphasis on coping skills used in processing, negotiating, and resolving life's difficulties. But, in terms of spiritual well-being, the competency evolves from beliefs in God's presence and activity. An added experience of competency is that of cultural capital expressed in deepening understandings of scripture, culturally and broad-based artistic expressivity, and global and multicultural awareness derived from exposure and service opportunities beyond religious settings.[45]

Spiritual well-being of young people is also experienced in terms of social and organizational ties wherein they connect with others cross-generationally, which offers them valuable information, resources, and opportunities through mentoring, trusting relationships beyond their families. Their involvement in a religious community interacts with relational networks that are key aspects in relational well-being. As part of their experience of social and organizational ties, young people's spiritual well-being is encountered in Christian Smith's description of network closure and extra-community links. The experience of well-being of youth through network closure occurs through their relationships with people in the religious community who pay attention to their lives, provide supervision, connect with parental figures, and encourage constructive life practices while, at the same time, discouraging destructive ones. Extra-community links become an experience of spiritual well-being as young people engage in a variety of activities and events beyond congregations, such as camps, retreats, para-church programs, mission projects, and service programs that expand their horizons, ambitions, knowledge, and competencies.[46]

---

45   Ibid., 24–25.
46   Ibid., 24–27.

6. Intellectual and Creative Well-Being

Young people experience intellectual and creative well-being through their ability "to imagine, think, and reason—and do things in a 'truly human' way informed and cultivated by an adequate education."[47] Youth further experience this form of well-being in various types of self-expression and re-creative endeavors that revitalize them, evoke laughter, reaffirm their gifts, and open avenues for fulfilling hope in other areas of life. Visual and performing arts as well as sports are high among these re-creative experiences. Moreover, intellectual and creative well-being occurs through young people's cultural enrichment, such as story sharing or exposure in the form of service projects found both within and beyond the bounds of their neighborhoods. This form of well-being extends to young people's ability to engage in critical reflection on life's journey, their vision for life ahead, and plans to make it happen. This perspective on well-being connects with economic and vocational well-being.[48]

CONCLUSION

It is understood that every facet of well-being needs to be operant in the lives of young people. Deficiency or absence in one impacts the others. Of equal importance is recognition that young people are not and must not be treated as passive actors in life's journey or in their own well-being. On the contrary, they must be regarded as decision makers with ideas, preferences, choices, and having potential for efficacious action.[49] Indeed, their desires for an active role in the affairs of life appear over and over again in the opening centering story: in the youth who spoke of hanging on and successfully being accepted on the football team; in the youth who adamantly confronted stereotypical views of Black students with the straightforward assertion, "But

---

47   See Sabina Alkire, "Dimensions of Human Development," 188.

48   Ibid.; Anthony Ong, "A Life Worth Living,"106.

49   The point is made that all persons must be regarded as active participants in the journey of life in Martin E.P. Seligman and Mihaly Csirszentmihalyi, "Positive Psychology: An Introduction," 8.

I am capable. I am doing well, and I am determined to keep doing it"; in the one who was determined to go with peers on a school trip and said, "I had to put a little of my own energy in the hope I had. That's what I mean by 'hope works when you work with it.'" We see from these examples that young people have positive traits that are shown not simply in their decision-making resourcefulness but in their gifts and talents, interests, creativity, hope, and courage. These traits also characterize resilience.

The capabilities and resilience of young people alongside hope and courage are particular human strengths that act as buffers amid tough realities of life that threaten well-being.[50] Previous attention was given to research that discloses ways in which young people's hopefulness, resilience, and ability to thrive are promoted and nurtured. We simply want to reiterate here the necessity of pathways and strategies of engagement to promote and nurture young people's well-being, which embrace courageous hope needed for courageous living. Moreover, the call is to do so from the perspective that youth are "placed at promise" rather than the all-too-often characterization of them as considered "at risk." That is, they are at promise to become active participants in families, schools, churches, communities, and wider society; and, therefore, as agents of change that are needed to promote well-being and hope.[51]

Key among the pathways to which we turn later, in part 2, are opportunities to share stories revealing experiences of well-being that point to hope (as well as stories that demonstrate experiential deficiencies that have occasioned a level of thwarted hope); other pathways explored include artistic expression, conflict transformation, and exposure to enrichment and service opportunities. There is also the necessity of considering what precisely is meant by *courageous hope that leads to courageous living.*

---

50 Ibid., 7–8.

51 American Psychological Association (APA) Task Force on Resilience and Strength in Black Children and Adolescents, "Resilience in African American Children and Adolescents: A Vision of Optimal Development" (Washington, DC: American Psychological Association, 2008), 24.

FORMING COURAGEOUS HOPE AND ENACTING COURAGEOUS LIVING

The courageous simply decide that a change is gonna come, and they will have to make the change themselves.

—Steven Barboza[1]

Rejoice in hope, be patient in suffering, persevere in prayer.

—Romans 12:12

[A CENTERING STORY]

Looking outward from the windows of the cafeteria, we, along with other leaders of a four-week Youth Hope-Builders Academy (YHBA) summer residential program, saw two of the academy's young men walking toward the building. Three White youth took turns approaching them from behind. Each of them held bananas, a couple of which they threw at the Black teens, and several others they attempted to place on the teens' shoulders. As the teens looked straight ahead and hastened their gait toward the building, we ran to meet them and stop the disrespectful onslaught. As we approached, the White teens ran in the opposite direction.

---

1   Steven Barboza, ed., with commentary, *The African American Book of Values: Classic Moral Stories* (New York: Doubleday, 1998), 65.

In moments of debriefing, we discovered that disparaging remarks, the "N" word, and other racial epithets had been verbally hurled at the YHBA teens on the grounds of the retreat center during the day. The banana incident that we just witnessed included the demeaning words "jungle monkeys." When we asked the teens about their silence and nonretaliatory response as we all walked toward the cafeteria, they said, "We know who and Whose we are." They said that they "did not want to create a scene and mess up their time here." One of the teens said, "We just thought 'Keep walking! Just keep walking!' So, we just let the stuff pass."

However, as leaders, we shared another view based on our own observations. One empathic leader commented, "Well, I would say it took a whole lot of courage to just keep walking and not strike back or punch 'em out!" Others of us affirmed this stance and added, "Under the circumstances, your response was admirable. You really showed what it means to be hope-builders." Of course, we also saw the incident as a blatant act of racism and set out to address head-on the egregious behavior of the White youth. We filed a complaint in the retreat center office and asked for a meeting with an official of the center and other leaders, the White teens who were implicated in the incident, and the YHBA young men. We didn't know whether the meeting would actually take place, and we were honestly anxious about what might happen in and beyond an actual meeting. However, the importance and gravity of the situation propelled us forward.

The meeting was arranged, and we asked the YHBA youth to tell the story of what had happened. We also invited them to share how it made them feel. In response, the leaders of the White youth said how embarrassed they were and apologized on behalf of their teens: "We've got a lot of work to do." They also asked each one of their youth to say how they would feel if they were on the receiving end of being attacked, belittled, and ridiculed. The White teens were instructed by their leaders to apologize. They were then told by the retreat center official that if anything like this happened again, they and anyone else involved would be instantly removed and barred permanently from the premises. Their leaders followed by insisting that their youth shake hands with the Black teens as a sign of apology and commit to respectful behavior in the future, that is, if the Black youth would agree to receive the handshake. The Black teens agreed. The retreat center official also expressed his apology to the entire YHBA group on behalf of the center and gave assurance of respect going forward.

MORE THAN HOPE

In the introduction, we highlighted hope as an essential answer to the question, "What does the soul want?" Amid a range of troubling realities, from life-threatening to life-taking events, young people yearn for a vision and a reason to move forward in life; they need affirming views of the self and images of life's possibilities. We further pointed to the need for more than hope. Often, tough events and the general havoc of life call for hope that is infused with courage. It takes both to help young people move beyond despairing attitudes and behavior and hold onto a surety of life's prospects. These questions emerge: "What's courage got to do with it?" "What does hope infused by courage mean anyway?" and "How can young people develop a courageous hope that combines both hope and courage in such a way that leads to fruitful ways of being and acting?" These questions are essential to discuss with youth.

THE CALL FOR COURAGE

The centering story exposes a specific situation that called forth a response from the young Black men in the Youth Hope-Builders Academy (YHBA) as well as action on the part of the Academy leaders, the leaders of the White youth, and the retreat center official. Were their responses courageous? Where did hope emerge? What evolved was a moral situation that threatened the value of and respect for human life given by God. It transgressed the principles of human dignity that center on protecting and enhancing life rather than negating it. This moral situation summoned the young men and others to consider what happened and then do something about it. We glean from the unfolding story that decisions had to be reached and options taken that felt right or were considered a necessary means of addressing the moral dilemma.

Rather than choosing physical means of defending themselves, the Black teens made a conscious choice not to respond physically, even though it was a viable option. They had reason not to choose a combative response because they did not want to spoil their retreat. Their actions may be described as morally courageous. They risked further attack. They wanted to do what was best, not simply for themselves, but for the positive outcome of the retreat as a whole. We also note that the young men did not set out to be courageous; nor did they see their behavior as bold or audacious. Clearly, they weren't out to prove any sort kind of "bigness" or bravado. While they were unaware of their exercise of courage, what they demonstrated was a courage that comes from a motivating or energizing push within the self to respond out of necessity to a particular challenge. Mark Nepo says it is something from inside us that we live into. He calls it "an applied art of spirit."[2]

It is further important to note that, even though the teens did not recognize their display of courage, there is no mistaking that the leaders saw in their behavior a particular kind of hope-bearing capacity that they identified as courage; and from the leaders' perspective, attributing courage to them in front of others was a way of highlighting the nature of hope infused with courage.[3] The teens' behavior and remarks also show that they had clearly made a choice to "keep walking" rather than respond to racial epithets and physical assaults based on their belief or "knowledge" about themselves as valued creations of God. In response, several leaders commented that the youth had actually demonstrated the internalization of a key goal of YHBA; that is, to heighten Black youths' awareness and embrace of their value given by God, thereby

---

2   Mark Nepo, *Finding Inner Courage* (Conari Press, 2011), 13.

3   Miller highlights the importance of assigning courage to those who act courageously even though they do not consider themselves as courageous. The reason for this assignment is for the sake of others knowing, preserving, and acting on the substantive virtues inherent in the courageous act. These views appear in Rielle Miller, "Moral Courage: Definition and Development" (Ethics Resource Center, March 2005), 19, http://www.emotionalcompetency.com/papers/Moral_Courage_Definition_and _Development.pdf.

claiming themselves as unashamedly Black with a clear sense of what Jacqueline Grant calls "somebodiness."[4] Stated another way, they exercised what Blagen and Yang call "the courage of self-affirmation." From their perspective, it is this courage shown in the present that leads to a sense of personal empowerment and ability to see and choose to exercise hope-filled responsibility and courage in the future.[5]

What the leaders did was also a morally courageous intervention based on their acute awareness of injustice. They made a choice to respond forthrightly to the harmful, degrading treatment of the youth. The necessary task was to focus attention on injustice with hopeful expectation that amends would occur. Their aim was what is called *morally conscious pro-social behavior.* Importantly, the leaders' efforts were met with responsibility-taking by the other leaders involved. As leaders, we all saw ourselves as moral agents; and in that role, we were committed not to turn away or to shield the White youth, but rather, to take responsibility to act for good in a way for all—both Black and White—to see and judge. Hope emerged in the remark of one of the White leaders, "We've got a lot of work to do." Optimism also appeared in the reconciling gesture of a handshake offered by the White leaders as well as the stern recitation of retreat center rules of conduct and apology given by the center official.[6] As a result, the incident ended with what may be reckoned as a moment of truth and reconciliation, because it pointed to the importance of developing courageous hope for the sake of a just and noble purpose.

---

4   The term *somebodiness* is central to the youth ministry framework proposed in Jacqueline Grant, "A Theological Framework," in *Working with Black Youth: Opportunities for Christian Ministry*, eds. Charles R. Foster and Grant S. Shockley (Nashville: Abingdon, 1989), 65–70.

5   See Mark Blagen and Julia Yang, "A Tool of Facilitating Courage: Hope Is a Choice," paper based on a program presented at the American Counseling Association Annual Conference and Exhibition, Charlotte, NC (March 2009), https://www.counseling .org/docs/default-source/vistas/vistas_2009_blagen-yang.pdf.

6   Exploration of the nature of moral courage appears in Silvia Osswald, Tobias Greitmeyer, Peter Fischer, and Dieter Frey, "What Is Moral Courage? Definitions, Explication, and Classification of a Complex Construct," in Cynthia L.S. Pury and Shane J. Lopez, *The Psychology of Courage: Modern Research on An Ancient Virtue* (Washington, DC: American Psychological Association, 2010); and in Rielle Miller, "Moral Courage: Definition and Development."

Of course, the situation at the retreat center is only one example of a circumstance calling for moral sensibility and response. Young people today are privy to, personally involved in, or observe on a daily basis a wide range of morally problematic circumstances. These include bullying, cheating, unfair treatment, discriminatory practices, and human rights violations that fracture trust in other humans, deepen anger, diminish hope, and in extreme cases, end life. Courageous hope is all about a posture of determination; to remain obstinate against forces that seem unbearable. Life brings with it trouble, danger, and pain; yet, as Martin Luther King Jr. declared years ago, courage is self-affirmation despite the ambiguities of life. It "requires the exercise of a creative will that enables us to hew out a stone of hope from a mountain of despair."[7] It is also true that, while courageous hope may indeed arise spontaneously in the heat of a difficult circumstance, it does not necessarily exist as an innate disposition or habit. It is important to highlight awareness of it and tend to the development of it through intentionally engaging young people in exploring what hope is, its necessity, and when it is called for. Moreover, it is important for young people to have role models who can demonstrate courageous hope and act as mirrors to help youth internalize hopeful habituations.

FORMING COURAGEOUS HOPE

The experience noted in the beginning of this chapter became part of an extensive dialogue with the entire group of YHBA teens. The discussion evolved into their recounting "soul stories" of hurt and injustice and the impact of these wrongs on who they perceive themselves to be, their decisions, and their overall understanding of courage and hope. The youth struggled, not simply with difficulties including experiences of racism arising in the larger societal arena, but with problems in their

---

7   This quotation is found in Martin Luther King Jr., "Antidotes for Fear," (chap. 14 in *The Strength to Love*) in *A Testament of Hope: The Essential Writings and Speeches of Martin Luther King Jr.*, ed. Melvin M. Washington (copyright by Coretta Scott King, Executrix of the Estate of Martin Luther King Jr., 1986; New York: HarperSanFrancisco, a division of HarperCollinsPublishers, 1991), 512. It is also found on: http://www.thekingcenter.org/archives/document/mlk-sermon-about-courage-and-cowardice.

homes, families, schools, neighborhoods, and peers. When asked about their responses or what they had done to address difficulties, the majority simply said that they had done nothing and had not, in fact, told anyone about their experiences. What typically emerges from youth are incredulous examples of negation of their human value and their all-too-often sense of aloneness and invisibility in their distress.[8] What also tends to come across is their deep need for a welcoming, listening presence and their yearning for something that will sustain and motivate them to keep going despite the very real stuff of each day's experiences, injustices, and life-threatening incidents.

A critical question invariably raised by teens in group discussions is, "What can I do with all of this?" Too often they think, "There's nothing we can do. That's just the way it is!" As Academy leaders, our hearing the youths' stories and longing for change, alongside questionable confidence in the possibility of a different future, reminds us that the issues faced by previous generations persist, often with tragic consequences and unresolved outcomes. Racism and racial injustice are still prevalent in too many places. It is well to recognize that the words of Martin Luther King Jr., penned in the 1960s, show an eerie resemblance to the portrait of current reality. Even then, he understood that the heritage of racial oppression is marked by critical insufficiencies in education, housing, health care, and employment opportunities. Further, a lack of recreational and job-counseling opportunities coupled with hostile police relations created a situation he identified as "social dynamite" or "a truly explosive situation."[9]

Of course, we cannot disregard the strides made by many Black people in a wider range of opportunities and middle- and upper-class status. However, in spite of some positive outcomes of the Civil Rights Movement, Black individuals and families as a whole have remained in

---

8   Martin Luther King Jr. tells of this very situation of Negroes who, over the course of time from the era of slavery forward "were not only grossly exploited but negated as human beings. They were invisible in their misery." See Martin Luther King Jr., "A Testament of Hope," an essay published posthumously in James Melvin Washington, ed., *A Testament of Hope: The Essential Writings and Speeches of Martin Luther King Jr.* (New York: HarperCollins, 1991), 313.

9   Ibid., 314, 324.

peril regarding racial stigmatization and profiling in the public square. As elsewhere, disparaging treatment of the young in schools exists in all communities alongside cultural pressures in the home for these young people to achieve, despite questionable options for equal access. Recall again the story of the youth in the centering story in chapter 1, whose high achievement ran counter to white classmates' low expectations of Black youth. In fact, suicidal ideation and attempts tend to be higher among middle-class Black youth compared to youth of other socioeconomic groups, as the result of external and internal pressures.[10] Moreover, the threat of downward mobility is real due to youth falling below their parents' income as adults. It is true that the various groups of middle-class Black families—lower middle-class to upper middle-class—necessarily differ in occupation, income, and residential location and may not, therefore, experience racial adversities similarly or to the same degree. However, there is no mistaking that the experience of the Black middle-class status is still different from that of the White middle class, in that the Black identity portends race-related perils.[11]

The point here is that King's views on the realities of Black life and on hope and courage continue to hold sway today. Moreover, part of the ministry with youth focuses on the requirement that they remember the stony road that Black people have already trod and view the nature of courageous hope as lived out by forebears.[12] In short, this requirement recognizes that young people are as challenged today with

---

10   Walter W. Shervington, "We Can No Longer Ignore the Rising Rate of African-American Suicide," President's Column, *Journal of the National Medical Association* 92, no. 4 (February 2000): 53–54 (54).

11   The term, "Privileges and Perils" to describe the particular situation of middle-class Black people appears in Mary Pattillo and Annette Lareau, *Black Picket Fences: Privilege and Peril Among the Black Middle Class*, 2nd ed. (Chicago: University of Chicago Press, 2013). Other studies on the Black middle class also reveal differences across the groups of those in this status while pointing out the common thread of the impact of racial identity on their sojourn in the United States. These studies are reported in Karyn R. Lacey, *Blue-Chip Black: Race, Class, and Status in the New Black Middle Class* (Berkeley: University of California Press, 2007); Joe R. Feagin and Melvin P. Sikes, *Living with Racism: The Black Middle-Class Experience* (Boston: Beacon Press, 1995).

12   This view of the difficulty of grasping hope appears in the text of the Negro National Anthem, "Lift Every Voice and Sing," written by James Weldon Johnson. A version of the Anthem appears in *African American Heritage Hymnal* (Chicago: GIA Publications, Inc.), #540.

the sting of racism as those in times past. Yet youth—and all of us for that matter—are not without resources that engender the hope and courage necessary to survive and thrive. Past stories provide mirrors or behavioral images of courageous hope for us to emulate. These mirrors are essential means of opening the way for well-being and flourishing.

HOPE INFUSED WITH COURAGE: HISTORY AS A TOUCHSTONE

It is well to state up front that, in this current era of rapid change, there tends to be an emphasis on what is happening now and may yet happen, with little attention to—or even indifference to—the past. As a result, youth are prone to be unattached to the stories of predecessors and, therefore, unaware of information, guides, and encouragement found in them. However, narrative materials detailing views, attitudes, and values, as well as spiritual, social, and artistic practices from the past, provide wise perspectives concerning hope infused with courage for such a time as this, when trouble seems all around. Black predecessors remind us that there is something of inestimable worth in what they knew all too well about the ups and downs of life and how to be hopeful and courageous. Stories and practices of forebears that reveal how they were able to live amidst crisis are important mirrors or means of revealing and shaping thoughts about ways of addressing issues in the present. These materials have the power to trigger critical thinking about currently held attitudes and views, the ability to perceive new perspectives, affirm existing practices, and embrace new and promising ones. Building on Zipes's views on the impact of story, it may be said that narrative cultural materials from the past have the power to work with young people, for young people, and on young people, "affecting what [these] people are able to see as real, as possible, and as worth doing or best avoided."[13]

---

13 Although Zipes focuses primarily on the role and impact of fairy tales on people's lives, his view that stories help to shape people's narrative selves and have the power to influence social practices is applicable to the uses of narrative materials from Black forebears with youth. Find his views in Jack Zipes, "The Cultural Evolution of Storytelling and Fairy Tales: Human Communication and Memetics," http://press.princeton.edu/chapters/s9676.pdf.

The veracity of remembering the Black cultural past is power-fully affirmed in Alice Walker's essay, "The Civil Rights Movement: What Good Was It?"[14] In the essay, she recounts the story of an old Black Mississippi woman who had been accused of disturbing the peace, arrested, and physically maimed by police brutality as she stood up for justice. She was asked to share her thoughts about the movement and whether she viewed the movement as dead. As she hobbled on her cane, the woman likened the movement to herself and said, "If it's dead, it shore ain't ready to lay down!"[15] In Alice Walker's words, the woman had been "beaten for singing Movement songs, placed in solitary con-finement in prisons for talking about freedom, and placed on bread and water for praying aloud to God for her jailers' deliverance."[16] The testimony of this Black heroine reveals an indefatigable and audacious hope that she carried out for the sake of justice in her generation and the ones to come. But her testimony signals more than that. Alice Walker goes on to say that persons like this woman satisfy the hunger of the young for sources—heroes and heroines—outside the self and home who turn them on and give wisdom and hope for living in times of terror and unease.[17] To the question, "What did the movement give us?" comes the answer—models of courage and strength, hope, a call to life.[18]

In essence, history matters. Making possible young people's immer-sion in and critical reflection on wise counsel from the cultural histori-cal past about meanings of hope and the nature of acting on it with unabashed courage provides mirrors for their creative imagining of how to move on anyhow amid the toughness of life. The stories and practices of forebears are what may be called *memes*, or cultural units of information that serve as mimetic or mirroring structures with po-tential for young people's seeing themselves in another light; allowing them to hear, consider, and adopt thoughts and ideas of what sustains

---

14   Alice Walker, *In Search of Our Mothers' Garden: Womanist Prose* (New York: A Harvest Book, Harcourt, Inc., 1983), 119–30.

15   Ibid., 119–20.

16   Ibid., 120.

17   Ibid., 122.

18   Ibid., 129.

and promotes hope-filled living and action they have not considered. Memes have relevance by virtue of their transferability from a past situation to a present state. The mirroring or mimetic power lies in the ability of the cultural units of information to evoke hope within youth; the kind of inner transformation that inspires them to initiate transformation in the world in response to difficult and unjust realities they and others confront.[19]

In short, wisdom from the past is not dated material that had a place then and must now be left to the pages of history. On the contrary, what Black predecessors have to say about hope infused with courage is akin to what Peter Gomes says about theologian Paul Tillich's *The Courage to Be* for the twenty-first century. It "has even more to say at the start of a new century than it had at the midpoint of the last. . . . We would like to make a life and not just a living, which—as we know from our own experiences and that of others—takes courage."[20] Moreover, youth require and hunger for external sources in whom they can see positive life patterns and receive encouragement.

The Transferability of Perspectives on Hope Infused with Courage

With particular regard to hope, the mid-twentieth-century Civil Rights leader Martin Luther King Jr. contended that hope resides in one's view of oneself as an actor on one's own behalf. It evolves from a person knowing that he or she has a choice and can decide on an optimistic course of life while, at the same time, recognizing the barriers life presents. Furthermore, choice is undergirded by an inner "sense of affirmation generated by the challenge of embracing struggle and surmounting obstacles."[21] Other writers echo this view. For example, Donald Capps refers to this kind of perspective within the self as an "attitudinal disposition"; that is, an attitude or belief in an open future that holds possibility. The self's disposition is one of hopefulness rather than

---

19   Zipes, "The Cultural Evolution of Storytelling and Fairy Tales," 20.

20   Peter J. Gomes, "Introduction," in Paul Tillich, *The Courage to Be*, 2nd ed. (1952; New Haven, CT: Yale University Press, 2000).

21   Tillich, *The Courage to Be*, 314.

despairing.[22] Within this frame of mind is what Capps also describes as "anticipation that sooner or later, one will find a way out."[23] Stated in other terms, choosing hope simply means claiming for the self the view "I'm gonna make it," or the psychological frame of mind that reflects the resilient self. Gillham and her colleagues further state that an optimistic view versus pessimistic orientation to life advances persons' motivation to engage in effective coping mechanisms in the face of adversity.[24]

The words of other Black forebears point to not simply hope but ways of being that reveal elements of courage. In responding to the stories she heard of older Black women, Maya Angelou remarked, "They have overcome the cruel roles into which they had been cast by racism and ignorance. They have wept over their hopeless fate and defied destiny by creating hope anew."[25] In the words of one, "In my day, life was not a journey for the weak or the fainthearted. From the word go, I've learned firsthand the fine art of prevailing."[26] Another said it differently, "Hope is the secret weapon of the soul that allows us to persevere when the facts seem troubling and the truth unbearable. Hope moves potential into power. Hope—it's what keeps me standing."[27] And still another made clear that, "Where there is hope, there is life, and I choose to live."[28]

For Mama,[29] Anne Wimberly's grandmother, the song "Life is Like a Mountain Railway"[30] said it all. It was not her singing the song that

---

22 Donald Capps, *Agents of Hope: A Pastoral Psychology* (Minneapolis: Fortress, 1995), 28.

23 Ibid., 14.

24 Jane E. Gillham, Andrew J. Shatte, Karen J. Reivich, and Martin E. P. Seligman, "Optimism, Pessimism, and Explanatory Style," in *Optimism & Pessimism: Implications for Theory, Research, and Practice*, ed. Edward C. Chang (Washington, DC: American Psychological Association, 2001), 67.

25 Maya Angelou, "Foreword," in Emily Herring Wilson, *Hope and Dignity: Older Black Women of the South* (Philadelphia: Temple University Press, 1983), xii.

26 See Dennis Kimbro, *What Keeps Me Standing: Letters from Black Grandmothers on Peace, Hope, and Inspiration* (New York: Harlem Moon, Broadway Books, 2003), 47.

27 Ibid., 80.

28 Ibid., 84.

29 This storied commentary to the song "Life Is Like a Mountain Railway" was a favorite and revered one told many years ago by Anne Wimberly's grandmother, Hazel Wilson, whom Anne called *Mama*.

30 The song is attributed to Eliza R. Snow, with further reference to M. E. Abbey in 1890. The words and attribution are found on: http://library.timelesstruths.org/music /Lifes_Railway_to_Heaven/.

punctuated its meaning. Rather, it was the wisdom conveyed by her commentary on the song. She shared in vivid detail the kinship of life's journey to the winding of a train around a mountain, through lowly emerald valleys, to a strenuous journey upward to heights that, once reached, would take your breath away. Along the way dangerous curves appear and ferocious storms threaten to derail the train. And on occasion, landslides cause abrupt stops, loss of time, and bone-chilling fear that the end is surely at hand. But Mama's next words hit at the core of what comprises a journey undertaken with courageous hope. She said, "Whatever happens, no matter where you are, or however difficult or frightful the circumstance, don't get off the train! And one more thing! Know who the engineer is, and that is God who will be with you all the way."

Mrs. Eva Roundtree's emphasis on the role of faith goes beyond Mama's reference to God as the engineer in her insistence that "without God, honey, we don't get too far. . . . You talk to the Lord and wait for an answer. And when you get to thinking about what the *Lord* can do, then you'll sing these songs. . . . You might get disturbed, you know. I just got disturbed last week, and I walked the length of this house and I said, 'I don't let nothing separate me from the love of God.'"[31] She later added, "I helped the Lord to make me what I am."[32] For Mrs. Roundtree, courageous hope for living is empowered by faith and sustained by her personal and creative sense of agency that takes the form of singing and her use of this gift on behalf of others. Similarly, Alice Walker says that "our mothers and grandmothers, *ourselves*—have not perished in the wilderness."[33] They sang. They imagined what was possible. They held onto a deep spirituality. These gifts are shown, for example, in the quilt portraying the story of the Crucifixion, which was created by an "anonymous" Black woman from Alabama and hangs in the Smithsonian Institution in Washington, DC.[34] Indeed, creative means of surviving

---

31 The story is found in Emily Herring Wilson, *Hope and Dignity: Older Black Women of the South* (Philadelphia; Temple University Press, 1983), 9.

32 Ibid.

33 Alice Walker, *In Search of Our Mother's Garden*, 235 (italics original).

34 Ibid., 239.

in the unknown and treacherous place they described as being "knee-bone in the wilderness," dates back to the beginning of Black people's sojourn in this country.[35] Original songs, dancing, shouting, and other religious expressions opened the way for lament, nurture, resistance, and the political commentary needed to survive. They were dominant ways by which enslaved forebears exerted personal agency and worth that countered performances coerced by their captors and views, readily heard by them, of their inferiority and deficiency based on their bodily appearance and complexion.[36] These means of expressing themselves were audacious, inventive practices of tapping into and passing on to others life-affirming strength and power. They stand as forerunners and affirmative promoters of current youth's originality in rapping, liturgical dance, stepping, mime, and spoken word.

Black predecessors present an understanding of hope infused by courage that is active, dynamic, and life affirming. It is neither a docile nor life-negating approach to life. This understanding provides a helpful foundation for conversations with young people about courageous hope and activities that help them act in positive and life-affirming ways. Four images of the nature of hope infused with courage emerge from the perspectives of Black predecessors. These images offer guidance for embracing four particular dispositional qualities that may be regarded as markers of courageous hope to be formed in young people:

---

35 References to the song, "Knee-bone in the Wilderness" appears in the volume that details the history of the ring shout among enslaved Black people in this country: Art Rosenbaum, *Shout Because You're Free: The African American Ring Shout Tradition in Coastal Georgia* (1998; repr., Athens: The University of Georgia Press, 2013).

36 Katrina Thompson provides extensive documentation of Black people being forced to perform music and dance as amusement for slavers during the middle passage, on slave ships from the African continent to what became known as the New World, as well as over the period of Black enslavement. From her perspective, music and dance were used as means of defining and subjugating Black people and of setting forth stereotypical and degrading views of Black people. Because of this emphasis, she does not give attention to the freedom taken and exercised by Black people in their self-created communal environments to create songs, dance, and other religious expressions that served as lament, nurture, resistance, and political commentary needed for survival. Thompson's history of performing arts and race is found in Katrina Dyonne Thompson, *Ring Shout, Wheel About: The Racial Politics of Music and Dance in North American Slavery* (Urbana, IL: University of Illinois Press, 2014).

Courageous Hope as a Choice

With regard to courageous hope as a choice, an earlier mentioned comment of a YHBA teen was that it takes courage to live. This sentiment was repeated by an older Black woman but included the emphatic notion of choosing life. Amidst hardship and sorrow, this optimistic bent toward life is itself an act of courage. Similarly, Martin Luther King Jr. addresses the choice of optimism in his own story of refusing to be overcome and hardened by the toughness of treatment from adversaries. Rather, he chose to embrace the struggle, knowing that it affirmed his purpose.[37] In other words, one bears witness to the possibilities that exist in one's own ability to act courageously.

At the center of courageous hope is one's view of oneself as an actor on one's own behalf. Courageous hope evolves from a person

---

37   Martin Luther King Jr., "A Testament of Hope," 314.

knowing that she or he has a choice and can decide on an optimistic course of life while at the same time recognizing the barriers life presents.[38] Such a choice, then, presumes an existing view of hope that centers on the psychological attributes of optimism and positivity. Donald Capps refers to this kind of perspective within the self as an "attitudinal disposition" or attitude toward life that things will work out in the unfolding of time. Within this disposition lies the belief in an open and hope-filled future that holds possibilities rather than despairing outcomes.[39] Further understanding of this perspective is set forth by Gillham and her associates, who cite an explanatory style that makes it possible for persons to maintain motivation amidst adversity, which promotes their ability to cope and continue on.[40]

Snyder and his associates also highlight a sense of choice to believe in a positive rather than negative outcome, which they place within a cognitive model of hope. They, too, emphasize a person's agency or "sense of successful use of energy in the pursuit of goals in one's past, present, and future."[41] However, in their model is the assumption of some clearly identified pathways to exercise or make one's agency come alive.[42] There must be ways to move from choosing to live, to actually living. In Tillichian terms, there must be the means to move from the courage to be, to being—which opposes nonbeing; and that means courage to affirm the self in spite of all that come against it and of doing it even in the face of anxiety and fear.[43] The key point is that choice resides in one's affirmation of one's value. But it also extends to

---

38 Ibid.

39 Donald Capps, *Agents of Hope: A Pastoral Psychology* (Minneapolis: Fortress Press, 1995), 14, 28.

40 Jane E. Gillham, Andrew J. Shatte, Karen J. Reivich, and Martin E.P. Seligman, "Optimism, Pessimism, and Explanatory Style," in *Optimism & Pessimism: Implications for Theory, Research, and Practice*, ed. Edward C. Chang (Washington, DC: American Psychological Association, 2001), 67.

41 C. R. Snyder, Susie C. Sympson, Scott T. Michael, and Jen Cheavens, "Optimism and Hope Constructs: Variants on a Positive Expectancy Theme," in *Optimism & Pessimism: Implications for Theory, Research, and Practice*, ed. Edward C. Chang, 101–2.

42 Ibid., 102.

43 Tillich explores courage as self-affirmation and the nature of fear and anxiety that threaten courage but can be faced. See Paul Tillich, *The Courage to Be*, 32–54.

asserting oneself in ways that affirm one's rightful being or "somebodiness" with all of the rights, opportunities, and resources that make for a fulfilling life in community. Young people must be involved in opportunities that stimulate or evoke their *choosing* to envision and reach for possibilities for their lives. There must be intentional recognition of young people's *agency* that is set in motion through uses of gifts and talents that build on and build up their leadership and decision-making potential and skills. There must be *hopeful thinking pathways* that engage young people in activities that accentuate positive emotions, choices, and achievable goals.

The courage to choose hope simply means claiming for oneself the view "I'm gonna make it," which is akin to having the psychological frame of mind that reflects the resilient self.[44] Of course, we recognize that in the case of difficult, dehumanizing, and traumatic life events or experiences emanating from racism, forms of abuse, or other means have the propensity to impede a sense of positivity and bring about a sense of pessimism. We also recognize that hope cannot be forced on anyone. People cannot be made to choose hope. The truth is that a person may accede to fatalism, as Capps notes.[45] On this basis, young people may hold fast to the earlier-mentioned statement: "There's nothing we can do. That's just the way it is." The role of leaders is to be agents of hope who find ways such as and beyond those included in chapters 4–7 of this volume, ways that seek to inspire, instill, and support courageous hope in young people.

Courageous Hope as an Empowering Attitude

In addition to being chosen, courageous hope also has an empowering capacity in young people's lives to the extent that they are enabled to envision goals that hold the potential of contributing to a hopeful outcome and are accorded pathways to move. Even amidst obstacles, this capacity makes possible an inner power that is reckoned as the wherewithal—or what we have already named as

---

44   See Capps, *Agents of Hope*, 14.

45   Ibid., 24–25.

human agency—and the mental energy or psychological verve to move toward an identified goal, however great or small, that might be quickly attained, delayed, or even unseen. The empowering capacity of courageous hope has at the center hope-filled positivity and the zest or the "push" from within that is likened to the byword of Barack Obama's 2008 presidential campaign: "Yes we can!" But it also requires the embrace of several key empowerment perspectives that may be called *weapons* against pessimism, passivity, and action that negates self-affirmation and human flourishing. First, it depends on *one's awareness of the dangers* that accompany an action to be taken and on one's acknowledgment of legitimate fears of what might or might not happen, including fear of failure.[46] Recall that the YHBA leaders had honest anxiety about whether a meeting would be granted to air the grievances of the young men and other Black youth who had been on the receiving end of hurtful, degrading behavior. However, the importance and gravity of the situation literally propelled us forward. Courageous hope, then, entails a movement to a form of "fearlessness" or contentment, an inner resolve to undertake action for the sake of an identified outcome.

Second, Goud points to *one's confidence* as a key aspect of empowerment that comes from paying attention to previous successful outcomes on the one hand and, on the other, engaging in a "strengths inventory."[47] Using Goud's recommendation with youth includes taking stock of "career, interpersonal, intellectual/academic, physical, and emotional traits as well as special abilities such as art, music, athletics, hobbies, and so forth. Without a conscious reminder of strengths, they tend to slip from one's awareness (therefore not available under conditions of challenge)."[48] The commentary shared by Mama on "Life Is Like a Mountain Railway" alludes to the very real fear of derailment.

---

46 In his discussion of the nature and development of courage, Goud presents three dimensions of courage, including fear, appropriate action, and a higher purpose. These dimensions appear in Nelson H. Goud, "Courage: Its Nature and Development," *Journal of Humanistic Counseling, Education and Development* 44, (Spring 2005): 102–16.

47 Goud, "Courage: Its Nature and Development," 110.

48 Ibid.

However, she was confident that the onward journey would be assured, because God is the engineer and must be recognized and counted on in that capacity. Moreover, Mrs. Eva Roundtree highlighted her dependence on God, as well as her own agency, in the form of singing that empowered her journey forward and her action on behalf of others. The writings of Martin Luther King Jr. also remind us that there is a decidedly spiritual dimension to confidence in the line of fire. In the face of obstacles, struggle, fear, and faltering he cites an incomprehensible strength that faith in God brings. And, for him, profound security comes through knowledge of God's love and design for humankind that goes beyond human failure.[49]

Third, courageous hope that empowers action on the part of young people includes wise consideration of the reason for action. In this regard, Goud makes the point that there must be awareness of specifically *why* an action is needed and undertaken.[50] From our perspective, the *why* has historically been and continues to be about human flourishing that affirms persons' human worth and value given by God and the assurance that persons have the wherewithal for this affirmation to be made concrete. In his historical analysis of the lives of enslaved Black people, Eugene Genovese wrote about their resistance to the oppression they were forced to endure. The *why* of their action was empowered by a religion of hope that countered the prevailing myth of their docility and made possible their imagining a way forward in life with a sense of freedom of mind and spirit as well as a vision of the day when they would be free bodily.[51] During the mid-twentieth-century Civil Rights Movement, the *why* centered on rectifying injustices, ensuring equal rights and protections under the law, and bringing about a beloved community. In this current era, the *why* persists as the assurance of actual life and breath, justice, human dignity, and the resources that support life.

The key point here is that the empowering function of courageous

---

49 King, "A Testament to Hope," 314.

50 Goud, "Courage: Its Nature and Development," 113.

51 Eugene D. Genovese, *Roll, Jordan, Roll: The World the Slaves Made* (New York: Vintage Books, 1976), 596–97.

hope has particular salience in young people's lives because, as it made possible Black forebears' courage to prevail and persevere in life, it engenders the belief in youth that they have both the physical wherewithal and mental energy to move toward and achieve an identified goal. Hope functions as an empowering capacity in young people in ways that allow them to see, reach for, and accomplish positive goals, even amidst obstacles. This view reflects Carl Richard Snyder's view of hope as "the perceived capability to derive pathways to desired goals, and motivate oneself via agency-thinking to use those pathways."[52] Empowering hope energizes what Dana Harley calls "self-talk" or the "push" from within to shout out, "I can do this! I'm not going to be stopped!"[53]

Courageous Hope as a Faith-Filled Posture in Life's Wilderness

What also comes across from the perspectives of the forebears is the centrality of faith in their embrace and practice of courageous hope. The perspectives of Mama, Mrs. Eva Roundtree, and Martin Luther King Jr. underscore the necessity of knowing and relying on God and of engaging in spiritual disciplines such as prayer. Moreover, a gift of forebears from the era of enslavement forward is the recognition of life as wilderness and wilderness as a "classroom" in which to learn and claim the ability to live and keep on keeping on, with courage and hope in life and even in the face of death.[54]

A faith-filled posture in life's wilderness must not be missed in the sojourn of today's youth. In fact, we contend that it is necessary to: explore a wilderness theology with young people by inviting them to openly and honestly name the painful places, struggles, and broken places of

---

52 Carl Richard Snyder, "Hope Theory: Rainbows in the Mind," *Psychological Inquiry* 13, no. 4 (2002): 249–75 (249). See also the perspectives of Snyder in "Hypothesis: There Is Hope," 3–24, and "Genesis: The Birth and Growth of Hope," 25–38 in C. R. Snyder, *Handbook of Hope: Theory, Measures and Applications* (New York: Academic Press, 2000).

53 Dana Michelle Harley, "Perceptions of Hope and Hopelessness Among Low-Income African American Adolescents," (PhD dissertation, Graduate School, The Ohio State University, 2011), 24, http://etd.ohiolink.edu/rws_etd/document/get/osu1313009132/inline.

54 The idea of wilderness as a classroom appears in Scott C. Hammond, *Lessons of the Lost: Finding Hope and Resilience in Work, Life, and the Wilderness* (Bloomington, IN: iUniverse, 2013).

their lives that characterize wilderness; engage them in lament before God; and involve them in spiritual practices such as communal worship, Bible study, praying, singing, liturgical arts, and service that provide openings for them to search for, hear, find God, and discern God's actions in their lives in the wilderness. The Bible is particularly rich in offering perspectives on the wilderness and stories of exemplars who journeyed in the wilderness and encountered God there. For example, the story of Hagar, a servant, reveals the difficult wilderness experience of being impregnated by and bearing a child, Ishmael, of her master, because of the failure of the master's wife to bear a child. Her abuse by the master's wife and subsequent abandonment in the desert made even more difficult her painful struggle. Yet, in her period of exile, God's existence became known in a spring of water and in God's voice of promise. In short, it must not be forgotten that, just as the dimension of faith was pivotal for past generations, so also it holds significance in the lives of the current generation of youth. Indeed, Philip Dunston and Anne Wimberly, in their discussion on the connection between hope and self-discovery, state that "there is no empowerment, growth, or transformation without recognition and appreciation for the transcendental force present in all life forms. Black youth need guidance, on how to effectively commune with and develop a relationship with God."[55]

Courageous Hope as an Ongoing Creative Sojourn

We are also reminded by the perspectives of forebears that past realities of life do not disappear completely with time. Rather, it would seem that each generation is met with concerns that are similar if not the same as previous ones. On the one hand, recognition of the repetition of issues over time raises questions about the germaneness of hope for transformation or change. On the other hand, while the ongoing presence of injustice threatens to overwhelm and stifle ongoing efforts to continue on the journey, creativity can become a remarkable

---

55 Philip Dunston and Anne E. Streaty Wimberly, "A Matter of Discovery," in *Keep It Real: Working With Today's Black Youth*, ed. Anne E. Streaty Wimberly (Nashville: Abingdon, 2005), 39.

and renewing pathway of meaning-making, survival, and inspiration for others, as indicated in the stories of Eva Roundtree and the anonymous quilt-maker. The ongoing creative spirit is further affirmed by Emilie Townes, who shared her own personal perspective, "Trying to understand racism and other forms of hatred has been one of the most formative things I've done in my life, and I have now come to realize that it will remain a challenge until I draw my last breath. I learned at an early age that I must learn how to survive the daily small and sometimes large indignities of racism by negotiating it with creativity, imagination, and sometimes humor while maintaining my integrity and sense of self."[56]

Reference has already been made to music, dance, and other artistic expressions as central to Black people's self-chosen expressions of agency. These expressions have been primary means by which a Black people's eschatology emerged. Central to their eschatological viewpoint was the religious assertion found in the music called *spirituals* that God had both a promised future for them and was working to bring an end to their oppression in the present. Black liberation theology emerged from this view of hope in divine emancipation. James Cone, the author of this distinctly cultural theological perspective, contended that the impact of the music of enslaved forebears lies in its authentication of a Christian hope that centers on a vision of "a new heaven and a new earth. Their hope is against the present order of injustice and slavery and for a new order of justice and peace."[57] Cone's assessment of the form of Black people's eschatology found in the music also points to the strong presence of courage, as noted in his statement that "according to the black spirituals, belief in God's future meant accepting the burden and the risk of escape to the North and later Canada."[58] In the heat of the mid-twentieth-century Civil Rights Movement, a sermon of Martin Luther King Jr. also made clear that "Trouble is a reality in this

56 Emilie M. Townes, "Teaching and the Imagination," *Religious Education* 111, no. 4 (July–September, 2016): 366–79 (367).

57 James H. Cone, *The Spirituals and the Blues: An Interpretation* (Maryknoll, NY: Orbis Books, 1972), 96.

58 Ibid., 95.

strange medley of life, [but] . . . These forces that threaten to negate life must be challenged by courage."[59]

MOVING FROM COURAGEOUS HOPE
TO COURAGEOUS LIVING

Like our forebears, young people today need an alive and courageous hope that has in it a concrete view of a changed here and now. As such, it is more than an abstract concept. It is a way of living courageously to be embraced. It extends to a vision of what or who can help them form and sustain it. As stated earlier, we also recognize that hope and courage cannot be forced on them or anyone. People cannot be made to see hope, choose hope, or act on hope. Nor can they simply be told to "Buck up! Be courageous!" and the behaviors will somehow magically occur. The role of leaders is to be agents of hope who find ways to inspire, instill, and support hope infused with courage in young people. The undeniable responsibility to be assumed by church leaders now is to set before youth a vision of courageous hope and a zest for hope-filled action that is infused with understandings of what constitutes courage in the heat of difficulty. But young people must be invited into it.

Consider, for example, the following idea. Invite a group of young people to answer the question: What is the most courageous thing you have done?[60] Ask them to tell the story to a partner or a small group. The dyad or small group is to create a space for young people's open story sharing and their becoming aware of their practices of courageous hope (e.g., youth may tell about choosing to speak up on behalf of a friend who was being bullied, or to keep walking as the youth did in the centering story, or of telling parents of disappointing news).

---

59 Martin Luther King Jr., "Antidotes for Fear" (chapter 14), in *A Testament of Hope: The Essential Writings and Speeches of Martin Luther King Jr.*, ed. James M. Washington (Copyright by Coretta Scott King, Executrix of the Estate of Martin Luther King Jr., 1986; New York: HarperSanFrancisco, A division of HarperCollins Publishers, 1991), 512. This quotation also appears on http://theKingcenter.org/archives/document /mlk-sermon-about-courage-and-cowardice/.

60 The question is frequently posed to guests by Dennis Rainey at the end of his radio broadcast program, *Family Life Today*, a CRU, Campus Crusade for Christ ministry, www.familylifetoday.com.

The following rubric is an example of a tool for leaders and youth to determine where youth are and where guidance and support may be needed in the four areas of practicing active, dynamic, and life-affirming courageous hope.

CHART 1. RUBRIC FOR RAISING COURAGEOUS HOPE THROUGH STORY[61]

Dispositional Qualities of Courageous Hope Awareness and Practice	Launching Beginning: Very little awareness and/or action	Rising Developing: Some awareness and/or action	Breaking Through Developed: Honorable awareness and/or action	Fully Embraced Well Developed: Exemplary awareness and/or action
A Choice Recognized and chose an optimistic course of action despite fear and anxiety				
An Empowering Attitude Used self-talk such as "yes I can"; modeled confidence, moving from fear to fearlessness; affirmed one's God-given human worth and value				
A Faith-filled Posture in Life's Wilderness Reliance on God; discipline of prayer				

---

61 The rubric builds on the one set forth in Craig A. Mertler, "Designing Scoring Rubrics for Your Classroom," *Practical Assessment, Research & Evaluation*, a peer reviewed electronic journal, 7, no. 25 (December, 2001): 1–8 (2), http://pareonline.net/getvn.asp?v=7&n=25.

Dispositional Qualities of Courageous Hope Awareness and Practice	Launching Beginning: Very little awareness and/or action	Rising Developing: Some aware-ness and/or action	Breaking Through Developed: Honorable awareness and/or action	Fully Em-braced Well De-veloped: Exemplary awareness and/or action
An Ongoing Creative Sojourn Negotiated issues calling for coura-geous hope with creativity; inspired to act for change on an issue of injustice and knowing why it's important to act				

Young people enter into the enactment of courageous living through the process of launching, rising, breaking through, and fully embracing the four dispositional qualities that are markers of courageous hope: a choice, an empowering attitude, a faith-filled posture in life's wilderness, and an ongoing creative sojourn. These dispositional qualities define dis-tinguishing traits that are deemed important in their formation of cou-rageous hope.

An added dimension refers to situational behaviors. These behav-iors pertain to specific actions young people undertake that reflect their enactment of courageous living. It includes actions called for in personal, familial, educational, cultural, communal, and societal situa-tions. They are behaviors that involve acknowledging and assessing threats to hope occurring in these situation environments, engaging in prosocial behaviors, and being hope-bearers. The following chart pro-vides descriptions of the situational behaviors, demands for action, and examples of courageous living in action.

CHART 2. MOVING FROM COURAGEOUS HOPE TO ENACTMENT OF COURAGEOUS LIVING

Situational Behaviors	Description	Demands for Action	Enactment of Courageous Living
Acknowl-edging threats to hope	This behavior refers to youth's awareness of threats to hope present in any of the situational environments of their lives.	On several occasions, Lakeisha and Amber have observed Sandy's being bullied by an older student. They have noticed the bystanders and were themselves bystanders on at least two occasions.	During a youth group meeting, Lakeisha and Amber raise the subject about the incidents of bullying in response to the youth ministry leader's question to the group: "What's happening in your world these days?"
Assessing the situation through the lens of courageous hope	This behavior refers to youth's ability to critically appraise their situation in order to envision pathways of hope infused with courage. Youth set goals (emotional, physical, social, spiritual) that align with courageous hope.	The need to stop the bullying of Sandy weighs heavily on Lakeisha and Amber. They agree that being bystanders is not acceptable if they own up to being Christians. They weigh the options of what might happen in addressing the situation.	In the youth group discussion, Lakeisha and Amber consider approaching the bully and going to the school guidance counselor. The leader affirmed their action and engaged the entire group in discussing bullying and responses to it.
Enacting courageous hope	This behavior refers to concrete decisions made by youth that move in the direction of courageous living.	The opportunity arises for Lakeisha and Amber to approach the bully during the lunch hour. The three step outside the cafeteria where a heated conversation takes place, but Lakeisha and Amber do not back down and indicate to the bully that they will be watching out for Sandy and reporting the bullying to the guidance counselor.	At the next youth group meeting, the leader inquired about what had happened. Lakeisha and Amber shared their actions. After further discussion on the role of Christians as hope-builders in the world, several youth committed to exploring group actions at their schools that included making signs declaring the school as a NO BULLY ZONE.

Situational Behaviors	Description	Demands for Action	Enactment of Courageous Living
Being hope-bearers	This behavior refers to youth's embrace of a way of both doing and being. They not only choose courage-infused pathways of hope for themselves, but they become bearers of hope that help other youth desire to live courageously.	Lakeisha and Amber recognize the need for their ongoing watch over Sandy and for their encouragement of others to move from bystanders to upstanders who know something's wrong and have the courage to make things right.	Youth's ongoing enactment of courageous living builds as they claim their role as God's ambassadors in the world and followers of Jesus Christ, and are encouraged as well as supported by leaders who are agents of hope.

We cannot overemphasize the significance of the role of adult leaders in young people's entering into courageous living. Note in chart 2 that, even though Lakeisha and Amber initiated their response to the bullying of Sandy, the youth ministry leader took on the role as an agent of hope, first by inviting young people's voices on the happenings in their lives. The role continued with the leader expanding the discussion of the issue of bullying with the entire group and the offer of encouragement and support of Lakeisha and Amber. As agents of hope, leaders will also have abundant opportunities to initiate conversation, engage youth in assessing situations, and encourage youth to enact courageous hope based on circumstances both they and youth identify. In a real sense, this role calls for courage on the part of leaders—an unhesitating willingness to take seriously and grapple with the real-life issues young people bring forward. It also requires tackling the issues leaders already know about, the same issues that young people are wary to bring forward because they suspect leaders will not tackle them. What is called for is a particular kind of environment within which to engage young people. This is addressed in the following chapter.

BEING AND BECOMING AGENTS OF COURAGEOUS HOPE

The movement of the Spirit of God in the hearts of [persons] often calls them to act against the spirit of their times or causes them to anticipate a spirit which is yet in the making. In a moment of dedication, they are given wisdom and courage to dare a deed that challenges and to kindle a hope that inspires.

— Howard Thurman[1]

Be strong, and let your heart take courage, all you who wait for the LORD.

— Psalm 31:24

[A CENTERING STORY]

As part of an evaluation process, a group of Youth Hope-Builders Academy leaders engaged in conversation around this question posed by Anne: "What have we learned about ourselves as leaders and from youth in the Youth Hope-Builders Academy (YHBA) ministry?"[2] An immediate response from one was:

> Honestly, answers to that question might fill a book. It really is not just what I've learned about myself. It's what I've learned from the youth. A lot of times, I feel like I've learned more from

---

1 Howard Thurman, "Introduction," *Footprints of a Dream: The Story of the Church for the Fellowship of All Peoples* (Eugene, OR: Wipf & Stock, 2009), 7.

2 This experience of journaling was part of a larger, culminating evaluation process undertaken at the end of every summer residential program of the Youth Hope-Builders Academy. The journal entries were completed anonymously.

> them than I've been able to teach them from what I know. Their lives—what too many of them are going through—is beyond anything I could imagine. They really need us to step up, hear their stories, and walk into the battlefield of life with them, whether it's in circumstances of injustice or in their trying to figure out who they are and where they're headed in life. It scares me! Like, if something isn't done that can help or make a difference, what hope is there for them? For all of us? Doing something? It's on me!

Another joined in:

> I agree, but my take on it is that youth today are looking for hope they can grab hold of. I see my job as a hope visionary who helps them to be the same. It's a heart thing! Honestly, sometimes, I've got to pull hard to bring hope out when I see all that's going on. No, it's not that I don't have hope. It's more a thing of knowing the muscle I've got to put in it to make a difference in what I do with youth. Well, I'll have to say that being with and relating to them, I get in touch with the genius that's in them and the need to make it shine. I see what's possible, and that gets me going.

In reply, a leader said:

> There's another point I want to make. Sometimes I forget how unique each youth is, how important their relationships are with each other, and how they struggle to "fit in." They remind me by what they do and what they say or don't say. Some are too shy to tell their story. There are tough ones who challenge me and everyone around them. Some seem to have it all together and ones who clearly don't. But make no mistake. They're God's children. I agree that they're talented, smart, beautiful, and handsome with a lot to give to the church and world. That's something I learn every time I'm with them.

Added thoughts about personal capacities for ministry and addressing challenges surfaced in the following interaction: "I realize that I deeply love ministry with young people. It's something that I feel deep down in my soul. I think that has always been the case, but I never put it in words before. Relating to them and being able to serve them gives me joy." A leader responded, "I agree, but this ministry is hard. The truth is, I've got some growing edges. I don't know everything. It's been helpful to see how others do it. I've learned from each of you."

Another leader added:

> What has been said is true for me too, especially the part
> about ministry not being easy. A lot of times, I struggle with
> how best to help young people and even whether I'm the
> one to do it. I've asked myself the question: What's right to
> say or do when a kid tells you someone in their family is ill or
> has died, or a friend has been killed, or they're being abused,
> or things aren't going well in school or at home? My first re-
> sponse is, I'm hurting for them. Gee, I've been through some
> of the same stuff. I feel like I need to—I've got to—fix things
> for them. But sometimes, all I can do is listen to their story, en-
> courage, or comfort. Sometimes, the only answer is to pray.
> I've developed greater ability along the way, but there's more
> I need to learn—like how to appropriately choose what to
> do, when to address something, and when to let it slide.

From another leader: "I don't always get it right. But I know that
each step prepares me for the next steps and helps me to grow." That
was followed by the statement of a colleague:

> The point I want to make is this: I've found that caring has
> to be a community thing where we are all in it together—
> where we support these kids, where we leaders help each
> other, and where we help these youth come together and
> support one another. I think we've shown it sometimes in re-
> markable ways, like one time when everybody, the whole
> group of youth and all of us leaders, created a huge colorful
> note of support on newsprint for one of the youth whose
> grandmom was gravely ill and not expected to live. And, by
> the way, the whole idea came from one of the youth. Mostly,
> it calls for thinking outside the box and knowing that we as
> leaders don't have to be alone in doing whatever is needed
> at the time.

A succession of comments followed: "For sure, there's no single
way of doing ministry with youth today. We need multiple directions
or courses of action; and we have to have what I call 'guts' to try them
out!" And:

> I've learned that knowing the *what* and *how* and *when*
> doesn't happen all at once. I've discovered a new level of
> patience. It isn't even about years of experience. New ques-
> tions come up in this new tech-connected and yet, in many
> respects, disconnected age that call for new answers. Young
> people today need to have their say—a chance to lead.
> So, I've learned to keep saying inside myself: "So let them!"

> Sure, I have to listen more intently to them, to colleagues, and others. I have to get in touch with far more resources than I used to.

The importance of a spiritual dimension became evident in other shared thoughts:

> God is key! Youth are looking for a spiritual dimension. I've also discovered over and over that it's not possible for me to get very far without God at the center. It's not just alright to be in conversation with God and in touch with Jesus in the nitty-gritty of youth ministry. It's necessary! In that conversation, I'm reminded of my calling to this work. I'm reassured that God has given me a hope and a future in youth ministry. I've also become even more convinced that too much is at stake to stop, especially in terms of the youth! I've got to act on my call no matter what! I also know I'm not in it by myself. God and others are on this journey with me.

The follow-up comment of another leader was, "Really, I also realize most profoundly that I'm called to it. But I also have found myself telling God that I'm not perfect. A lot of times I 'miss the boat,' like expecting too much or too little from the kids. But God reminds me of things I need to work on and lets me know, too, that even in my imperfections, I can be used as a vessel for good." Another leader followed:

> Having that spiritual dimension is true for me too. I confess that there have been moments of personal need when an answer to more than one of the youth's hardship was in short demand. I just had to call out loud the name of Jesus. But I also yelled "Hallelujah! Thank you, Jesus!" to unexpected and really great outcomes in more than a few tough situations. Somebody said before that they're not in it by themselves. That's an important word. I know God and others are on this journey with me. But my part counts! So does my hope for youth and my hope in God. The word for me every day is that "hope does not disappoint us, because God's love has been poured into our hearts through the Holy Spirit that has been given to us" (Rom. 5:5).[3] That's my favorite verse. My hope is that walking with them through the storm of their life will help restore lost hope.

---

3   This reflection originally appeared in a larger article in Anne E. Streaty Wimberly, "Preparing for a Vocation of Hope," A Message from the Director, *The Hope Messenger* 7, no. 2 (Summer 2009): 1.

REFLECTION ON THE SELF AS LEADER

In the introduction, we emphasized the importance of young people's voices, of adults listening to young people and taking them seriously so that the "biographies of the soul" can be revealed and responses can be given. Yet, in this chapter, we have begun with the voices of youth ministry leaders. We are aware that much happens inside us and other leaders in the process of interacting with youth as we negotiate our role of engaging young people in ways that raise hope within them. Because of this awareness, we contend that there is a key place for the voices of youth ministry leaders and other adults who work with youth or have a role in guiding their lives. What we have found is that their reflections on their experiences reveal how they are formed by what they do and the impact of this formation on how they lead.[4]

This chapter is an invitation to you, the reader, to explore your present or anticipated role as youth ministry leader. Our invitation is to center your reflection on the role of leader as an agent of courageous hope. So we begin with the function and necessity of reflection followed by sections on attitudes and behaviors that mirror courageous hope. Undergirding this invitation is the premise that courageous hope is an essential core value, an attitude and action for leaders. Indeed, the leadership role cannot be fully realized if courageous hope is missing in the lives and ministry of leaders.[5] This emphasis is also guided by the longing and need of young people for an attitude and behavior from leaders that press for justice, invite mourning of life lost, and affirm

---

4   Youth ministry leader Elizabeth Corrie refers to the shaping process that occurs within youth ministry leaders as "the staff effect." In her discussion of its meaning, she makes the claim that "leaders tend to receive the formation they want for their youth; every teacher knows that we teach best that which we most need to learn." Her discussion of this effect appears in Elizabeth W. Corrie, "Becoming Christ's Hands and Feet in the World: The Vocational Formation of Staff," in *How Youth Ministry Can Change Theological Education—If We Let It*, eds. Kenda Creasy Dean and Christy Lang Hearlson, (Grand Rapids, MI: William B. Eerdmans Publishing Company, 2016), 233–34.

5   This view aligns with the assertion of Capps that "the basic and fundamental role of the clergy is to be providers or agents of hope, and it is terribly difficult, if not impossible, to be an agent of hope if one has oneself lost hope." See Donald Capps, *Agents of Hope: A Pastoral Psychology* (Minneapolis: Fortress, 1995), 3.

remaining life and self in opposition to disaffirmation or feelings of non-being.[6] Youth are seeking from us as leaders the kinds of attitude and behavior that help them move through and beyond anxiety, fear, and, in increasing incidences, the reality of death.[7] They are calling for leaders who have hope and can help them both see the same for their lives and act on it with courage. They also need leaders who consciously decide to assure the provision of pathways that have transforming potential, knowing that the reality facing them may be insufficient settings, finances, and human resources. Nonetheless, "courageous 'called' leadership requires boldness, confidence, fortitude, stamina, fearlessness, and a spirit of adventure and achievement."[8] Yes, this requirement is a demanding one, but it can be no less, given the seriousness and enormity of current-day ministry with young people that must assure their courageous living.

Entering into Self-Reflection

What it means to tend to this kind of leadership role is to draw attention to the importance of ongoing self-reflection in every aspect of ministry. Of course, in doing so, we are aware that time overflows with the fullness of life in general and caring for specific actions that promote vital nurture of youth. Consequently, occasions for reflection may simply slip by us. Yet reflection alone and with others is important. Credence to the need for reflection on courageous hope by leaders appears in Sandra Walston's article "Courage in the Workplace." In it, she points to the tendency of workers to carry more and more responsibilities and spend longer and longer hours in work-related activities. In these situations, workers tend to give primary attention to *what* they do rather than to the self they bring to their work. Walston highlights the real need to "step back and gain perspective," in order for workers to arrive at the pivotal

---

6   Tillich makes the claim that courage is behavior that affirms the self in spite of what has happened or is happening that is disaffirming. See Paul Tillich, *The Courage to Be*, 2nd ed. (1952; New Haven, CT: Yale University Press, 2000), 32, 54–57.

7   Ibid., 36–39.

8   James Henry Harris, *The Courage to Lead: Leadership in the African American Urban Church* (Lanham, MD: Rowman & Littlefield Publishers, Inc., 2002), 40.

starting point of seeing *who* they are in what they do rather than simply *what* they do.[9]

When honest and open reflection happens, as it did with leaders in the centering story, discovery or rediscovery of needed insights about the role of leadership in the lives of young people emerges. Times of reflection are, in fact, revelatory occasions for agents of courageous hope to examine what has been done or must yet be done in ministry with youth that is helpful and hopeful or in need of change. Moreover, hope-bearing ministry with young people that is infused with courage—or *guts*, as one leader in the centering story called it—impels us as leaders to seriously consider who we are and what we bring to it: our motivation, attitudes, capacities, and spirituality. Insofar as we are called to be agents who make possible youths' formation of courageous hope, the need is for our honest reflection on the presence of this same kind of hope in our lives.

Connecting the Self to Ministry Action

Self-reflection is not the end, however. What we discern in that process must connect with how we actually carry out ministry with youth. Consequently, the selves we bring and what we do in youth ministry go hand in hand. We must be mindful of how we relate to youth, how they relate to one another, what our expectations are of their relationship to us, and what this relational element means for our role as agents of courageous hope. Moreover, we must not forget how we relate with other leaders and adults who are part of the lives of young people. This aspect centers on the relational bridges we build and the strategies we use that result in their positive involvement in pathways designed to bring about their courageous hope. One added comment also needs to be made about the value of leaders' self-reflection. This same activity that we as leaders undertake should be offered to youth. It is important that young people are invited to look at—to notice—the need and nature of courageous hope in their lives and what is involved in their acting on pathways of courageous hope.

---

9   Sandra Ford Walston, "Courage in the Workplace," *Chief Learning Officer* (December 2011): 22–25 (23), http://www.clomedia.com/2011/12/08/courage-in-the-workplace/.

COURAGEOUS HOPE AND THE LEADERSHIP ROLE

In this era of ongoing life-and-death challenges and change in the sojourn of Black youth, we want to reemphasize at this point that hope infused with courage, called *courageous hope*, is a necessity for all those who lead and guide them. This quality of hope centers on a person's will or conscious choice to confront a difficult situation, no matter what, alongside a resolute expectation of a positive outcome.[10] We understand courageous hope to be a moral disposition or attitude, held deep within the heart and spirit, that propels an individual to act on behalf of the best interest of another in spite of very real or apparent risks. This nature of courageous hope that we want young people to develop is also needed in the lives of leaders. In what follows, we will expand on this notion.

Based on our own ministries with youth and what we've gleaned from other leaders, courageous hope of youth ministry leaders is a soul-deep response triggered by what may be called *disruptive awareness* of the realities faced by youth and *courageous commitment to act in spite of anxiety*. Moreover, this sojourn of ministry with youth cannot happen without both a deep connection with and calling upon God, the Source of courageous hope. Consequently, we will give some attention to the nature of a practical spirituality of courageous hope.

SOUL-DEEP RESPONSE TO LIFE'S REALITIES

In the introduction to this book, we mentioned youths' "biographies of the soul" that reveal their thoughts, deep emotion, and the predicaments of their everyday lives, where the question for far too many is, "Will I live to see tomorrow?" We have continued to highlight the need for hope-filled pathways and agents of hope that make possible young people's courageous determination to claim life tomorrow and act on that claim. Making this happen requires leaders to give what we call "soul-deep response." Our reference to this kind of response is meant to

---

10   This quotation is found on: http://www.thekingcenter.org/archives/document/mlk-sermon-about-courage-and-cowardice.

call attention to a kind of courageous hope that must be present deep within us as leaders.

In the centering story that opens chapter 1, one youth defines hope with the following phrase: "to believe and wish for something with all your heart, body, and soul." In the opening story in this chapter, a youth ministry leader refers to discovering a love for youth ministry that is felt deep in the soul. Another leader targeted the need for hope within the self's heart, which often requires strength beyond the self's knowing; and still another told of the need to have "guts" to try out multiple directions in ministry. We draw from these comments particular import for leadership centered on courageous hope.

In particular, this emphasis on the heart connects with the definition of courage that draws from the French root word *couer*, meaning "heart." Courage is a matter of the heart. Use of the term *soul* adds another dimension. It is a central concept in the Black community that points to an identifiable quality of Black life that is captured in traits such as "emotion," "spontaneity," and "creative expressiveness."[11] *Soul* also refers to more than these traits. It speaks to Black people's tenacious affirmation of life-giving breath and generating spirit in spite of all that points to or makes for our nonbeing. Moreover, it speaks to a historical sense of peoplehood expressed in family—both blood kin and non-kin across generations—and to a loyalty for one another that evokes within the self the requirement to respond with and on behalf of one another to oppressive circumstances and hostile environments. *Soul* further embraces the notion of interconnectedness found in the Akan proverb, "I am because we are, and since we are, therefore I am."[12]

When applied to ministry with youth, the notion of peoplehood, family, and interconnectedness as "soul" qualities combine to form an

---

11   Description of the metaphor *soul* in the Black community appears in a source on ministry to African American older adults. Although the meanings of *soul* are applied to this ministry, they are, nonetheless, applicable to ministry with youth. The description is found in Anne Streaty Wimberly, "What Honoring Elders Means: A Call to Reenvision the Church and the Soul Community," in *Honoring African American Elders: A Ministry in the Soul Community*, ed. Anne Streaty Wimberly (San Francisco: Jossey-Bass, 1997), 10–12.

12   The proverb is presented in John S. Mbiti, *African Religions and Philosophies* (New York: Doubleday and Company, 1970), 14.

understanding of "we-ness" that includes young people as a valued part and ministry leaders' solidarity with them. This quality is shown in the leader's statement in this chapter's centering story "that caring has to be a community thing where we are all in it together—where we support these kids, where we leaders help each other, and where we help these youth come together and support one another." A critical part of this attitudinal understanding of *we-ness* is the leaders' view of young people as welcomed members of the community and as contributors with valuable and multiple capabilities. It also means that we as leaders see them and us as partners in conversations and story sharing. This community is considered essential in examining the stuff of life and not simply envisioning but deciding how to act on new and preferred life possibilities. In this "soul community" the "soul stories" get told and re-storying happens.[13]

Recall also in the centering story the reference of leaders to young people as "talented, smart, beautiful, and handsome with a lot to give to the . . . world." This soul-oriented perspective of Black people is critical, because it stands in defiant opposition to perplexing, deficient, and demeaning views of Black people in general and Black youth in particular, which are experienced in attitudes, treatment, and media in wider society, and to which earlier references have been made.[14] Such a stance further propels leaders' forthright guidance and support of young people that affirms and sustains their valued identity and hope-bearing sojourn amidst racism and other distressful life circumstances.[15]

The quality of soul that defines the courageous hope of leaders extends to a sense of solidarity or we-ness with young people based on first-hand comprehension of or shared experiences of racial discrimination.

---

13 Edward Wimberly explores the importance of community in the process of re-storying in Edward P. Wimberly, *Claiming God, Reclaiming Dignity: African American Pastoral Care* (Nashville: Abingdon, 2003), 98–103.

14 Barnes and Wimberly make clear that this stance reflects a critical asset-based orientation of the African American community that carries out the role of "village." See Sandra L. Barnes and Anne Streaty Wimberly, *Empowering Black Youth of Promise: Education and Socialization in the Village-minded Black Church* (New York: Routledge, 2016), 17.

15 The importance of the Black collectivity or communal solidarity called *village* in the lives of youth is highlighted in Anne E. Streaty Wimberly, ed., *Keep It Real: Working with Today's Black Youth* (Nashville: Abingdon, 2005), xvii–xix.

For example, in the centering story, a leader made the statement, "I'm hurting for them. Gee, I've been through some of the same stuff." Tommie Shelby pointedly describes this sense of we-ness in terms of

> bearing the weight of the stigma attached to looking and acting "black"; being subject to the vicissitudes of a racially segmented labor market; suffering discrimination on the basis of presumed incompetence; enduring the systematic exclusion from certain neighborhoods, schools, and social circles; recognizing that one is often the object of unjusti-fied hatred, contempt, suspicion, or fear; feeling powerless to change one's inferior racial status; functioning as the pe-rennial scapegoat for social problems and economic crises; and living with the knowledge that one is vulnerable to be-ing victimized, at almost any time, by an antiblack attitude, action, social practice, or institutional policy.[16]

Still another attitudinal view of we-ness is captured in the word *empathy*. In this regard, even if leaders have not had the same experi-ences of young people, there is a sense of feeling or experiencing what the young feel or experience as though it is the leader's own feelings or experiences. The leader senses the hurt (or pleasure) of youth, per-ceives the causes as they do, as though the self of the leader experi-ences it. This empathic presence is understood as a state of being.[17] But it is also referred to as a process in which the leader is sensitive to the world of the youth and their feelings that connect with that world. The leader's role becomes one of checking out the accuracy of the self's feelings with the youth without making judgment.[18]

---

16 Tommie Shelby, "Foundations of Black Solidarity: Collective Identity or Common Op-pression," *Ethics, An International Journal of Social, Political, and Legal Philosophy* (Jan-uary 2002): 231–66 (260), http://www.tommieshelby.com/uploads/4/5/1/0/45107805 /foundations.pdf.

17 This understanding of empathy is set forth by Carl Rogers, "A Theory of Therapy, Per-sonality and Interpersonal Relationships, as Developed in the Client-Centered Frame-work," in *Psychology: A Study of Science*, vol. 3, ed. S. Koch, (New York: McGraw-Hill, 1959), 210–11. The material also appears in Howard Kirschenbaum and Valerie Land Henderson, "A Theory of Therapy, Personality and Interpersonal Relationships," in *The Carl Rogers Reader* (New York: Houghton Mifflin Co., 1989). Kohut points to a similar view in his reference to thinking and feeling oneself into the inner life of another. See Heinz Kohut, *How Does Analysis Cure?* (Chicago: The University of Chicago Press, 1984), 82.

18 Carl Rogers, "Empathic: An Unappreciated Way of Being," *Counseling Psychologist* 5 (1975): 2–10 (4).

Of course, it is one thing for leaders to know about and accede to this understanding of we-ness and to have had personal experiences, past or present, akin to the ones just mentioned, as well as feelings about those experiences. It is another thing to move from this stance to an actual mobilization of ministry pathways that contribute to hope-bearing change in young people and in the situations faced by them. We propose here that leaders have to be moved or prompted to provide these kinds of pathways by what we call *disruptive awareness*.

Disruptive Awareness

In the publication, *The Courage to Teach*, Parker Palmer revisits the story of Rosa Parks, the revered Black matriarch whose courageous refusal to relinquish her seat to a White passenger in Montgomery, Alabama in December 1955, sparked a movement for justice. What Palmer places upfront is the depth and integrity of Rosa Parks' inward spirit that prompted her to stay in her seat. He cites her words, "People always say that I didn't give up my seat because I was tired, but that isn't true. I was not tired, physically, or no more tired than I usually was at the end of a working day. I was not old, although some people have an image of me as being old then. I was forty-two. No, the only tired I was, was tired of giving in."[19] A similar sentiment of being "sick and tired of being sick and tired," propelled Civil Rights activist Fannie Lou Hamer toward response to the hate and violence perpetrated against Black people.[20] We use these examples here to highlight a similar "tiredness" of heart and spirit that the disparaging events in the lives of Black youth must now evoke in us as leaders. We point to this kind of "tiredness" that must stimulate our will—our courage—to be both available to young people and to find the wherewithal to provide

---

19   The quotation of Rosa Parks appears in Parker J. Palmer, *The Courage to Teach: Exploring the Inner Landscape of a Teacher's Life*, Tenth Anniversary Edition (San Francisco: John Wiley & Sons, 2007), 176. The original source of the quotation is Rosa Parks, *Rosa Parks: My Story* (New York: Dial Books, 1992), 116.

20   Fannie Lou Hamer's words appear in Kay Mills, *This Little Light of Mine: The Life of Fannie Lou Hamer* (New York: Penguin Books, 1993), 93.

pathways so desperately needed for their formation and enactment of courageous hope.

Here, however, we reframe *tiredness*, and instead use the term *disruptive awareness* to denote what must move us as leaders to soul-deep, hope-bearing, courageous action with and on behalf of youth. *Disruptive awareness* may also be described as an impassioned response that emerges from leaders' seeing and feeling what is happening in the lives of youth. This response brings us as leaders to the point of saying, "Enough!" Disruptive awareness arises from leaders coming face-to-face with the situation of young people and of having our thinking—our very souls—disturbed enough that we cannot sit still. We cannot refuse to act; we must find ways to address real circumstances. This stance is captured in a leader's words presented in the centering story, "Their lives—what too many of them are going through—is beyond anything I could imagine . . . It scares me! Like, if something isn't done that can help or make a difference, what hope is there for them? For all of us? Doing something? It's on me!" At this point, the role of agent of courageous hope is fully embraced. The leader must then carry through on the tug within the self to act. This brings us to the next point—that real youth ministry requires genuine commitment that often must go forth amidst anxiety.

Courageous Commitment to Act in Spite of Anxiety

Honestly, as leaders, the "scariness" of what we see in the lives of young people that prompts prodigious action can also have the effect of provoking anxiety. Fear bubbles up with the awakened reality of all that happens in the process of choosing wisely, preparing for, and implementing the kinds of pathways of courageous hope for youth we think are needed. Note the statement of a leader in the centering story, "I struggle with how best to help young people." In this case, the leader "developed greater ability along the way," but added, "I need to learn—like how to appropriately choose what to do, when to address something, and when to let it slide."

As leaders, we may be anxious or fearful of meager or nonexistent human and financial supports. Worry may surface about the location, adequacy, or even safety of the ministry setting. In truth, concerns may rise within us regarding who, how many, or whether the young people we are trying to reach will actually show up or that we're doing the right thing to reach them. We submit that all of these concerns of the inner self and outer realities are part of youth ministry, are permissible, and yet require attention. But here, we invite attentiveness to the attitude of courageous commitment that allows us to act in whatever way we can in the throes of anxiety fraught by whatever our circumstance may be. This attitude is constitutive of what it means to be and become—or persist in being—agents of courageous hope in the lives of youth.

In his discussion about leading from within, Parker Palmer sheds more light on the predicament of anxiety by pointing to fear as a "shadow among leaders" that forms in response to "the natural chaos of life."[21] He further describes this shadow as the need of leaders for order and the removal of all complicating or perplexing matters.[22] Even though Palmer is writing for leaders in corporate cultures, he offers an insightful response that is applicable to youth ministry leaders. His rejoinder is that "chaos is the precondition to creativity."[23] In fact, what he seems to suggest is that there is a place for chaos because this quality of the endeavors of leaders opens the way for new and more vital efforts.[24]

As youth ministry leaders and curriculum writers, we, the authors of this resource, can personally attest to the veracity of Palmer's suggestion during the time when we were developing curricula to be used with young people in congregations in the United States and Africa. One of us was working on an identity and vocation curriculum and the other on a conflict resolution curriculum. We were fearful that what we included in the curricula might not address either appropriately or well the concerns or issues occurring in the variety of settings. We tried and tried again to craft and re-craft our writing in order to cover all the bases. The results of hands-on uses of the curricula proved that

21   Parker Palmer, "Leading from Within," in *Spirit at Work: Discovering the Spirituality in Leadership* (San Francisco: Jossey-Bass, 1994), 36.

22   Ibid.

23   Ibid.

24   Ibid., 37.

we had both fallen woefully short of fully addressing every contextual situation. But we received remarkable reports of leaders' creative embellishments and suggestions for curricular changes based on their innovation and young people's responses. Their replies energized us and opened for us new and imaginative possibilities for curricular additions and revisions. In this instance, we learned the meaning of Palmer's assertion that "there is vitality in the play of chaotic energy."[25]

The statements of youth ministry leaders in the centering story also draw attention to the growing edge that is part of ministry challenge: uncertainty and fear. Recall the words of one leader, "I've grown in my understanding that ministry takes you in many different directions. I don't always get it right. But I know that each step prepares me for the next steps and helps me to grow." A colleague mentioned discovering "a new level of patience." This latter reference to patience is particularly important because of the current unpopularity of this strength in our fast-paced, instantaneous needs-fulfillment age. But, to this predicament of current-day living, Donald Capps presses the point that patience is, in essence, choosing hope. The embodiment of patience is the courage not to give up.[26]

None of us is alone in our leadership endeavors. There are others on the journey of being and becoming agents of courageous hope in the lives of young people. Recall the words of a leader in the centering story, "I've learned . . . I have to listen more intently to [young people], to colleagues, and others. I have to get in touch with far more resources than I used to." Parker Palmer also reminds us that "ours is not the only act in town. Not only are there other acts in town, but some of them, from time to time, are even better than ours. . . . We can be empowered by sharing the load with others, and that sometimes we are even free to lay our part of the load down. We learn that co-creation leaves us free to do only what we are called and able to do, and to trust the rest to other hands."[27]

---

25 Ibid.

26 Donald Capps, *Agents of Hope: A Pastoral Psychology* (Minneapolis: Fortress, 1995), 153–54.

27 Palmer, "Leading from Within," 36.

The characteristic of commitment is part of the leader's embrace of hope infused with courage. Commitment in the behavior of the leader is, in fact, a mirror of what is hoped for in young people. As indicated in chapter 2, it is daring to engage in the "fine art of prevailing"[28] or simply persevering through and around troubling facts and unbearable truths.[29] In this way, commitment further reflects a soul response. It is a way of asserting what we described earlier as the tenacious affirmation of life-giving breath and generating spirit in spite of all that points to or makes for nonbeing. The key here is that a hopeful view of life is necessary for us as leaders, and the youth ministry we lead. It should be "grounded in eternal hopefulness," to use Donald Capps's words.[30] But, more than this, the need is to add the quality of courage that further defines the depth of our commitment—our heart and spirit—in all we undertake with and on behalf of youth.

A PRACTICAL SPIRITUALITY OF COURAGEOUS HOPE

There is a spiritual dimension to leaders' embrace and action on hope that is infused with courage. We now turn to reflecting on this dimension that we call a practical spirituality of courageous hope. Practical spirituality is what we believe and how we live it—practice it—in our daily lives and ministry out of response to God's presence, calling, and ongoing activity.[31] Here, we invite reflection on four aspects of a leader's practical spirituality: ministry calling, valuing

---

28 See Dennis Kimbro, *What Keeps Me Standing: Letters from Black Grandmothers on Peace, Hope, and Inspiration* (New York: Harlem Moon, Broadway Books, 2003), 47.

29 Ibid., 84.

30 Donald Capps, *Agents of Hope*, 3.

31 McDermott describes practical spirituality in terms of the expression of the authentic self that responds to and is inspired and filled by God's Holy Spirit. It is the response of self to God who "offers God's self to be noticed and responded to both in the external world that surrounds us and the inner world of our psychological life." This description is found in Brian O. McDermott, S.J., "Partnering with God: Ignatian Spirituality and Leadership in Groups," in Jay A. Conger and Associates, *Spirit at Work: Discovering the Spirituality in Leadership* (San Francisco: Jossey-Bass Publishers, 1994), 134. Bill Grace defines *spirituality* as "the practice of aligning our daily activities with our internal animating force . . . that can make better leaders" in Bill Grace, *The Spirituality of Leadership* (Seattle, WA: Center for Ethical Leadership, 1999), 10.

youth, courageous hope offered by God, and ongoing connectedness with God.

Ministry Calling

A leader in the centering story tells of a reminder of being called in conversations with God. Here, we want to stress the importance of a vocation of hope at the center of the calling to serve young people today. We believe that heeding this call is nonnegotiable. Embracing this calling doesn't negate what we've said in the foregoing section on commitment and anxiety. These qualities, which are part of engagement in ministry, can trigger questions, not simply about the surety of dedication to continue in ministry with youth, but about a sure sense of calling to it. The questions are deeply spiritual ones that demand courage—the will—to stay in conversation with God, seek direction from God, and respond to that direction. The direction that appeared in the words of a leader in the centering story was of being "reminded of my calling . . . God has given me a hope and a future in youth ministry." The leader goes on to say, "I've also become even more convinced that too much is at stake to stop, especially in terms of the youth! I've got to act on my call no matter what! I also know I'm not in it by myself. God and others are on this journey with me." The point we want to make here is the necessity of the leader's clear embrace of a practical spirituality that has its source in God and relies on the direction of God's yes to a vocation of hope with and on behalf of youth or that honestly says, not right now, or no.

Valuing Youth

A focal point of youth ministry leaders' spirituality of courageous hope, which is carried out in a vocation of hope, is the belief and faith in God's for-us-ness that is evidenced through the breath of life given each human being by God and made in God's image. This life given by God signifies God's love for each person as a being with the same worth as all others, and love, therefore, that is not limited to a particular person or group. This view of God by us as leaders results in attitudes and actions revealing a deep valuing of youth. Here we note again the attitudinal disposition of the leader in the centering story that Black youth are God's valued creation with definite positive attributes. This valuing stance is buttressed by the biblical theological view of God's creation found, for example, in the psalmist's words:

> For it was you who formed my inward parts;
> you knit me together in my mother's womb.
> I praise you, for I am fearfully and wonderfully made.
> Wonderful are your works;
> that I know very well. (Ps. 139:13-14)

When this treasuring of the worth of young people is held deep *within* the hearts of leaders, it gets exerted in action, no matter who they are or the circumstance in which they are found. This treasuring is the inner assertion of and outer regard for the value of human life given by God, which is seen in young people and evidenced in relationships with them. A leader in the centering story reflected this relational quality in action terms, "My hope is that walking with them through the storm of their life will help restore lost hope." Relating to young people and serving them is a mark of valuing them that another leader simply says "gives [her] joy." Valuing young people also forms the basis of the declaration that "Black lives matter" in order to make clear that the lives of Black youth are unmistakably and irrevocably included in the avowal that "all lives matter."

Courageous Hope Offered by God

The leaders in the centering story shared an unabashed awareness that their part in being agents of hope counts. As one has said, "It's on me!" But we also get the clear sense that courageous hope comes from God's hope, which "does not disappoint us, because God's love has been poured into our hearts through the Holy Spirit that has been given to us" (Rom. 5:5). In his chapter, "On Christian Hope," Jean-Louis Chretien's exegetical insights on Romans 5:1-5 provide a helpful view of the Source of courageous hope for youth ministry leaders' reflection.[32]

---

32   The exegetical insights are found in Jean-Louis Chretien, "On Christian Hope," in Jean-Louis Chretien, trans. John Marson Dunaway, *Under the Gaze of the Bible* (New York: Fordham University Press, 2015), 69–84.

Chretien makes the point that the hope God offers is provoked within us in the heat of combat with the trials of life. We cannot shelter the hope we claim to have. Hope is more than an idea, and this idea is weakened even more by our protecting it as an idea. Rather, hope becomes active or acted upon and strengthened when it is exposed or attacked. Chretien says that it is "nourished by what attacks it."[33] He also describes it as "hope against hope," that is connected to unfailing faith in the promises of God (Rom. 4:18-20). Building on Chretien's insights, courageous hope in youth ministry demands leaders to relinquish inert—lethargic, passive—hope and activate vigorous, dynamic hope that makes possible our helping youth to press through trouble and peril, buttressed by faith in God's promised presence and activity.[34] Moreover, in this process, we as leaders recognize that active courageous hope is offered by God and becomes active by God's love placed within our hearts by the Holy Spirit (Rom. 5:5).[35]

Agents of Hope as Conduits of Joy

In the preface, we discuss that pathways are those experiences that serve as channels for young people's well-being and environments for joy. Mary Moschella says that joy is "a counter-cultural emotion and a spiritual path that can strengthen our resolve to transform unjust social arrangements."[36] Importantly, it is the case that agents of hope contribute to young people's joy through the guidance they give that raises hope. As with hope, leaders' attention to joy evolves from recognition up front that there is much that inhibits the lives of Black adolescents. But, for these youth, joy becomes an outgrowth of hope they experience as a deep knowing that their lives are given by God; that they are valued, affirmed, nurtured, and have a purpose given by God. Joy becomes a deep manifestation of their surety of God's love that does not come by

---

33 Jean-Louis Chretien, "On Christian Hope," 77.

34 Chretien actually states that hope "is not a hothouse flower that must be kept sheltered in our inward parts. It must go out and serve. Ibid.

35 Ibid., 78.

36 Mary Clark Moschella, Caring for Joy: Narrative, Theology, and Practice (Boston: Brill, 2016), xiii.

simply saying to them, "There's reason to be joyful! So, be joyful!" Rather, the conditions for joy begin to emerge when caring others frankly notice, to use James Weldon Johnson's words in the Negro National Anthem, that "hope unborn had died" in more than a few of the lives of young people.[37] A joy-promoting environment proceeds when caring adults—agents of hope—hear and invite their stories of lament and become the incarnational presence of Christ who sit, walk, share, support, and encourage youth; and engage them in rituals of blessings, communion with God, and service.

As conduits of joy, the role of agents of hope extends to that of praying for and finding ways to take action in the church to assure young people's rightful participation in the public sphere and to ensure their well-being. A public theological stance occurs, for example, when a congregation adopts a school that includes providing mentors for youth, supplies for needy students, and support and celebration for teachers; sponsors forums for youth and parents with police to forge positive relations; and advocates for neighborhood or church-sponsored health clinics to promote physical well-being. These actions press for a hope-bearing future for young people. They reflect a pastoral theological perspective that, to use Mary Clark Moschella's words, shows "hope is as important as the action. Hope might be considered a form of anticipatory joy. Experiences of hope have a future-oriented focus that can support our capacity to imagine new and better worlds."[38] For young people, the aim is for them to arrive at the point of saying, "I get it! I know that God knows me and God has placed God's hands on me!" When agents of hope also become conduits of joy, young people are placed in a position to claim the kind of joy Black forebears sang about to which we referred in the preface, "This joy that I have . . . The world didn't give it to me and the world can't take it away."[39]

---

37   James Weldon Johnson, "Lift Every Voice and Sing," *African American Heritage Hymnal* (Chicago: GIA Publications, Inc.), #540.

38   Moschella, *Caring for Joy*, xiii, 225.

39   This anonymous gospel hymn became prominent through the performances by gospel singer, Shirley Ceasar. Lyrics to the song appear at http://www.elyrics.net/read/s /shirley-ceasar-lyrics/this-joy-lyrics.html.

Ongoing Connectedness with God

We have learned from youth ministry leaders that a practical spirituality of courageous hope includes the spiritual disciplines, most particularly prayer. Leaders in the centering story reveal their reliance on prayer as noted in the statement of a leader in the centering story, "Sometimes, the only answer is to pray." In a survey of youth ministry leaders in 833 Black congregations, 96.9 percent identified ongoing connectedness with God through prayer as an indispensable endeavor in ministry pre-paredness; for gaining support, strength, and courage to persist; and for clarity in ministry practices and renewing hope.[40]

It is also true that, while this connection with God is a conduit to courage and hope, it also requires activated courage. Entering into con-versation with God requires us as leaders to have the courage to be honest with ourselves and God, as shown by leaders' claims in the cen-tering story, that ministry is hard. Honesty exposes imperfections and the need for growth and continued learning. Yet from an ongoing con-nectedness with God comes the reminder from God that, even amidst imperfections, we as leaders can be used as vessels for good.

Actually, it takes the courage of intentionality to maintain connection with God—to create time to choose and persist in spiritual disciplines that may include and extend beyond prayer to scripture study, medita-tion, journaling, fasting, and the liturgical practices of worship including singing and involvement in other artistic endeavors. Frankly, the courage to be personally engaged in the spiritual disciplines is important for an-other reason. Our goal as leaders is to make it possible for young people to see in us the significance of the spiritual disciplines, to desire these practices for themselves, and to become eager to engage them, not only because of our invitation to them, but because they desire them.

---

40 These findings resulted from a research effort entitled "Vision Quest: A Study of Efforts, Challenges, and Needs of Youth Ministry Leaders in Black Congregations," sponsored by Interdenominational Theological Center (ITC), and carried out through a national telephone survey of leaders in youth ministries in 833 Black churches across the de-nominational spectrum. The results became the basis of the book in which the ref-erence to prayer appears: Anne E. Streaty Wimberly, Sandra L. Barnes, and Karma D. Johnson, *Youth Ministry in the Black Church: Centered in Hope* (Valley Forge, PA: Judson, 2013), 98.

[PART 2]

ENTERING PATHWAYS TO COURAGEOUS LIVING

STEPS TOWARD PATHWAYS TO COURAGEOUS LIVING

I hereby command you: Be strong and courageous; do not be frightened or dismayed, for the LORD your God is with you wherever you go.

—Joshua 1:9

God, we have pushed so many of our children into the tumultuous sea of life in small and leaky boats without survival gear and compass. Please forgive us and help our children to forgive us. And help us now to build that transforming movement, to give all of your children the anchors of faith and love, the rudder of hope, the sails of health and education, and the paddles of family and community, to keep them safe and strong when life's sea gets worse. Thank you for your witness.

— Marian Wright Edelman[1]

[A CENTERING STORY]

What an amazing gathering. We were entering the first day of a multi-week summer retreat for youth participants in the Youth Hope-Builders Academy (YHBA). The mix of excitement and nervousness was palpable as we were about to enter into the "releasing ceremony" where parents would release their sons and daughters to the care of trusted

---

1   Marian Wright Edelman, "Lessons from Noah's Ark," The WIP (The Women's International Perspective), posted October 5, 2010, http://thewip.net/2010/10/05/marian-wright-edelman-lessons-from-noahs-ark/.

leaders.[2] We, other leaders, youth, their parents or guardians, and other family members were assembled together in one room. The youth sat with their families. The youth ministry leaders stood in the front of the room facing them. Anne thanked everyone for this time together and then shared gratitude to the families who, in a short while, would release the youth to the leaders' care. She spoke of the African heritage of the "village" from which the extended family emerged in this country as a circle of shared responsibility for the young. With this message, we were being called on this beginning day of the retreat into a ceremony of consciously affirming the expanding family circle. But it was more than simply ushering in a widening family circle. It was a ritual by which the leaders personally acknowledged their responsibility for inviting youth into a time of living and learning together as God's family and as Christians. They spoke of being present with and caring for youth in ways, which these young people would also adopt, to care for one another during the retreat, then serving others after their departure. The leaders told of their role — guides with the purpose of presenting opportunities for young people to affirm themselves as valued people of God, as Black unashamedly, as Christian unapologetically, and more fully as what it means to be Christ's followers in everyday life.

The ceremony followed with the leaders' collective question to the young people's parents or guardians and family members: "Will you entrust us with the responsibility of inviting, being present with, and guiding your youth in the ways we have described?" With the answer of "Yes, we are willing," the youth were asked to come forward and stand with the leaders. Upon the invitation to parents or guardians and other family members to respond, the father of one of the youth rose, and said, "I expect my son to show respect at all times and to come away knowing exactly what you said he should know." A mother's statement was, "This is my daughter's first time away from home. I'm going to miss her maybe more than she misses me. But I know she's in good hands. So I'll be all right, and I know she will too." A final comment from

---

2   The summer retreats, called *summer residential programs*, were planned overnight events where teens and leaders stayed onsite at a retreat center over periods ranging from two to four weeks.

another mom came as she called her son by name and simply said, "You'd better behave yourself!" The leaders then responded in unison, "We receive these young people from you as gifts with gratitude for the trust you have placed in us. We accept our responsibility for them and will carry out our duty to the fullest and best of our ability in the name of Jesus Christ, who called us to this honored role." A closing prayer was followed by concluding moments of family and youth connecting and then the families' departure.

A FOCUS ON READINESS

Up to this point in the book, we have called attention to leaders' reflection on the self's identity and role as agents of courageous hope, as well as the necessity of this role in young people's forming and acting on hope infused with courage amidst the toughness of life. We have invited reflection on courageous hope as soul-deep response to the life realities of young people, evoked principally by *disruptive awareness* of these realities and *courageous commitment to act in spite of anxiety.* We invited further consideration of a practical spirituality of courageous hope that affirms the Source of courageous hope and supports and sustains it in youth ministry efforts. But we have also said that the self-reflection we invited on courageous hope that leads to courageous living happens through the necessary involvement of young people in pathways designed to bring about this outcome. In the introduction, we described pathways to courageous living as programs, opportunities, and experiences that help young people to sort out what is going on in their lives and provide direction from a Christian faith perspective. Pathways are further understood as creative and nurturing endeavors that engage young people in imagining hopeful ways forward in life and that build courage within them to act on these ways. In the next four chapters, we present four pathways to courageous living for Black youth that center on young people's engagement in: story sharing; artistic expression; conflict transformation; and exposure aimed at enrichment, life direction, and contribution to church community and the world. The chapters build on experiences undertaken with young people in the Youth Hope-Builders Academy (YHBA).

Entering these pathways requires guidance on the part of the leaders and their readiness to use *triggers or strategies* that result in youths' active participation in the pathways and the leaders' positive interaction with them. Three strategies are distinguishing marks in the pathways of courageous hope presented in upcoming chapters. They include *invitation, guidance,* and *presence,* energized by youth ministry leaders' valuing youth in the same manner that God values them. As indicated earlier, this valuing is an essential quality of the leader's spirituality of courageous hope. In short, as agents of courageous hope, leaders express this valuing in the three distinctive relational strategies.

INVITATION

The use of invitation in pathways of courageous hope builds on invitational education theory. *Invitation* derives from the word *inviting,* which comes from the Latin word *invitare,* meaning "to offer something beneficial for consideration." But it points further, to "an ethical process involving continuous interactions among and between human beings."[3] The theory privileges pedagogy based on the value of youth, their potential for forming and acting on courageous hope in their own creative ways, and their taking responsibility for their actions. Principally, leaders recognize that young people seek acceptance and affirmation as valued, capable, and responsible human beings, and desire to be treated accordingly. As leaders, we respond to this desire of young people regardless of their background, situational circumstance, gender, sex, or other diversity factor, maintaining a view of them as important, valuable, and capable; and we strive to create a respectful, trusting, and optimistic relational environment that affirms and invites the development of their human potential.[4]

---

3 This definition is found in "Invitational Learning," http://teorije-ucenja.zesoi.fer.hr/doku .php?id=instructional_design:invitational_learning. It is drawn from William Watson Purkey, "An Introduction to Invitational Theory," *Journal of Invitational Theory and Practice* 1, no. 1 (1992): 5–15.

4 Assumptions and fundamental beliefs undergirding invitational theory appear in John J. Schmidt, "Diversity and Invitational Theology and Practice," *Journal of Invitational Theory and Practice* 10 (2004): 27–46 (27–28); Melanie Hunter and Kenneth H. Smith, "Inviting School Success: Invitational Education and the Art Class," *Journal of Invitational Theory and Practice* 13 (2007): 8–15 (9).

Invitation is central to this effort and takes place as we "graciously call upon" youth to open themselves to new ideas and experiences directed toward developing their self-concept, hope-bearing attitudes, and the courage needed to act on them.[5] But their openness to new ideas does not discount the stories of their daily lives. Inviting the personal narratives gives them voice and calls forth leaders' and peers' courage to care on the spot and engender hope in ways that we want them to practice in their daily lives. The point is that youth are active participants in the process of invitation and are free to share their authentic selves and creative expressions.

Because courageous hope is a Christian way of being and acting, invitation also involves youths' immersion in scripture. This immersion is directed toward young people linking their life experiences with particular qualities found in scripture, of hope-bearing, Christian life that demands courage, and imagining and deciding what these qualities mean for their forward sojourn. It includes imagining and deciding how they can deal with identified issues they face personally on a daily basis and what their role is in contributing to hope-bearing family and community life. In this way, invitation-centered pathways of hope become "fundamentally an imagination of hope."[6]

PRESENCE

Black youth yearn for acceptance amidst experiences of feeling unacceptable. Bishop Desmond Tutu says it well: Young people are "desperate to know that someone in this world finds them lovable no matter

---

5   Reference to the act of "graciously calling upon" individuals "to develop physically, intellectually, socially, spiritually, and emotionally" is found in Hunter and Smith, "Inviting School Success," 13.

6   This descriptor of pathways of hope draws from the work of Purkey and Novak to describe education. But its use is intended to draw attention to the need to develop awareness of and responses to the broader social and political context. The reference appears in Gabriela Welch and Ken Smith, "From Theory to Praxis: Applying Invitational Education Beyond Schools," *Journal of Invitational Theory and Practice* 20 (2014): 5–10 (9). The original source of the descriptor is W. Purkey & J. Novak, *Inviting School Success: A Self-Concept Approach to Teaching and Learning*, 3rd ed. (Belmont, CA: Wadsworth, 1996).

what."[7] We recognize the reason for this hunger in the experiences of rejecting attitudes and actions described in previous chapters. Likewise, we see the frustration, anxiety, and anger of youth resulting from these events. The observation of a leader, recounted in chapter 3's centering story, also reminds us that young people deal with what happens to them in differing ways, "[There are] some [who] seem to have it all together and ones who clearly don't." Sometimes, the stories themselves and the way youth handle them are difficult for us as leaders to receive. The impact revealed in young people's low self-esteem, self-hatred, lack of trust, depression, anxiety, withdrawal, and cautious participation in hope-bearing endeavors is difficult to see and to know how to respond. The stories of young people may also remind leaders of troubling events in our own lives that, truthfully, require care for the caregiver for the sake of hope-bearing leadership.

Nonetheless, young people's need for real relief, hope, and courage is paramount. The practice of guidance can promote this response. But this practice also requires the caring, relational presence of leaders who are able to receive young people's stories, questions, and expressed or unexpressed feelings with an attitude of deep respect for the hard truths as well as for the youth who suffer from them. This attitude of presence is exemplified by getting in touch with young people, including their distresses and hostilities, with an attitude of "unprejudiced objectivity."[8] Added to this understanding of presence is the incarnational view of Christian presence that centers on the purpose of sharing the love, hope, and peace of God that was shown in Jesus Christ to others. This presence requires our commitment as agents of courageous hope to reach out to, welcome, and tend to the needs of the young in youth ministry endeavors. It also extends to our willingness to be exposed to and participate in the lives of youth beyond group meetings and the physical bounds of church. At times we may be silent witnesses, as in our supportive attendance at family, community, or school events.

---

7   Desmond Tutu and Mpho Tutu, *Made for Goodness: And Why This Makes All the Difference*, ed. Douglas C. Abrams (London: Rider, 2010), 182.

8   Johnson emphasizes this nature of presence in Paul E. Johnson, *Psychology of Pastoral Care: The Pastoral Ministry in Theory and Practice* (Nashville: Abingdon, 1953), 115.

At other times, we stand with or on the behalf of youth in a situation calling for peace, justice, and reconciliation.[9] Whenever it is expressed, this incarnated nature of presence called "showing God's love, peace, hope, and courage with skin on"[10] creates a pathway for this same quality of God to become incarnated in young people to the extent that they are able to extend it to others.

GUIDANCE

The use of guidance in implementing pathways of hope is not separate from the practice of invitation. Like invitation, guidance happens with the leader's understanding of the importance of youth, the life stories they bring, their need for and right to receive respectful treatment, and the leader's role in creating an interpersonal environment that is conducive to their forming and acting on courageous hope. At the same time, guidance comprises several distinctive characteristics—including active listening, questioning, facilitating critical thinking, and inspiring decision-making—that result in young people's building, acting on, and maintaining hope infused with courage in their lives.

Active listening is regarded as indispensable in the practice of guiding young people. It bears repeating that they have stories to share about happenings in their lives, and both need and want someone to hear them, especially in light of a world where they frequently feel both unseen and unheard. When agents of courageous hope listen, they carry out what Michael Nichols calls "bearing witness to another's experience."[11] This occurs when we, as youth ministry leaders, step out of our own frame of reference into that of young people. In that process, we affirm and validate them. In fact, when we hear them, we take

---

9   A description of incarnational presence is presented by Gabriel Fackre, "Presence, Ministry of," in *Dictionary of Pastoral Care and Counseling*, ed. Rodney J. Hunter (Nashville: Abingdon, 1990), 950–51.

10 Archbishop Tutu uses the phrase "showing God's love with skin on" in Desmond Tutu and Mpho Tutu, *Made for Goodness*, 183.

11 Michael Nichols, *The Lost Art of Listening: Learning to Listen Can Improve Relationships*, 2nd edition (New York: Guilford Press, 2007), 15.

them seriously.[12] Sometimes hearing the narrative disclosures of youth is enough. In this case, their desire is simply cathartic or to get a story of catastrophe or celebration "off their chests." However, in many more instances, a young person is after far more; and in those instances, the need for story sharing is critical because hope and courage may well be in jeopardy, in need of affirmation, or celebrated in community.

Encouraging young people to take the risk of sharing requires an inviting space where listening happens without judgment. In this regard, Nichols reminds us that "a good listener is a witness, not a judge."[13] But this kind of listening is not passive. As a means of helping youth grapple with the stuff of life that tugs at their hope, the leader takes on a *questioning* role. Here, we are not referring to questioning that makes youth feel as though they are in an interrogation room and being challenged to defend themselves. Rather, questioning is to invite thoughts on what they understand is happening in their story, how they feel about it, and more they would like to share. It is, in essence, to invite their internal dialogue or "the whispering self."[14] This invitation to youth's further vulnerability may also open up an opportunity for the leader's collaborative sharing, wherein the leader reveals personal stories akin to those of the youth and adds the element of hope and courage that was called for to either resolve a struggle or celebrate a success.[15] One young person stated it this way, "Leaders must be willing to be vulnerable enough to share. That's what we call 'being real.' Those are the leaders we want to go to and tell our deepest thoughts." Previous chapters have drawn attention to the presence of both pain and promise in the lives of young people. In this regard, it is important to highlight the necessity of leaders' not simply being aware of this reality, but of receiving both types of stories, and helping

---

12   See Michael Nichols, *The Lost Art of Listening*, 15, 18.

13   Ibid., 18.

14   This term is found in Daniel E. Shaw, Betty L. Siegel, and Allyson Schoenlein, "The Basic Tenets of Invitational Theory and Practice: An Invitational Glossary," *Journal of Invitational Theory and Practice*, doi: 19920130:30–42 (35).

15   Descriptions of the role and processes of listening are found in Anne Streaty Wimberly, "Give Me Mentors: Pedagogies of Spiritual Accompaniment," in *How Youth Ministry Can Change Theological Education—If We Let It* eds. Kenda Creasy Dean and Christy Lang Hearlson (Grand Rapids, MI: William B. Eerdmans, 2016), 90–91.

young people to process what is occurring in the stories in order to bring greater depth to their engagement of meanings of hope and courage.

Of course, we will discover in upcoming chapters on pathways to courageous living that oral story sharing is not the sole manner of inviting narrative disclosure. Artistic expressions are creative narratives through which young people communicate realities of their lives in a way not possible in words. As agents of courageous hope, we "bear witness" to these expressions of the heart by allowing our hearts to hear what the ears cannot. Importantly, the expressions of youth, whether in the form of spoken or pictorial narrative, communicate to us concrete experiences, thoughts, feelings, and responses they need. Their expressions reveal their search for guidance. The role of the leader as guide is to *facilitate their critical thinking* about the meaning and impact of life experiences on their emotions and actions. The endeavor of critical thinking also entails what Charles Gerkin calls "interpretive guidance." In our role as agents of courageous hope, we carry out this quality of guidance by facilitating and interpreting youth's inquiry and dialogue around the Christian story contained in scripture and its connection to their lives and the enactment of courageous hope in life.[16] Ultimately, guidance is meant to *inspire decision-making* on the part of youth on what is needed for hopeful living, what risk or courage is needed for hope to come alive for them, and what is needed to assist this direction. This activity extends to providing opportunities to enact courageous hope that hold potential for their becoming agents of hope.

THE PIVOTAL ROLE OF THE LEADER IN PATHWAY PURSUITS

In chapter 3, we emphasized the reflective and active processes that are undertaken in being and becoming agents of courageous hope in the lives of young people. At this point, we turn briefly to specific matters pertinent to the leadership of agents of hope in engaging young people in pathways to courageous living. We refer here to the need for leaders to acknowledge the nature of our leadership role, remember

---

16   Charles V. Gerkin, *An Introduction to Pastoral Care* (Nashville: Abingdon, 1997), 114.

the Source of our role-taking as leaders, connect with parental figures in the lives of youth, and be aware of the particular qualities of each of the pathway's implementation strategies.

Acknowledge the Nature of the Leadership Role

Use of the relational strategies needed to carry out the pathways con-notes leaders' acknowledgment and embrace of responsibility given them by God to fulfill the special and demanding ministry with young people in times of both pain and promise. Acceptance of the role as leader further signifies the recognition of themselves as principal actors in ensuring the kind of "village" care described in this chapter's centering story. In this position, leaders have a central part in the village of helping to make concrete the extended family of God that demonstrates the qualities of care that are central to Christian community. Indeed, the central characteristic of valuing young people, caring for them, and showing the meaning of Christian community by what is done is pivotal, given the cry of Black youth "for a sense of belonging that they can feel and claim with caring others. They search for it in youth ministry."[17]

Be Aware of the Source of Leadership Role-Taking

In the efforts of leaders to provide effective guidance that may feel, at times, beyond their personal abilities, the reminder of the biblical story of Joshua is pertinent. In that story Joshua is called to prepare for and then lead the people through the pathway across the Jordan River to the Promised Land. He is told three times by God to "be strong and courageous" (Josh. 1:6–7, 9), with the added words in verse 9, "do not be frightened or dismayed." But he is also encouraged with the words, "I will be with you; I will not fail you or forsake you" (Josh. 1:5), with added assurance of God's presence "wherever you go" in verse 9. Alongside this message, we call attention once again to the emphasis in chapter 3 on leaders' recognition that courageous hope

---

17 Anne E. Streaty Wimberly, Sandra L. Barnes, and Karma D. Johnson, *Youth Ministry in the Black Church: Centered in Hope* (Valley Forge, PA: Judson Press, 2013), 183.

is offered by God, is buttressed by faith in God's promised presence and activity and by an ongoing connectedness with God through the spiritual disciplines.

Connect with Parental Figures in the Lives of Young People

In the role of leadership in pathway pursuits, it is important for agents of hope to remember that the responsibility we accept is also a promise that necessarily should be made to parents or guardians or other adults raising teens. Effort should be made, not to leave adult caregivers out, but to create opportunities, through meetings like the one in the centering story, visits to homes, or phone calls, to create awareness of the processes in which their young people will be, or are already, involved, and the outcomes. An important closing event to the Youth Hope-Builders Academy retreats took the form of a reincorporation ceremony in which the parents or guardians and other adults raising teens, as well as family members, assemble with their youth and the retreat leaders. As part of this ritual, the youth summarize the retreat experiences in oral and creative artistic presentations. The leaders affirm the young people's presence and accomplishments by giving them awards. A capstone of the ritual occurs in the form of the leaders' unified statement of honor and joy in becoming extended family members to the youth and their familial kin. This statement is followed by their announcement of the time to release the youth back to the families from which they have come. The question is posed to the families, "Are you ready to welcome your youth back with you and hear more stories from them of their retreat experiences, knowing that the prayers of all the leaders will follow you along with our willingness to answer your call to us when needed?" With their answer of "We are ready," the ceremony concludes with a reception.

It is important to add that when parental figures show little discernible interest in the activities of teens or when making contact with them proves difficult, we must persist in endeavors to connect, with the understanding that these family members matter and hold potential for emerging interest. We also recognize that there will be instances when young people's involvement in the endeavors of pathways will function for them as an experience of home away from home. Indeed, the outcome of efforts of agents of hope to create a caring community may well be young people's formation of views, expectations of, and decisions about the nature of family they will press for when they become adults.[18]

Particular Qualities of Pathways Implementation Strategies

Because of the unique direction of each of the four pathways to be presented in the following chapters, the strategies of invitation, presence, and guidance will necessarily include qualities beyond those indicated earlier. In *narrative pathways*, for example, evidence of the special character of each strategy will be seen in the repeated use of all of the strategies in every activity, from the ones where youth share their stories, to those in which they connect with biblical wisdom, link with wisdom from Christian faith exemplars, and discern the self's posture and action on courageous hope in everyday life. The point is that the effectiveness of leaders in engaging youth in each activity in narrative pathways depends on the recurring uses of invitation, presence, and guidance.

We understand the *artistic pathway* as a creative means of young people's truth-telling through story sharing. In the implementation of this pathway, the leaders' invitation to young people to freely enter into creative expression requires openness to the interpretation of those expressions and desire to comprehend what may be unfamiliar and sometimes difficult to understand. Presence becomes the leaders' act of bearing witness to deep feelings. Guidance calls for the leaders' triple actions of observation of what sometimes goes unnoticed, creating spaces of experimentation with creative expression, and engaging youth in examining meanings of their artistic expressions for their lives.

The *conflict-transformation pathway* requires leadership that makes communication, particularly listening, central to invitation; recognition of the human need for acknowledgment, belonging, and participation as vital to leaders' presence; and young people's restoring peace

---

18   The varied roles of parents in ministries with youth appear in Anne E. Streaty Wimberly et al., *Youth Ministry in the Black Church*, 178–92.

with self, reconciling relationship with others through truth sharing, and renewing intimacy with God through lament as the goal of guidance.

The strategy of invitation that is needed in a *pathway of exposure* underscores the necessity of the leaders' provision for and welcoming of youth in opportunities that enable their cultural, spiritual, social, relational, civic, or academic enrichment. Invitation extends to the acceptance and nurture of youth in activities that promote active listening, physical safety, and affirmation. The leaders' presence with youth in a pathway of exposure is marked by roles that are undertaken as mentors who are supportive agents; institutional agents who mediate young people's connection and access to life-enhancing social, relational, and cultural networks; and protective agents who provide trusted advice and direction. The mentoring role is carried over into the strategy of guidance that centers on mentoring conversations that affirm young people's strengths, evoke youths' critical self-appraisal, and promote life-skills orientation, involvement, and development.

CHAPTER 5

SHARING THE SOUL'S STORY: A NARRATIVE PATHWAY

What a priceless possession is the gift of speech! To be able to make sounds, convey specific meanings and deliberate notions, to be able to put at the disposal of another the feelings that nestle within the inner life, to be able to reveal one's self in symbols which make clear and do not betray—this is the miracle and the gift of the spoken word.

— Howard Thurman[1]

*The hearing ear and the seeing eye—
the LORD has made them both.*

— Proverbs 20:12

[A CENTERING STORY]

On an occasion of worship during a retreat for youth, I (Anne) served as primary leader. After the teens and the leaders ended moments of silently placing ourselves in the presence of God, I gave each individual a marker and a rock. I indicated to the group that the rock was a symbol of God[2] and that they were invited to write a word or short phrase to God on the rock that represents a personal story of pain, promise, or other words that are most pertinent to their story. They were then

---

1   Howard Thurman, *The Inward Journey: Meditations on the Spiritual Quest* (Richmond, IN: Friends United Press, 1977), 52.

2   References to God as *Rock* appear in the Old Testament in 1 Sam. 2:2; 2 Sam. 22:3; Pss. 18:31; 28:1; 31:2-3; 89:26; 95:1; Isa. 30:29; 44:8. *Rock* as a symbol of Christ appears in the New Testament in Matt. 16:18; Rom. 9:33; 1 Cor. 10:4.

113

to place the rock on the altar. I continued by saying, "Each of us has a story that is particularly our own; our stories are important because they are part of the lives we live that connects us to God and to others. So, as we worship today, we are invited to share stories before God and one another."

I further commented that some stories are of deeply felt pain because of difficult, hurtful, negative things that have happened or are now happening to us and haven't yet gone away. Some of us have stories of pain that have good endings, which make them stories of promise; or we may have stories of celebration—a joyful event, an amazing accomplishment; or it might be a story of admiration for someone whose life is an inspiration. I made it clear that they may feel free to choose any word or phrase that reflects their particular story.

Upon assurance that all had responded to the invitation, I told of printing the word "possibility" on my rock. I went on to tell of a happening during my adolescence:

> I had considered myself ugly and awkward in the way I walked and talked. Hostile attitudes of some of my peers toward me worsened my feelings about myself to the point that, at times, I simply wished I could disappear. But my best friend and a teacher helped me to go on in spite of overwhelming negatives. When, on occasion, I dissolved into tears, my best friend switched my thoughts toward another picture of myself. The picture was one of beauty and the gift of "smarts" that my friend said had allowed me to get good grades and be on the honor roll. A teacher—I still remember her name, Mrs. Mulvihill, with whom I maintained contact into my adult years until she died—persisted in giving affirming words and encouragement to me to go to college. These two people helped me to see promise in myself and possibility for my life in spite of everything.

I ended by saying that it didn't happen all at once, that it took awhile; but it happened. When I concluded my story, I laid my rock on the altar.

In advance of guiding group members in story sharing, I indicated that story sharing may bring out deep feelings in us. These times open the way for us to offer affirmation, support, and encouragement to others and to enter into conversation with God individually, or with or on behalf of someone else. I then invited group members to say the word that was placed on their rock followed by their story. After several moments of silence, a flurry of teens volunteered to disclose the inscriptions on their rocks, tell their stories, and then place their rocks on the altar. Some of them chose only to place their rocks on the altar.

Inscriptions on the rocks ranged from "pain," "promise," and "praise' to "disappointment," "angry," and "things must get better"; to "denial," "I have hope," "grateful," "happy," "Life is hard," "Where was God?" "Gonna make it," "inspired," and "Jeremiah 29:11" to name a few. The youth told stories of pride in making it this far in school, of attaining various accomplishments, and of past and upcoming events of celebration. Others told of traumatic experiences of family issues and fears of what would happen to them, instances of being bullied, struggles with self-esteem sparked by labeling and taunts of others, instances of being an observer or victim of violence, instances of being racially profiled, name-calling, and of struggling with next steps in life.

One particular story, shared by a young man, stuck out because it was not his personal story, but of a friend, which made him write the word "inspired" on his rock. The friend had been stopped by police a short while after leaving track practice at school. He was told that a robbery had taken place a few blocks from where he was stopped and that he fit the thief's description. When he tried to tell the officers that he had just left track practice and was on his way home and then to church where he was part of a peer-mentoring program, he was shoved to the ground and told, "Shut up nigger, and put your hands behind your back." He was arrested and taken, handcuffed, to the police precinct. He was allowed to call his mom and told her to call the track coach. Both showed up, corroborated his story and timing, and demanded validation that nothing in his backpack remotely connected him to any robbery. He was later released without apology. Together, he and his mom filed a complaint about the officer's treatment.

The young man who told the story was inspired because, in his words: "I probably would have lost my cool, mouthed off after being told, 'Shut up nigger!' and resisted being handcuffed, which could have ended up with my being beaten by the police or even worse." In his words, "Every time I think about what happened, I've wondered, 'How did he get through that situation and keep on going in his life?'" He also said that inspiration came from his friend's insistence on calling the church after it was all over to let them know why he had not shown up to mentor the youth to whom he was assigned and "because they didn't let things slide. They filed a complaint. Of course, no action was taken after it. But they filed it."

During the time of sharing, youth cried and were consoled by their peers. All of the retreat leaders were available to individuals needing care or who wanted to talk. Youth were also told that they could reach out to any of the leaders as need arose.

In the next portion of the story-sharing experience, I called the group's attention to the story found in Psalm 139:1-14 by saying that it was a song written by an Israelite who was in a tough situation. I asked them to close their eyes and picture themselves in the room with the psalmist as they listened to what this writer said. I then conveyed that the writer had been laboring under the weight of a falsehood hurled by someone else. What the lie was and who said it is not known. As the story goes, somebody "bad-mouthed" the psalmist. The writer also felt deeply along with other community members the painful memory of their people who had been deported forcefully from their own community and had lived difficult lives in a foreign territory. But it wasn't just the memory of those days that had passed. Present circumstances were tough. Setbacks and persecution brought unthinkable pain and hardship. They had a story of struggle.[3] I asked, "What questions do you suppose the people raised about who and where God was in their situation? What would you feel, think, or do if someone lied about you?" In moving on, I wanted the group to know that a twist in the story was coming in what the psalmist wrote.

I followed by asking the group to listen to the psalmist's words. After reading the verses, the group was asked to listen only to the words of verses 13 and 14: "For it was you who formed my inward

---

3   See J. Clinton McCann Jr., *Great Psalms of the Bible* (Louisville: Westminster John Knox, 2009), 124.

parts; / you knit me together in my mother's womb. / I praise you, for I am fearfully and wonderfully made. / Wonderful are your works; / that I know very well." Group members were then asked to repeat each verse after me and to insert their own name in the place of the words "my" and "I" in the scripture (e.g., "For it was you who formed [Anne's] inward parts; / you knit [Anne] together in [Anne's] mother's womb. / [Anne] praise[s] you, for [Anne] is fearfully and wonderfully made. / Wonderful are your works;/ that [Anne] know[s] very well"). I then said, "God knows you. God is with you wherever you are. God created you. You are God's masterpiece. God values you. God loves you. And, let me add, 'I love you and so do the leaders who are with you in this room today!'"

Following the scripture reading, I particularly wanted to draw attention to the use of the racial epithet in the young man's story about his friend's incident with the police, because the word *nigger* not only appeared in other stories but had surfaced in prior sessions with the youth. I also drew attention to the remarkable stand taken to file a complaint against the police officers. I invited the group to sit forward in their chairs in preparation for an imaginative journey, as though in a time capsule, to an era in which Black people lived long ago. I indicated that, upon arrival, they were invited to imagine themselves in the presence of noted theologian Howard Thurman, during the time of his youth, at his grandmother's home; and in that setting, they would overhear the message his grandmother gave to him at a time when racial epithets hurled at Black people were common.

After announcing our arrival at the home of Howard Thurman's grandmother, I began with her words: "Howard, there was a minister who held secret meetings with others who were enslaved like him. He gave me a message that I want you to have." Before her next words, I alerted the group that they need to be prepared because her voice is going to get louder and louder and louder. She's going to use what is called in music a crescendo as she talks. I added to the group to take note that, as her tone increases, the intensity will become so forceful that we'll see her grandson start to tremble, and he will noticeably shake as his grandmother's voice rises to a near deafening shout. I said, "Listen to what she is saying." Then I spoke her words, getting louder and louder: "You are not niggers! You are not slaves! You are God's children!"[4]

After allowing for moments of silence, I gave words to return to our present space; and in that reinhabited location, I said: "I have a question for you, to enter into conversation about in a follow-up retreat session, talk with some others, or journal after leaving this time of worship: 'What went on inside you as you heard the message of Howard Thurman's grandmother to him?'" To evoke further thought about views of self and behaviors emerging from these views, I asked the group to add to follow-up conversations or journaling: "What did both the biblical message and grandmother's words say to you about who you are and who those around you are? Remember the story about the young man and his mom who filed a complaint against the police officers. What views do you have of yourself in a tough situation, and how will you act on it?"

Following the questions, the group was guided into a circle where another leader and one youth offered a closing prayer.

RECEIVING AND OFFERING THE GIFT OF SHARED STORY

In the introduction, we said that the voices of young people today are windows to the real stuff of their lives. Moreover, through careful listening, adults become privy to young people's "biographies of the soul" that reveal their thoughts, deep emotions, life predicaments, and profound insights with daring forthrightness.[5] This chapter is about story sharing, story listening, and tending to the stories of youth. It is about engaging them in hearing and reflecting on their own and others' stories as a pathway to their formation of courageous hope; knowing that this hope is about their finding meaning in life by living out the multi-dimensions of human flourishing that we outlined in chapter 1.

---

4   The material is a paraphrase of Thurman's account presented in Howard Thurman, *Jesus and the Disinherited* (Richmond, IN: Friends United Press, 1981), 50.

5   Here, we draw attention again to James Hillman's reference to "the biography of the soul," which speaks of a vital, inner experience of a real feeling self with "inner images and feelings" or "soul-stuff." See James Hillman, *Healing Fiction* (Barrytown, NY: Station Hill Press, 1983), 24–49.

We enter this chapter by asserting that the stories young people share with adults is a gift. What they share allows adults to be connected with them. As a gift, their stories open opportunities to "bridge the space" that all too often exists between them and teens.[6] As such, the shared stories of teens have shaping power in the lives of those who are older than they are. They have the power to deepen and enrich cross-generational relations as well as youth-peer relations as youth hear, learn, affirm, and encourage one another. In the wide-ranging content of stories that surely includes both pain and promise, the gift of story given by young people has the power to nudge listeners toward hope-bearing response and wholeness for all. Their shared stories point toward the creation and re-creation of the currently and immensely needed ethnic-cultural "village" that is reflected in the previously mentioned Akan proverb, "I am because we are, and since we are, therefore I am."

Another pivotal side of the gift of shared story must be placed at the center of a pedagogy of narrative expression. The stories of young people are supposed to mean a lot to grown-ups. And, insofar as they do, adults accept the gift. This is actually the stance that is expected of agents of hope. These leaders must not be simply sincerely appreciative of the stories of youth as a gift; they must actually invite and listen to them. Indeed, receiving the gift of story from young people is the expectation of adults who claim the role of agents of hope. Receiving their stories as a gift confirms a sense of mutuality—of adults being part of their lives and their being part of the lives of those who lead and care for them. This latter action is among the greatest gifts adults can give to youth. When agents of hope invite the stories of youth and are fully present to hear them, what is offered is the gift of awareness of the value of youth. Receiving every aspect of their sharing gives them the gift of acceptance, which brings relational closeness. Welcoming and remaining present with youth as they struggle to convey difficult

---

6   Psychologist Michael Nichols highlights the mutuality that is part of the story-sharing and listening process. For him, "Mutuality is a sense not merely of being understood and valued but of sharing—of being-with another person. Here it isn't just I but we that is important. Our experience is made fuller by sharing it with another person" (Michael P. Nichols, *The Lost Art of Listening: How Learning to Listen Can Improve Relationships* [New York: The Guilford Press, 1995], 33).

realities of their everyday lives presents to them the gift of patience. Guiding them in reflecting on their stories, the stories of others, and God's story offers them the gift of hope-filled imagination. Readiness to facilitate young people's seeing God's promise for their lives and ways to act on it grants them the gift of courageous hope. When agents of hope stand with them and kindle in them both faith and skills that help them re-author their stories in constructive ways, they activate in them the gift of courageous living.[7]

This does not mean that achieving this understanding of the gift of story sharing is easy. In truth, there are barriers that must be surmounted. Not to face them is to accept them and to dismiss the very gift that must be honored. Thus, we will turn to several dominant barriers.

NAMING BARRIERS TO THE GIFT OF STORY SHARING

It bears restating that honoring the gift of story that young people bring to adults, and the honor of receiving that gift, are obligatory if young people are to form and act on courageous hope in their everyday lives. This reciprocal sharing of gifts is also needed, we might add, if we as adults are to claim the same hope and stand with young people in making it concrete. Moreover, honoring the gifts is an indispensable response to the very present and heart-tugging criticisms of young people that adults do not listen to them. The critique of Black youth—about this barrier to sharing that is constructed by nonlistening adults—is all the more serious because this group of young people tends to be both unseen and unheard in a variety of ways. By *unseen*, we refer to the valued selves that are hidden behind preconceived and stereotypical portrayals of them that have persisted in wider society over time and continue in modern media. Hiddenness also results from distant communication on social media. Recall our reference in the introduction to

---

7   In his prelude to the book on the church's necessary engagement in the ministry of listening, Robert Brizee describes listening as a gift. He goes further to describe caring listening as the gift of awareness, listening with acceptance as a gift of healing, patient listening as the gift of freedom, and reverent listening as the gift of grace. Here we build on and go beyond these descriptions. Brizee's typology of the gifts of listening appear in Robert Brizee, *The Gift of Listening* (St. Louis: Chalice Press, 1993), x.

empirical data that corroborates the distorted portrayals of Black adults and youth, particularly Black men and boys, in mass media, which create problematic understandings and attitudes in such a way that these images are taken as reality.[8] We also called attention to the danger in social media of creating a slanted or less-than-authentic self-image by conveying pictures and stories that are not wholly true or real. In short, these instances are examples of how the hiddenness of Black youth occurs.[9]

Our reference to young people's state of being *unheard* derives, in some respect, from an authoritarian view of adult-child relationships, which assumes the child's silence as a sign of respect, even though this view diminishes the child's formation of agency and denudes attention to more fruitful understandings of respect. Associated with this perspective is the case that Black students tend not to raise questions in school because they are dissuaded from asking questions at home. A similar scenario tends to be repeated at church.[10] But the situation in the church may also be attributed to the expectation of conformity that is described in *Not Safe for Church*. The authors, F. Douglas Powe Jr. and Jasmine Smothers, describe the groups who form the post–Civil-Rights generation as those who think critically and hold to their own views and reasoning to come to a particular stance. Their observation is that the church wants "out-of-the-box" persons to fit into a conformity-centered environment.[11] To this degree, the conformity-centered church is a silencing church where young people are concerned. The fact is that young people want, need, and deserve to tell their stories, which

---

8   See Topos Partnership, with consultants Janet Dewart Bell and Elani Delimpaltadaki Janis, "Opportunity for Black Men and Boys: Public Opinion: Media Depictions and Media Consumption," *The Opportunity Agenda* (A Project of Tide Center, October 2011), 14, https://opportunityagenda.org/explore/resources-publications/opportunity-black-men-and-boys-public-opinion.

9   Marilyn Price-Mitchell, "Disadvantages of Social Networking: Surprising Insights from Teens," *Roots of Action.com*, http://www.rootsofaction.com/disadvantages-of-social-networking/.

10   Black Youth Project Staff, "Black Youth Dissuaded from Asking Questions?" *Black Youth Project* (January 31, 2012), 1, http://blackyouthproject.com/black-youth-dissuaded-from-asking-questions/.

11   See F. Douglas Powe Jr. and Jasmine Rose Smothers, *Not Safe for Church: Ten Commandments for Reaching New Generations* (Nashville: Abingdon Press, 2015), 34.

include the broad range of realities of their lives, from issues of family and peer relations to school, employment, racism, sexism, sexuality, health, violence, death, incarceration, and juvenile justice. They desire, need, and deserve to raise questions, engage in serious dialogue on the answers, and decide their roles forward in ways that model courageous hope and courageous living undergirded by a strong faith. When this is not granted, silence prevails. Their hope is in danger of being thwarted. And the church remains stuck in its unyielding conformity mode.

In another respect, young Black males and females experience what Gregory Ellison II calls *"muteness* and *invisibility,"* the effects of which result in severely reduced opportunities to participate in and speak out about life affairs, as well as a deficit in the attention of responsible adults who could attend to the critical needs faced by them. Participation in society, by which people are seen and heard, is stifled by previously mentioned realities, such as truncated schooling and incarceration, as well as resistance to and unavailability of helpful services and supports for disproportionate numbers of Black youth.[12] Ellison further shares his observation that when young people are ignored, they may rightly question their worth, life's meaning, and raise the question, "What if I didn't exist?"[13] In fact, evidence of their answer of no to life is found in the rising suicide rate among Black youth and instances of young people's destructive behaviors toward self and others to which we referred in the introduction.

Here, we raise again another outcome of social media that is found in young people's yearning for the caring listener. While people have come to rely more and more on varieties of available means of distant communication—and seemingly accept it as necessary, advantageous, and simply "the way it is"—there is also an admission of

---

12   Reference to muteness and invisibility, particularly of young Black males, appears in Gregory C. Ellison II, *Cut Dead but Still Alive: Caring for African American Young Men* (Nashville Abingdon Press), xiv (italics original). Also see H. Roy Kaplan, *The Myth of Post-Racial America: Searching for Equality in the Age of Materialism* (Lanham, MD: Rowan & Littlefield Education, 2011), 110–12, 117–27, 141–48, 159–72. Throughout his book, Kaplan draws on empirical data to explore in detail the realities of negative attitudes by White people toward Black people and thoughts about race by both, difficult issues in schools, and inequalities in the workplace and society at large.

13   Ellison II, *Cut Dead but Still Alive*, 24.

something missing. This point is highlighted in the words of an individual appearing in the book *Soul Stories*: "We are craving up-close 'in the flesh' telling and listening partners. We aren't finding them in our families at home. We are missing them in our communities where neighbors don't know, trust, or speak with one another. There is no substitute for up-close relating."[14] We hasten to add, however, that up-close, in-person, oral, story sharing in no way precludes the uses of story sharing in organized chatrooms, blogs, on Skype, or in digital storytelling forms that incorporate sound, still images, and video. These are legitimate assisters and promoters of qualities of appreciation of the self and others not otherwise possible.

THE HOPE-BUILDING POWER OF STORY AND STORY SHARING

The truth is that story and story sharing have hope-building power. Like adults, young people's lives are an evolving narrative, or story, that takes shape from all that happens around them. Their lives have a past, present, and future, which they think about and want to talk about. Opportunities to release the features, pieces, thoughts, and feelings of the self's story have the potential of bringing relief. Story sharing can become a cathartic event; moreover, the mere sharing of a story may bring about an "epiphanic learning moment"[15] or "aha" experience, as in the case of a teen in the Youth Hope-Builders Academy who, in the process of sharing a particular part of a story about a troubled friendship, blurted out: "Oh! I never gave a thought before about what I just said happened at school. I didn't think about her side. Maybe I need to think again about our friendship!" Story sharing has insight-giving power, and with these insights comes new or renewed hope or the embrace of new possibilities. We have

---

14 Anne E. Streaty Wimberly, *Soul Stories: African American Christian Education*, revised edition (Nashville: Abingdon Press, 2005), 2.

15 An "epiphanic learning moment" is an experience of new insight—an epiphany—that is brought into awareness on reflection. It is described in Frances Crawford, Julie Dickinson, and Sabina Leitman, "Mirroring Meaning Making: Narrative Ways of Reflecting on Practice for Action," *Qualitative Social Work* 1, no. 2 (2002): 170–90 (177).

mentioned above some of the topics in stories young people want to share. But it is helpful to be aware of primary attributes of people's lives that give shape to their stories. It is important to invite and listen to the stories of young people that also bear these intersecting attributes, including:

- *Identity in the Shaping World.* This relates to young people's perceptions of themselves as well as the world they live in that has helped to shape their view of self as in the case, for example, of the teen who told the story of being ridiculed because of her size and spoke of hating herself.

- *Social Context of Everyday Engagement.* This refers to young people's involvement in and thoughts and feelings about where they live and work, their school and church, which appeared, in part, in the story of the young male who shared a story of profound disappointment; he applied for and was turned down for a summer job that he desperately needed in order to buy school clothes for the upcoming school year. In another story, a young woman was sent home from school because her afro hairstyle was considered against the dress code, even though a blonde classmate whose hair contained purple streaks was allowed to remain.

- *Interpersonal Relationships.* This includes the nature of and opinions about everyday relationships with peers, parents, relatives, teachers, police, and others, as noted in one young man's recollection of his friend's experience with police, which appears in the chapter's centering story.

- *Situations in the Unfolding Journey of Life.* This refers to positive and negative events in the lives of young people, from celebrations and times of joy to crises and incidents that have caused uneasiness and challenge, as noted in the centering story of chapter 1 about the youth who expressed pride in advancing and doing well in school.

- *Meaning-making and life direction.* This pertains to young people's notions about meaning and purpose in life and how they are now acting on or intend to act on these views, as indicated by a youth who told of already exploring colleges that would best prepare him for law school.[16]

It is important to add that youth bring more than stories containing these attributes. They come with deep questions about happenings in their lives. They bring an inquiring self, which indicates a profound interest in hope-bearing answers to carry them forward in life. It further speaks to their interest in evaluating the stuff of life confronting them, which is all about critical thinking. Note in this chapter's centering story the question raised by the youth who told the story of his friend's encounter with the police: "Every time I think about what happened, I've wondered, 'How did he get through that situation and keep on going in his life?'" We see further significance in questioning by youth in the following interchange between Sarah, the coauthor of this book, and a group of Youth Hope-Builders Academy youth during a summer retreat. A group session called "What's Goin' On?" focused on how group members understand the presence of God in their lives. Sarah asked the group, "What stories would you tell of some things that brought you awareness of God's presence or that made you question who and where God is?" After several moments of silence, one youth stood up and said, "I'll share. There was a time when I was diagnosed with a serious illness. It could have taken my life. I don't remember praying about it, but I knew others were. To make a long story short, I got better; and here I am." In response, one of his peers said, "I know there is a God and that God can answer prayers. I believe that. I can see that in what you just said. But with all the stuff that's going on around us, it's enough [the youth hesitates]—well, it's hard. I've got a question. What are we supposed to think when we pray for God to help and nothing happens?" Another comment came, "You asked us about something that made us question who and where God is? Well, there's a lot of negativity out there. Peer pressure. Being afraid of what other people think. And, like, I wish my dad spent more time with

---

16   A discussion of the power of story and the content of stories appears in Wimberly, *Soul Stories*, 3–4, 27–29.

me. Honestly, sometimes I look in the mirror, and I don't even know who *I* am. What am I supposed to do with all that?"

To the invitation for added thoughts, one teen walked to the front of the room and assumed an authoritative posture before saying:

> It's true a lot of stuff is happening. But you've got to block the negatives from your heart and mind so you can hear God. I know life isn't easy. Do you think mine's easy? It isn't. We have to surround ourselves with positive things, and don't conform to the ways of this world. Sometimes, my own immaturity gets me in trouble. I can't blame God for that. It's up to me to get anger out, forgive, and get rid of fear. Now, about prayer. Prayer helps, even when we don't get the answer we want. Maybe we're not supposed to get *that* answer, or get it at *that* time.

This lively exchange showed young people in search of solutions to challenges in their lives. In their search, they demonstrated critical thinking, which has to do with a quest for understanding, to discover answers to the unknown out of recognition that there is something they do not know, or to quell confusion. A youth's insertion of the words, "What am I supposed to do with all that?" pointed further to the quest for the ideas of others that, in this instance, came from a peer group member.[17] The point we want to make here is that young people have the capacity to engage in the critical reflection on their everyday stories that is pivotal to their stance and action on courageous hope. In fact, Vincent Ruggiero, pioneer in uses of creative and critical thinking in schools, emphasizes that, without the quest for answers, persons are not free. Rather, they are slaves to their circumstances.[18] What we glean from this is the necessity of inviting the questions that emerge from the stories young people live every day, hold within them, and which are silenced if no one asks to hear them.

At the same time, questions posed by leaders help to facilitate young people's further inquiry and evaluation. Categories of questions appear

---

17 Vincent Ruggiero, pioneer in the movement on creativity and critical thinking in education, highlights critical thinking as an engagement in evaluation. It is a search or quest for answers. His discussion on critical thinking is found in his book, *Beyond Feelings: A Guide to Critical Thinking*, 9th ed. (New York: McGraw-Hill Education, 2011), 19–22.

18 Ibid., 22.

in Dennis Palmer Wolf's article, "The Art of Questioning."[19] Of particular relevance in our work with youth are existential questions, which are not included among ones proposed by Wolf; others presented by him include inference questions, interpretation questions, transfer questions, reflective questions, and predictive questions.

- *Existential questions* get at the heart of current-day happenings in the lives of youth. The intent is to open the conversation and welcome recent occurrences or those in progress that young people want or need to share. An existential question may be open-ended, such as: "What's been going on in your life this week?" or simply "What's up?" More directive existential questions focus on particular aspects of young people's lives, such as: "How are things at school? At work?" or "What's the most important thing that's happened to you recently?"

- *Inference questions* seek answers beyond the obvious or are designed for youth to fill in or propose possibilities about missing information. For example, in the centering story, background information on Psalm 139:1-14 was followed with an inference-centered query: "What questions do you suppose the people raised about who and where God was in their situation?"

- *Interpretation questions* call for youth to assess consequences or outcomes. For example, a culminating question raised within the group in the centering story was aimed at interpretation: "What did both the biblical message and grandmother's words say to you about who you are and who those around you are?"

- *Transfer questions* are designed to take youth in new directions, including imagining themselves in someone else's circumstances. In the centering story, the group was asked this kind of question in the inquiry that called them to place themselves in the situation of the people and writer referred to in the biblical text: "What questions do you suppose the people raised about who and where God was

19   Dennis Palmer Wolf, "The Art of Questioning," *Academic Connections* (Winter 1987): 1–7, https://www.exploratorium.edu/sites/default/files/pdfs/ifi/Raising_Questions.pdf.

in their situation? If you were in the writer's shoes, what feelings would you have if you knew of lies being said about you?"

- *Reflective questions* are intended to engender in young people thoughts and feelings about their lives and the impact of information they have received, as well as the stories/experiences of others on their views of self, others, and life. In the centering story, two questions were directed toward reflection. One was connected with the situation of the psalmist: "What would you feel, think, or do if someone lied about you?" The second occurred after Howard Thurman's story: "What went on inside you as you heard the message of Howard Thurman's grandmother?" and the related question, "Remember the story about the young man and his mom who filed a complaint against the police officers. What views do you have of yourself in a tough situation, and how will you act on it?"

- *Questions about hypotheses* invite predictive thinking. The centering story did not include this form of questioning. However, in response to the psalmist's message, a hypothesis-centered question to youth could be raised: "What would you say might happen if you placed the words of Psalm 139:13-14 on Facebook, and said, 'This is a word for today!' Who would respond? What would they say? How would you respond to what they say?"

ENGAGING YOUNG PEOPLE IN THE NARRATIVE ENDEAVOR

Narrative pedagogy is about engaging young people in story sharing that results in assuring their embrace of courageous hope and determining ways to act on it. Whether in a worship setting, youth meeting, youth workshops, retreats, or special, intergenerational story-sharing events, the role of the agent of hope is pivotal in carrying out the engagement processes described in chapter 4. This role centers on extending an *invitation* to young people to enter story-sharing endeavors, being a caring *presence* throughout each activity, and providing *guidance* in the narrative endeavor. To make it happen, we present here specific activities wherein youth share their stories and then reflect on them in light of scripture and past and present Black exemplars in the Christian faith. Reflection is to lead to their expressed thoughts and beliefs about courageous hope in their lives and ways in which they intend to activate it.[20] Four key activities are useful in this endeavor:

- **Activity One.** Share the individual story (or it may be a group's story);

- **Activity Two.** Revisit the story. The intent is to uncover important details, such as key highlights, issues, and concerns, that appear in it as well as feelings and questions that surfaced at the time of the story, during the moment of sharing, and in the recall of details;

- **Activity Three.** Connect with biblical wisdom on one occasion and inspiration from past or present exemplars of the faith on another occasion. Biblical materials and the stories of exemplars are resources for answering the questions raised above. They serve as mirrors for youth to look for thoughts, messages, values, and actions that reflect qualities of courageous hope and courageous living considered worthy to emulate; and

- **Activity Four.** Discern the self's posture and action on courageous hope. Young people evaluate their own embrace of courageous hope and decide ways to act on it.

Each of the activities will be described more fully in the following sections and will include the three engagement strategies of invitation, presence, and guidance outlined in the preceding chapter. We will draw on this chapter's centering story and other materials to illustrate the activities.

ACTIVITY ONE: SHARE THE STORY

Recall that Activity One is about sharing the individual's or a group's or community's story.

---

20 What is presented here builds on the story-linking process that is outlined in Wimberly, *Soul Stories*, 24–35.

Invitation

In the centering story, youth entered into story sharing following an invitation to them to write on a rock a word or short phrase that represented a personal story of pain, promise, or other words most pertinent to their story. Further invitation took place through requesting individuals to share their stories and, upon sharing them, to place their rocks on the altar.

Presence

Young people's entry into the process of sharing stories depends on a caring, nurturing youth agency-centered environment. The stories of youth are welcomed. It is an endeavor where relationships matter and where persons become present to one another. In the centering story, this understanding was conveyed through an emphasis on presence carried out through offering affirmation, support, and encouragement to one another and reference to the availability of and care given by the leaders. Presence was also shown in the leader's shared story. A leader's willingness to self-disclose is a way of showing our own vulnerability as well as indicating that our lives include stories that contain elements, not simply with which young people can identify, but that show the unfolding of life's journey and surely includes both pain and promise. It also points to the value of cross-generational sharing.

Guidance

In story sharing, guidance is about opening the pathway for young people to freely tell what is important in their lives and facilitating their exploration of meanings in what they share and discernment of direction beyond it. At the center of the process of guidance is the agency of youth, which has to do with giving them freedom to share. At times, this may take the form of simply asking the existential question cited earlier, "What's been going on in your life over the past week?" "Today?" This open-ended question provides opportunity for story sharing without parameters.

In the centering story, teens were guided in presenting stories focused on either of the two themes of pain or promise. Within that structural framework, they were free to choose any word or phrase that reflected a particular life experience. This kind of structure for story sharing is used in the guiding process in order to elicit young people's recall of past, present, or anticipated stories, and to get in touch with the range of feelings that accompany life's experiences as well as recalling untold stories. In this way, leaders also gain awareness of the sojourn of youth that may not be readily known.

Guidance carried out by the leader is to bring about young people's as well as the leader's awareness of and attention to the storyteller's feelings, concerns, insights, questions, and direction. In the centering story, the youths' care for one another was appended by the actions of the retreat leaders. These leaders were prepared to reach out to youth who were in deep emotion, to attend to or be present with them empathically, be ready to receive further words from them, and, where called for, to either suggest or receive requests from youth for later discussion.

ACTIVITY TWO: CONNECT WITH BIBLICAL WISDOM

The Bible is vital in ministry with youth. This is particularly the case in what is termed a post-Christian era of waning influence of the Christian faith on increasing numbers of young people and their unfamiliarity with scripture.[21] In his book, *The Next American Spirituality*, George Gallup Jr. describes the current situation of young people whose spirituality is bereft of a biblical foundation they can articulate.[22] Yet we also know that youth are searching for openings through which to envision "more" in life than the troubles of the world they are currently experiencing. We are

---

21 For a description of "post-Christian," see Harold Bloom, *The American Religion: The Emergence of the Post-Christian Nation* (New York: Simon & Schuster, 1992). However, the reference here applies to the documented trend in declining numbers of the US population who describe themselves as Christian, and the rise in those who are religiously unaffiliated, found in Gregory Smith, primary researcher, "America's Changing Religious Landscape," *Pew Research Center Report* (May 12, 2015), www.pew forum.org/2015/05/12/americas-changing-religious-landscape/. See also Charles G. Gallup Jr., *The Next American Spirituality* (Colorado Springs, CO: Victor, Imprint of Cook Communication Ministries, 2002). A discussion on the growing incidence of biblical illiteracy also appears in George Barna, *Transforming Children into Spiritual Champions* (Ventura, CA: Regal Books, 2003), 28–42.

22 Gallup Jr., *The Next American Spirituality*, 7.

aware of young people who are reaching out for the resources of faith and connections that can give answers to gripping questions the experiences of life evoke in them and for a hope-bearing reason and purpose to continue in life. Connecting with scripture opens them to the opportunity to discern wisdom from stories/texts that inform hope-bearing choices and decisions. In the context of worship, presented in the centering story, the activity of connecting with scripture was made with Psalm 139, and included the following uses of invitation, presence, and guiding.

Invitation

Group members were invited to hear the words of Psalm 139:1-14 and to position themselves in the presence of the psalmist. This was done by inviting the group to hear background information on the text followed by the transfer question: "If you were in the writer's shoes, what feelings would you have if you knew of lies being said about you?" An inference query was also raised: "What questions do you suppose the people raised about who and where God was in their situation?"

Presence

Reference to the struggle of the psalmist resulting from past and present trials and tribulations was an intentional means of moving young people outside themselves in a way that they could perceive the suffering of others who had gone before them and identify with the circumstance of others. In this sense, a particular aspect of presence had to do with the formation of empathy in youth that comes from imagining the feelings of those in the Bible story, which readies them for empathic presence today. But more than this, situating the youth in the biblical context by posing the reflective question, "What would you feel, think, or do if someone lied about you?" was designed to prepare them to discover how the writer dealt with adversity.

Guidance

Guidance consisted of directing the group's connection to the words of the text. They were to listen to all of the identified verses followed by

Psalm 139:13-14, which focuses directly on identity. Listening drew attention to the twist in the story. The request to group members to repeat the two verses with the insertion of their name guided them into an experience of self-talk that was to bring about self-confirmation of their God-given value. Self-talk is considered to be an internal monologue all of us engage in—a talking to ourselves—about a particular matter that affirms or changes the way we think about or act on that matter. The language we use is what prompts our thoughts or actions. It has been used as pedagogical and counseling methods to regulate young people's thoughts about themselves and their potential as well as in addressing specific personal and life issues.[23] Use of the self's name that appears in the centering story is in line with cognitive-behavioral strategies described by Kross and his associates, which suggest that using one's own name and non–first-person language is beneficial as a regulatory mechanism in confronting life's challenges.[24]

ACTIVITY THREE: CONNECT WITH WISDOM FROM CHRISTIAN FAITH EXEMPLARS

Engaging twenty-first-century young people in connecting with past exemplars is essential because of the hopeful disposition and actions found in the exemplars' stories. As indicated in chapter 2, connecting young people with past cultural narratives has the power to work with them, for them, and on them in ways that affect what they are able to

---

23 See Ethan Kross, Emma Bruehlman-Senecal, Jiyoung Park, Aleah Burson, Adrienne Dougherty, Holly Shablesh, Ryan Brenner, Jason Moser, and Ozlem Ayduk, "Self-Talk as a Regulatory Mechanism: How You Do It Matters," *Journal of Personality and Social Psychology* 106, no. 2 (2014): 304–24; Anita Jones Thomas, Devin Carey, Kia-Rai Prewitt, Edna Romero, Marysa Richards and Barbara Velsor-Friedrich, "African-American Youth and Exposure to Community Violence: Supporting Change from the Inside," *Journal of Social Action in Counseling and Psychology* 4, no. 1 (Spring 2012): 54–68 (62); Philip C. Kendall, "Cognitive-Behavioral Therapies with Youth: Guiding Theory, Current Status, and Emerging Developments," *Journal of Counseling and Clinical Psychology* 61, no. 2 (1993): 235–47 (239–40, 243).

24 Kross and his associates determined that the way persons think about themselves is informed by the language they use. Moreover, using one's own name and non–first-person language is beneficial. See Kross, et al., "Self-Talk as Regulatory Mechanism," 304, 317, 319, 321–22.

see "as real, as possible, and as worth doing or best avoided."[25] Our interest here is on what the stories of predecessors convey to youth about courageous hope and how to live it. The centering story reflects a way of making this happen.

Invitation

In the centering story, the group was invited to imagine themselves in a previous era of Black history. This invitation was to prepare them to enter an imaginative role as participant observers in a personal story of noted theologian Howard Thurman when he was a youth.

Presence

Engaging young people in an imagined "on location" storied moment functioned as a time of practicing what may be called *historical presence*. This kind of presence connotes a form of "being with" others who have gone before in a way that allows young people to experience a cultural connection and cognitive and emotional awareness of themes occurring in the past that are also currently present. In this view of presence, history is not composed of dissociated events. Rather, the past is still present in important ways and can offer young people mirrors of courageous hope and courageous living to internalize and act upon.[26]

Guidance

In the centering story, the group was guided to imagine overhearing

---

25　Although Zipes focuses primarily on the role and impact of fairy tales on people's lives, his view that stories help to shape people's narrative selves and have the power to influence social practices is applicable to the uses of narrative materials from Black forebears with youth. His views are found in Jack Zipes, "The Cultural Evolution of Storytelling and Fairy Tales: Human Communication and Memetics," http://press.princeton.edu/chapters/s9676.pdf.

26　Views on history as presence are found in Roy Rosenzweig and David Thelen, *The Presence of the Past: Popular Uses of History in American Life* (New York: Columbia University Press, 1998), 7–10; Ethan Kleinberg, "Prologue" and "Presence in Absentia," in *Presence: Philosophy, History, and Cultural Theory for the Twenty-first Century*, eds. Ranjan Ghosh and Ethan Kleinberg (Ithaca, NY: Cornell University Press, 2013).

Howard Thurman's grandmother and observing his response to what he heard her say. This strategy was aimed toward heightening young people's consciousness of the significance of the story's message to them. In her fervent shout, "You are not niggers! You are not slaves! You are God's children!" Grandmother also placed before young people a forceful self-talk message. The language used and how it was conveyed was meant to prompt bold resistance to the negative assertion of identity and to claim resolutely the valued self, given by God. Guidance ended with the reflective questions: "What went on inside you as you heard the message of Howard Thurman's grandmother?"

ACTIVITY FOUR: DISCERN THE SELF'S POSTURE AND ACT ON COURAGEOUS HOPE

As indicated earlier, it is important for young people to critically consider the meanings they assign to courageous hope and what constitutes the behaviors that will translate this hope into courageous living. This evaluative activity necessarily entails reflection on what they have gleaned from engaging scripture and wisdom of exemplars. Several questions raised in the centering story were to evoke thoughts about actions. In connection with the situation of the psalmist, the reflection query calling for thoughts about future action was: "What would you feel, think, or do if someone lied about you?" A second question occurred after the story of Howard Thurman's grandmother: "What views do you have of yourself . . . and how will you act on it?" This centered on what youth claim and articulate as their view of self and what this profession of the self means for how they live their lives. In recalling the story about the young man and his mom who filed a complaint against the police officers, the question was asked: 'What views do you have of yourself in a tough situation, and how will you act on it?"

Because an experience of story-centered worship was the context in which the centering story took place, the questions were not answered. As follow-up, leaders in the Identity and Vocation Exploration sessions engaged the young people in exploring answers to the questions. Discussions around lies evoked further stories from them about personal instances of lies about them and their varied responses from anger and withdrawal to physical altercations. They were reminded of the audacious twist in the psalmist's story, and were asked about kinds of bold twists that could be made in their stories going forward. In an instance when youth entered into an exploration of ways their lives connected with the Lukan account of the parable of the sower (Luke 8:4-15), a teen named Malik Jones responded with an extraordinary poem:

In this game called life

Filled with so much pain and strife,
We must call on the Gardener
To plant the seed in us of everlasting life.
A Cultivator, Cultivator, that's what we need
A Cultivator, Cultivator, to care for the seed,
To help it grow, provide nutrients to keep it strong,
To keep us rooted to Him, where we belong.
As bold believers in Christ, we must embrace our faith as one.
We should give thanks to our God who gave Jesus, the Son.
We must be unashamed and bring more people to the Word,
We must tell all those who still haven't heard.
As faithful servants of Jesus Christ
We should put God's plan before our own
And spread the news to all his people
That He is God and God alone.[27]

We have learned that scripture has the power to both inform and transform the stories of youth. Through Bible stories/texts, young people get in touch with the trials and tribulations of people long ago and God's activity in former times that provide a vision of God's presence and activity today. They are enabled to see themselves, as did people long ago, "in an unfolding story that is undertaken on faith and in faith, and in faithful, hopeful cooperation with God's direction."[28]

The story of the young man and the police officers who used the word *nigger* centers on cross-cultural intergroup and intragroup

---

27   The poetic story was written by Malik Jones when he was fourteen years old and a participant in the Youth Hope-Builders Academy program. Used by permission.

28   Wimberly, *Soul Stories*, 25.

settings where that term is used. Attention was on youth's actions when people who are not Black address them in that fashion. Moreover, they were asked to make a decision regarding their own use of the term with one another. The response regarding actions to take when they are addressed by that term or by any racial epithet was, "It depends." They agreed that they would act by lodging complaints with appropriate authorities in situations involving police, teachers, other public servants, in department stores or malls, or if their houses were spray painted. Such a response was deemed by them to be a justice issue. In other instances, such as slurs yelled from a car or passer-by, they indicated that it's simply better to "keep moving." Regarding their own use of the term with one another, a pre-test and post-test were given so that both young people and leaders could evaluate the decisions youth made. The pre-test showed that nearly half considered their use of the term to be acceptable and indicated that they did not see a conflict between the in-group use of the term and the positive value they placed on themselves. However, when exploring in the sessions the history of the term as a derogatory and devaluing expression and its current use in wider society, which is increasingly accompanied by demeaning and even life-threatening behavior, the post-test showed that nearly all the youth decided not to use the term and indicated their intent to dissuade peers from using it. The few who maintained their intent to continue using the term indicated that their use, in the medium of rap, is to call attention to its abusive intent.

In these responses, we see the potential impact of focused attention on the pathway of story sharing in young people's formation of courageous hope and their action on it.

NARRATIVE PEDAGOGY: SOME ADDED CONSIDERATIONS

Two added critical matters must be considered in carrying out a narrative pedagogy with Black youth: concern for stories of lament and celebration as well as attention to the selection of biblical and exemplar materials.

Lament and Celebration

The tragedies of police killings, death resulting from Black-on-Black violence, and a whole host of other crises that emerge in the stories of
youth demand response to deep grief that often comes out in deep
theodicy questions: "Why is this happening to us?" "Why is life so hard?"
and even, "Who cares?" The answer to the question has erupted in the
Black Lives Matter movement, which is being carried out largely by
Black youth and young adults, even as they are criticized for using that
metaphor in their efforts to confront racial justice issues that have been
ignored. Three young women, Patrisse Cullors, Opal Tometi, and Alicia
Garza, who are identified as progenitors of the movement, tell of being
courageous enough to call it what it was and give it "an aspirational
message: Black lives matter."[29] The movement of "justice seekers" has
become the Black Lives Matter Global Network, a coalition of forty-two
autonomous chapters focused on protesting racism, unlawful killing,
and other inequities, negative attitudes, and treatment.[30] This movement reflects the experience of lamentation among Black people that
has historically "included elements of grief, protest, and hope fully integrated in the personal, familial, and communal rituals of response."[31]
In this regard, we want to emphasize the necessary role of agents of
hope in creating spaces that engage rituals of lamentation beyond
protests, including inviting the stories of suffering young people, being
present with them in their expression of grief, and engaging *with them*
in determining guiding actions. Recognizing their agency is acutely important since young people have clearly articulated their awareness of
church leaders' and adults' absence with them in protest activities. As a
result, they have ideas to bring to the table about the nature of courage
needed to act. They want adults with them; and they want adults to
listen to them.

---

29 The story of these women appears in Collier Meyerson, "The Women behind Black
    Lives Matter," *Glamour* (December 2016), 218–19, 241.

30 Ibid., 241.

31 Peter J. Paris, "When Feeling Like a Motherless Child," in Sally A. Brown and Patrick D.
    Miller, *Lament: Reclaiming Practices in Pulpit, Pew, and Public Square* (Louisville: West-
    minster John Knox Press, 2005), 113.

In efforts to engage youth in addressing life challenges through story sharing, creating times for stories of celebration and responses to them must not be forgotten. Young people have stories of achievement, graduations, promotions, academic improvement, finding a job, being accepted to college or other programs beyond high school, special days in the lives of family members and friends, or other joys of life they want and need to share and for which recognition, affirmation, and praise are warranted.

Selection of Biblical and Exemplar Materials

The book *Soul Stories: African American Christian Education* cites helpful ways of selecting biblical stories/texts for use in story-sharing experiences by first drawing materials used over time in Black churches. This is called a historical-cultural approach to choosing scriptures that exemplify courageous hope and courageous living amidst tough realities of life.[32] These materials would include Old Testament freedom stories, such as: the stories of Moses and the freedom struggle of the Israelites, Joshua, Daniel, David and Goliath, the three Hebrew boys (Shadrach, Meshach, and Abednego), and Jonah.[33] In addition, examples of Bible stories/texts with theodicy themes to assist experiences of lamentation are Psalm 22:1-11; Psalm 13; Jeremiah 8:22.[34]

Bible stories/texts to assist young people in exploring the nature of, and decisions to enact, courageous hope in everyday life include Jeremiah 29:11; Matthew 5:13-16; Luke 12:4-12; Romans 12:1-21; Galatians 6:1-5; Ephesians 4:11-16; Hebrews 10:23, 35-39; 11:1. Other resources are the International Sunday School Lessons (ISSL) Uniform Series that presents a six-year plan for biblical study based on identified themes with planned lessons and culturally relevant materials[35] and books such as Romal Tunes's *God's Graffiti*, which presents stories of Moses, Rahab,

---

32 Wimberly, *Soul Stories*, 109–19.

33 Ibid., 110–11.

34 Ibid., 113.

35 See International Sunday School Lessons (ISSL) Uniform Series at https://standardlesson .com/scope-sequence/.

Jephthah, Ishmael, Hagar, Esther, Joseph, and the boy with the evil spirit found in Mark 9:14–29.

Young people are quick to say that limiting stories of exemplars to repetitive references to a few from the Civil Rights Movement is insufficient. While these leaders must not be forgotten, since their lives concretely demonstrate courageous hope in attitude and action, agents of hope are challenged to present a range of past and present men and women from those referenced in chapter 2 to youth in the Civil Rights Movement and others less mentioned, such as: aviator Bessie Coleman; writer Margaret Abigail Walker; biologist Ernest Everett Just; inventor and entrepreneur Garrett Morgan; astronaut Guion Stewart; Kathleen Johnson, Mary Jackson, and Dorothy Vaughan, whose vital role as "human computers" in the US space program is documented in the movie *Hidden Figures*; and navy veteran and construction worker Wesley Autry who, in 2007, was internationally recognized for saving Cameron Hollopeter, a film student who fell onto a New York subway track after suffering a seizure.

The importance of narrative expression as a pathway to the formation and expression of courageous hope cannot be overestimated. Yet it is but one of several pathways that are worthy of consideration. In the next chapter, we turn to artistic expression as a significant pathway to courageous living.

ARTISTIC EXPRESSION: A CREATIVE PATHWAY

Any form of art is a form of power; it has impact, it can affect change—it can not only move us, it makes us move.

—Ossie Davis[1]

My heart is stirred by a noble theme
as I recite my verses for the king;
my tongue is the pen of a skillful writer.

—Psalms 45:1 (NIV)

[A CENTERING STORY]

In a re-creation of the historic religious/sacred dance of Black enslaved forebears—the *ring shout*—Donna Walker, a Youth Hope-Builders Academy leader and dancer, began drumming on an African drum while leading youth participants and staff in a summer retreat through the woods to the secluded location of the retreat center labyrinth. During our walk through thick underbrush and trees, she gently nudged some with slower pace to move faster and whispered to all of us to move quietly and hurriedly in a manner that was indicative of enslaved forebears in their trek to a clandestine place of worship. Upon arrival at the labyrinth, we anxiously awaited Donna's instructions after being told that we would carry out a contemporary reenactment of the ring

---

1   The quotation by Ossie Davis—noted Black stage, screen, and television actor, director, writer, and playwright—appears in Joslyn Pine, ed., *Book of African-American Quotations* (Mineola, NY: Dover Publications, Inc., 2011), 43.

shout. She described the ring shout as a ritualized dance that originated in Africa. But, during their enslavement, Black people "stole away" quietly to secret locations—so as not to disturb the slave master—in order to engage in worship and group-affirming activity. In their chosen space, they engaged in expressive movements of clapping, dancing, and singing songs that often carried biblical messages and moved people to shout. They moved in a counterclockwise circular pattern that resulted in their entry into a state of ecstatic worship.

As Donna continued to drum, she invited us to enter the ring shout. She beckoned to us to form a circle and move our feet and bodies rhythmically in a counterclockwise direction. She invited us to add clapping, then rhythmic sounds with our mouths. As the experience unfolded, we were led in religious songs called *spirituals*, some of which everyone knew. Others were sung to the youth by the adults while everyone continued the counterclockwise dance. We were encouraged to move our bodies freely and improvise the motion of our feet. Youth and leaders alike laughed with delight as our actions became part of a communal experience. During moments when we were asked to stand silently in the circle, we listened intently to stories of enslaved forebears who would steal away to brush arbors in order to worship outside the gaze of the slave master. Following the storytelling, individuals were invited to create rhythms on drums given to them as they were summoned to the center of the circle. They were then asked to share heartfelt stories of struggle and triumph. Donna invited the group of youth to name artistic ways Black youth express themselves amidst contemporary struggles. They named gospel songs, hip-hop lyrics, liturgical dance, and break dancing as examples. She also asked them to consider the effect of these expressions on them in order to get in touch with what the ring shout likely prompted in forebears. The youths' responses included, for example, "getting in touch with God," "community togetherness," "being encouraged," and "getting inspired to go on in life."

The group's rhythmic movements in the reenacted ring shout, shared memories of Black history and contemporary stories, and thoughts about artistic expression during trying times transformed the space in which we gathered. Our time as a group evolved from what began as a reenactment performance space to a space of courageous hope formation, where the youth—and adults, for that matter—could affirm our sense of self in the world. The time together closed with shared singing, hand-holding, and turning on battery-lit candles as a symbol of bringing light into life's dark places. Upon conclusion, Donna invited youth to remain longer at the labyrinth if they chose and to walk silently back to our common meeting room. The invitation was for youth to become aware of the presence of God and the Holy Spirit and to listen for the voice of God.

As the group slowly gathered back in the common meeting room, we noticed a liveliness that we had not seen before. One young man who returned to the room looked as though he had been crying; yet his face bore a sense of sheer joy and excitement. We could tell he was eager to share about his experience. To our invitation for youth to share from where they sat in a circle, this youth, in particular, talked about how the experience of the ring shout and personal reflection enabled him to receive a clear pastoral call to ministry. He is currently a pastor as well as a regional music coordinator because of this formative experience. Other young people shared about the ways God spoke to them. One by one youth told of their encounters with God. Many talked about the sense of affirmation given to them during this time about their identity as valued beings.

ARTISTIC EXPRESSION FROM PAST TO PRESENT

Art is an expression of the human spirit. The leader of the ring-shout experience functioned as an agent of courageous hope who drew on an historic arts medium to engage young people in their expression of the human spirit.[2] This activity was a form of creative expression and

---

2   Observed first in the mid-1800s among enslaved forebears in coastal South Carolina, Georgia, and Florida, the ring shout is considered the oldest performance practice among Black people on the North American continent. A thorough description of its origin, description, and degree and place of use appear in Art Rosenbaum, *Shout Because You're Free: The African-American Ring Shout Tradition in Coastal Georgia* (Athens, GA: The University of Georgia Press, paperback ed. 2013), 1–52. Specific references to the ring dance appear in Katrina Dyonne Thompson, *Ring Shout, Wheel About: The Racial Politics of Music and Dance in North American Slavery* (Chicago: University of Illinois Press, 2014), 7, 114–16.

worship that, in reality, invited youth into an experience of embodying the kind of courageous hope forebears developed through artistic
expression. The historic ring shout represented one form of artistic liturgical expression that demonstrated and promoted enslaved Black
people's personal and communal agency and connected them with
God, whom they knew created and valued them. Despite dehuman-
ization, they dared to enact hope. Their "stealing away" to a culturally
defined place and carving out a space where they could affirm their
self-hood and faith in God energized their "capacity to move ahead *in
spite of despair.*"[3]

Their dual involvement in song and dance represented a unique
form of creative truth-telling. As they moved, danced, and sang, their
bodies told the truth of their existence. The body became a confes-
sional text of the self's value.[4] Black people were connected to a co-
herent cultural community, or world, and a God that transcended their
current situation. As text, their bodies communicated resistance to sub-
jugation through their movements. The more they moved and sang,
the more ecstatic their expression of worship. Even when missionaries
sought to stifle these African-derived dances, enslaved peoples would
continue to dance.[5] The ring shout practiced in the brush arbors, and
later within Christian churches, ultimately demonstrated a form of resistance. It allowed Black people to not only resist hopelessness, oppression, and despair but also literally transform the space. As Renee
Harrison notes,

> Ring shouting transformed oppositional spaces into momen-
> tary spaces of freedom, providing women a sense of au-
> tonomy, relief and ownership of their bodies. Ring shouting
> connected them to the spirit world, their roots, and to one

---

3   Rollo May, *The Courage to Create* (New York: W.W. Norton, 1975), 12–13 (italics original).

4   Building on the essays of Poulsen, we recognize that the body of enslaved Black
    people as *text* tells, not simply of its biological reality, but of itself as a mode of po-
    litical expression and of crucial awareness of human agency with the wherewithal
    to continue on life's sojourn. Poulsen's essays that provide thoughts on the body as
    biological, political, and crucial text are found in Richard C. Poulsen, *The Body as Text:
    In a Perpetual Age of Non-Reason* (New York: Peter Lang, 1996), 1–23.

5   Renee K. Harrison, *Enslaved Women and the Art of Resistance in Antebellum America*
    (New York: Palgrave Macmillan, 2009), 203.

> another. It allowed them to enter a shared alternate space,
> a space where they could shake off the pain and become
> inspired to move toward a permanent life of freedom.[6]

In other words, these ritualized expressions, described as liturgical theology[7] by some and rituals of resistance[8] by others, invited enslaved Black people to transform their bondage-infested space into a space that they could inhabit, if even for a moment. Artistic liturgical expressions like the ring shout transformed the space by promoting a sense of community and continuity between and among slaves. Dance offered a sacred gathering space, which allowed slaves to connect with God and their ancestral spirits. It often functioned "as a space for reawakening and re-centering; a space for gathering oneself and letting go."[9] The ecstatic movements communicated a wide spectrum of emotions, from joy to hope and sorrow imbued with courage. They invoked a spirit of resilience that enabled slaves to value their identity as cherished creations. This spirit of resilience manifested in slave revolts, in courageous hope, and in self-affirmation.

Art remains a powerful tool of activating hope within the Black community. The leader in this chapter's centering story relied on this rich heritage of expression and resistance to invite, be present with, and guide youth as they experienced their own bodies in motion. The involvement of youth in the ring-shout experience illustrated the important point in chapter 2, that artistic practices from the past provide memes or mirrors of wise perspectives on forming hope infused with courage for use at such a time as this, when trouble seems all around. Whether through historic experiences, such as the ring shout, or other artistic expressions, the arts are generative means of forming courageous hope in youth. When youth create, they affirm their *Imago Dei*. They embrace their God-given identity as creators. Moreover, the push toward their positive self-definition within the context of art pedagogy falls within the

---

6   Ibid., 204–5.

7   Traci C. West, *Disruptive Christian Ethics: When Racism and Women's Lives Matter* (Louisville, KY: Westminster John Knox Press, 2006), 112–40.

8   Harrison, *Enslaved Women and the Art of Resistance in Antebellum America*, 196–205.

9   Ibid., 203.

evocative method, whereby agents of hope stir up within young people an intrinsic valuing of self through evoking ways of thinking of the self positively, viewing the self through the eyes of God, and working to build others up within community.[10]

THE POWER OF ART PEDAGOGY IN THE LIVES OF BLACK YOUTH

The arts are important in the lives of Black youth. As in the past, the arts are highly expressive and creative mediums through which Black people across the ages/stages have continued to be powerful forces for cultural consumption and enrichment, locally and globally. But here, we focus on the spirit of resilience and courageous hope that can become manifest in intentionally planned, creative, arts-infused endeavors of young people that serve as pathways to courageous hope. By artistic endeavors, we are referring to a variety of artistic modes of expression ranging from visual arts to dance and song. These endeavors can be pathways for bringing forth young people's bold embrace and expression of hope with their voices, bodies, and other creative means that spur courageous action in everyday life.

For teens in the Youth Hope-Builders Academy and in other youth contexts in which we've been involved, it was not uncommon to find youth engaged particularly in dance. Often, *krumping* was the art form of choice. With great skill and flexibility, youth would take turns krumping in competition with one another. *Krumping* is a free flow, interactive, participatory dance that requires ample movement and expression.[11] Scholars identify this "complex expressive matrix of joy, disappointment, ownership, ecstasy, and danger" embedded in the dance as kinetic effect, whereby the space of dance connotes affective engagement

---

10 Anne Streaty Wimberly, *Nurturing Faith & Hope: Black Worship as a Model for Christian Education* (Cleveland: Pilgrim Press, 2004), 64–65.

11 Krump dancing, also known as clowning, emerged in South Los Angeles. The performance includes both the dancers and the audience. For example, in response to the dance moves, the audience cheers the dancers on. Dancers solicit participation from the audience to join the performance as a dancer. As new dancers join the movement, the dance intensifies.

between the body and community.[12] Dancers would battle or have dance-off competitions against one another. This unsolicited, somewhat competitive form of artistic expression often emerged spontaneously. To outsiders, the competitive nature of the art may seem too aggressive. For engaged Black youth, however, the art gives way to a freedom of body and voice not often found in other spaces. Scholars argue that krumping is a response to feelings of dispossession, violence, and alienation within the city.[13] Youth's unsolicited desire to move and engage demonstrates the need Black youth have to experience creative well-being that contributes to a revitalized self.

Both the historical-liturgical expression of the ring shout and the current, unstructured, contemporary krumping emphasize the way creative artistic expression opens the door for deeper connection and understanding among adolescents and communities of color. The interactive nature of krumping calls for improvisation and community participation that may also extend to intergenerational involvement. For example, we have been in contexts where youth have challenged adult staff members of varying ages and stages to participate in krumping. Staff members typically responded creatively. Some mimicked the krumping dance. Others danced with more familiar "old school" movements. All participated in the communal encounter that centered on creative artistic expression.

In what follows, we will give specific direction for the use of art pedagogy in implementing pathways for forming and maintaining courageous hope in youth. In doing so, we will build upon art endeavors used in the Youth Hope-Builders Academy (YHBA) as an example of artistic expression as a pathway to courageous hope in youth. YHBA took something that is germane to many youth—art—and integrated it as a major component, called Arts Express, in the summer programs or "retreats" that lasted for two to four weeks. Arts Express was a structured activity in the program that provided space for leaders to engage

---

12   Stephanie L. Batiste, "Affect-ive Moves: Space, Violence, and the Body in Rize's Krump Dancing," *The Oxford Handbook of Dance and the Popular Screen*, ed. Melissa Blanco Borelli (New York: Oxford University Press, 2014), 2.

13   Ibid., 2–5.

youth in a range of artistic modes of expression. Art, as both a *performative activity* and *observational activity*, became a key feature of creating a courage-infused, hope-forming pathway for youth in YHBA because of its capacity to enable creative truth-telling, confident expressions of resistance, and imaginative possibilities. Ultimately, the artistic process of creating and sharing art makes possible the kind of joy youth can experience in spite of the adversity they may encounter. As pedagogy, leaders who are the agents of hope use art as a teaching and learning endeavor through which courageous hope becomes evident in young people's resilient behaviors, initially described in chapter 1, and repeated as the expected outcome of narrative pedagogical pathways presented in the previous chapter.

Art Pedagogy Helps Young People Claim Their Voices Through Creative Truth-Telling

The activity of truth-telling about the very lives they live and courageous ways of being and acting in the world is required for young people to form and act on courageous hope that becomes evident in the aforementioned qualities. Yet, often, Black youth are relegated to silence. For this reason, art becomes a pivotal, self-revealing endeavor. To express one's self honestly, fiercely, and some would even say prophetically, is the gift of artists. Dancing, singing, miming, drawing, and acting reveal truths of self and life in creative ways that are impossible in spoken language and that counter destructive violence toward self and others. Art pedagogy practices that engage youth in these artistic gifts create a space for them to participate in creative truth-telling.

Specifically, artistic expression through which youth are the presenters is a creative truth-telling endeavor. It is rightly called a *performative activity* of creative truth-telling whereby youth reveal their personal, local, and community realities in innovative, communicative modes found in a variety of art forms. Inherent in creative truth-telling is the ability to release personal feelings, identify those contexts and events that both prevent and reveal joy and flourishing, and ultimately participate in a community's recognition of experiences. When youth create a dramatization of their thoughts and feelings about police shootings; or read and dramatize the biblical story of the apostle Paul and the shipwreck in Acts 27, and then share stories of their own "shipwrecks"; or when they sing and apply to their lives the words to the gospel song that begins: "You don't know my story / all the things that I've been through," and end with the words, "because my worship is for real"[14]; they engage in truth-telling. Truth-telling surfaces again as they sing, create a mime, or dance to words of the R&B song "Lovin' Me," which tells of the movement of a Black person's view of self from a place of feeling ashamed because of the views of others to a place of self-worth revealed in the words: "I found me a place, / and it don't even matter / what nobody else thinks."[15]

Art pedagogy is a critical resource, especially for youth in contexts of adversity, because it provides a cathartic space where they can release their pain and express joy. We are aware that their ways of expressing truth as they see it are not always pleasing to adults. Adults may reject the outright expression of rage that comes through various art forms, such as rapping; but when listening closely, they will hear that some expressions of art are actually a truthful commentary on life's difficult realities and a cry for help and change. These expressions also create opportunity for open and honest conversation about meanings of the commentary and ways the truth they share reflects a wider communal truth. Of utmost importance is the point that art provides a space for youth to vent; and they must be both invited and allowed to do so.

The image of a *vent* is one of a small opening on the wall, releasing air or heat into the room. A closed vent fails to provide the type of release necessary to shift or bring balance to the atmosphere. Much

---

14   Bishop Larry Trotter, "My Worship Is for Real," (Tyscot, 2001).

15   The lyrics go on to highlight negative views others have of Black bodily image (curves); media choices of who is considered a winner and loser, which results in one's relinquishing of personal power, and being dismissed because of the dark color of one's skin. But the refrain continually returns to finding a place of loving the self. Belle Johnson, G'Harah Lenvardo V. Degeddingseze, and Nichole Lynette Gilbert, "Lovin' Me" (Universal Music Publishing Group). The song was recorded by Faith Evans as the theme for the television series *R&B Divas* and appears on her album, *R&B Divas* (Prolific Music and E1 Music, October 2, 2012). Richelle White cites this song as "an anthem of empowerment that addresses the issues of body image and self-esteem among Black women." She also presents questions for use in theological reflection with youth (Richelle B. White, *Repertory with Roots: Black Youth, Black History, Black Culture, Black Music, and the Bible* [Xulon Press www.xulonpress.com, 2016], 50).

like the structural, architectural use of a vent, venting that takes place in art-centered, creative truth-telling often becomes an opening in a person's soul. This opening enables the individual to release emotions and passions that would remain pent-up or acted out counterproductively if not otherwise shared. Art becomes the "vent" or cathartic release of the "biography of the soul" that counters discouragement, sadness, rage, and thwarted hope by allowing individuals to purge or cleanse the soul from negative emotions. Art as *vent* makes possible youths' negative and positive release, their sharing of both pain and joy. Or, as Erwin Raphael McManus says, art "touches both our pain and our hope."[16] In this regard, art creates space for adolescents to release their emotions. This release of emotions found in creative truth-telling recognizes that how they feel is not wrong; rather, what they feel is human.

The importance of art as a space for young people to name truths about their lived reality and the injustices within it cannot be overemphasized. Artistic expression opens a space for them to vent about those experiences and publically share their emotions with others. The earlier reference to dramatizing thoughts and feelings about police shootings is an example. Another case in point is found in this chapter's centering story, which actually continued in follow-up sessions for the teens to vent about their own current-day experiences. We found that, most assuredly, more is called for than simply young people's release of emotions. In the particular instance with youth in the centering story, our attention was on moving the teens toward describing every detail of a specific event that had brought anguish, sadness, a sense of devaluation, or anger; then inviting them to dramatize, create bodily movements or dance, rap or other artistic means to convey these details. We reminded them that our forebears had created the ring shout as means of telling about and, in fact, working through the reality of their horrendous circumstances; but we indicated to the youth that they were free to create their own way into truth-telling. In one case, a teen who had been bullied in school entered into movements of withdrawing

---

16   Erwin Raphael McManus, *The Artisan Soul: Crafting Your Life into a Work of Art* (New York: HarperOne, 2014), 171.

and shielding herself followed by raising her arms as though to ask "Why?" Then, with arms outstretched, she pointed around the room in a manner she said later was her signaling to her peers at school her awareness that they did not help or come to her defense. She ended her dramatization by recoiling on the floor as a symbolic portrayal of her acquiescence.

Our point here is that art also exists as a vent for youth to artistically name the complexities and challenges that contribute to their emotions. This naming may include, but not necessarily be limited to, young people artistically describing fearful and troubling circumstances, their constructive and destructive responses to situations, and what they fear might yet happen to them that may either heighten fear or bring positive closure. Whether venting negative or positive emotions or naming difficult or happy circumstances, art provides spaces for self-affirmation, acknowledgment, visibility and support, recognition, and encouragement from peers and leaders.

In the case of the teen who had been bullied, the group surrounded her with care, affirmation of her giftedness, and their joy in her presence. In addition, the teen who had been bullied later said that her dramatization gave her courage for the future to tell about her experience to a school teacher whom she trusted. Her shared story also resulted in group members' acceptance of their role as more than bystanders. So we also want to add here that, when young people enter into the act of naming through artistic expression, they actually engage in an act of resistance against adversity. Their naming demonstrates their desire for and motivation toward flourishing. Augusto Boal, Brazilian educator known for his work with Theater of the Oppressed, says that "theater is a weapon, and it is the people who should wield it."[17] In this sense, art becomes a powerful tool to rehearse courageous ways of being and acting in the real world. In art, youth rehearse with daring their ability to name their reality through body, images, and words, even in, or in spite of, an unaccepting or difficult world or public.

---

17   Augusto Boal, *Theater of the Oppressed* (New York: Theater Communications Group, 1985), viii.

It bears repeating that what adolescents openly share in their creative expression is not always easily accepted by adults. The "in-ya-face" content of the local story, revealed through visual representations, vivid metaphors, rhythm, and dance, sometimes comes with such force that leaders in the faith community seek to squash the truth inherent in its message. The sentiment is that if youth want to communicate their personal feelings, they must do so with a degree of respectability. Art devoid of this respectability gets easily dismissed as ghetto, violent, or useless. Yet these stories hold great value. Art documents the human experience of individuals and communities. It narrates their emotions, triumphs, struggles, and joys. In this sense, art is a form of narrative that preserves the sacred stories of youth. For the art that many youth embrace in contexts of violence and poverty, these sacred stories are not just one's own story; they are often the stories of local communities. Such a story captures the struggle to hope that youth and their parents face on a daily basis. It captures violence navigated, the poverty endured, the stereotypes combated. It captures familial support, friendship, and solidarity. It captures both hope and thwarted hope experienced in the human village. Further, these candid expressions, made visible through art, counter the negative hypervisibility that reveals and labels youth as violent and fearful.

Overall, the "name-vent-publically share" triad that takes place in creative truth-telling serves as a way for young people to articulate their personal or neighborhood stories. Nevertheless, we want to make clear that creative truth-telling is not just about revealing realities in order to denounce individual and societal transgressions called *sin* (systemic or personal). It is also about announcing God's grace, hope, and power in the midst of brokenness. It is arriving at a hopeful end of the story, as noted in the earlier-mentioned lyrics of "My Worship Is for Real," which begins with the words, "You don't know my story," that infer struggle, but ends with the testimony of the realness of worship resulting from God's hope-giving activity. The very announcing of possibility amidst violence is a counterintuitive act of resistance that urges the faith community to shift focus from what is not to what can be so that this shift becomes evident in youth. Creative truth-telling within *performative artistic activity* has great potential to move youth toward envisioning possibilities of human joy and flourishing and evoking within them questions around their lived experience. But it also has the power to bring about not simply their courageous hope but their readiness to act on it, thereby making possible a future reality of courageous living.

Art Pedagogy Helps Young People Reclaim Agentic Space

Art pedagogy serves as a pathway to young people's courageous hope by opening spaces that move them from passivity to action. It allows youth to get in touch with the world as it is and invites them to shift how they think about and will act in the future. Artistic expression is embodied agentic activity in that it is youth-involved and youth-created activity. Moreover, it has the power to bring about their inner resolve and physical and mental wherewithal to resist the world as is. While there is an awareness of danger in the world as is, embodied acts of resistance can occur in art that help youth to reflect on, visualize, and act on hope-bearing views of the world. Through artistic expression, youth resist the temptation to simply accept things as they are, to assume that nothing can be done, or to allow anger and frustration to turn into destructive behavior—turned inward toward self or outward toward others.

Thus far, we have given primary attention to the significance of art as a *performative activity* undertaken and carried out by youth. In performative activity, they are the art presenters. Here, we move to art as *observational activity* and the interplay between it and performative activity that contributes to the agency of youth. Listening to music for the images found in it, observing dance, and seeing visual art are examples of art as observational activity. The emotional energy and sense of urgency provoked by these forms of art activity are meant to move young people from passivity to action in ways similar to performative activity. This activity creates, as described in chapter 3, a disruptive awareness that challenges the status quo while subsequently building space for young people to gather around the object of interest. When the musician/mentor in the Youth Hope-Builders Academy presented the song, "My Worship Is for Real," the initial invitation was for the group to listen to it on a CD, and while listening, they were asked to read silently the words from the sheets given to them. This was followed by the questions posed by the musician/mentor: "What story(ies) do you suppose are not known?" "What are your untold stories?" "Where does this song end?" "Why?" After a passionate discussion around the questions, the musician/mentor invited the group to read aloud together the words of the song as though the words were their own. The group then sang the song. As a final guiding question, the musician/mentor gave a personal testimony of the meaning of the song followed by asking the group simply to consider what their testimony might be if they found a place of healing and hope, and, if so, where would it be? Upon finding it, who would they say made it possible? The group was asked to journal their responses as they listened once again to the song on CD.

In this instance, there were two objects of interest. One was the untold story. The other was the storytellers coming to a place of testifying about worship or coming into the presence of God as a place where healing and hope were found. This experience brings to awareness that guiding young people in embodying the intersection of the realities of life and art is actually immersing them in a dynamic process whereby they claim or reclaim a vital space for transformation.[18] To this extent, youth participation in art forms must extend beyond "mindless entertainment" or passive diversion. Rather, as integrally tied observational and performative activity, youth involvement in art forms must enable them to both envision themselves in and create or re-create spaces where they are actors, instead of assenting to spaces where they have been seen as the passive recipient.[19] In this case, youth moved beyond the role of passive receiver. Art that is heard or seen must be used to evoke young people's insights and critical reflections on life's realities; however, it must also stir them to become givers of beauty and truth. For example, the youth who were led by the musician/mentor sang the song as part of their youth-led worship service.

---

18   Arlene Goldbard, *New Creative Community: The Art of Cultural Development* (Oakland, CA: New Village Press, 2006), 43.

19   Harrison, *Enslaved Women and the Art of Resistance in Antebellum America*, 203.

The reclamation of space that takes place within art is critical, particularly in the case of devalued and commodified bodies, such as the Black female body. Young women's ability to express themselves authentically is liberating. Even more, art as an authentic expression of the truest self allows youth to see themselves and their gifts as contributing to the community rather than worsening the community. This repositioning of agency is generative and has the power to not only promote hope within youth but also in communities. In this sense, youth participation in art is itself an act of resistance, transforming space while at the same time building community.

Art Pedagogy Helps Youth Reclaim Communal Space

In a world geared toward individualism and competition, art pedagogy emphasizes a "village ethics," which centers on community and interdependency. Art pedagogy, then, is intended to engage youth in moving beyond privatized spaces to an embrace of community spaces. The power of art to transform space is well known within community-based art efforts, specifically what has come to be known as "community cultural development." Art is viewed as a cultural practice that produces cultural capital for the purpose of restoring community. Practitioners adopt principles that highlight active participation, diversity, cultural equality, and change agency.[20] Those who work with youth can learn a lot from community-based arts project workers who seek to reclaim and transform spaces rife with thwarted hope into spaces that build and exude hope. Community-initiated, arts-based projects privilege the role of art as *transformative activity* for the sake of the community, making art a valuable partner in building hope in communities often depressed by many forms of injustice.

William Cleveland, a pioneer of arts-based community development (ABCD), defines ABCD as "arts-centered activity that contributes to the sustained advancement of human dignity, health, and/or productivity within a community," including activities that educate and inform,

---

20 Goldbard, *New Creative Community,* 43.

inspire and mobilize, nurture and heal, and build and improve people and communities.[21] ABCD builds communities through the use of art in economic, architectural, cultural, and human development. Researchers have begun to document the impact of arts-based community development initiatives throughout the United States. These initiatives, for example, seek to transform physical space, solve community problems, advocate for policy change, increase awareness, build the capacity of communities, and encourage community engagement.[22] Employing principles of ABCD in art pedagogical practices affirms the pivotal goal of art to build community through reclaiming and transforming spaces that have been deemed a wasteland.

For example, in a study of ten economically disadvantaged schools who rely on arts as a tool of school reform, researchers Lauren Stevenson and Richard J. Deasy discovered the tremendous effects within and beyond schools. Key findings point to art's ability to promote student visibility in a way that increases their sense of self-worth, builds student's efficacy and sense of ownership in the learning process, and fosters student's ability for flexibility and adaptability in situations.[23] What we find most intriguing, however, is the organic way in which art facilitates engagement between and among groups of people. This study, in particular, emphasized the way art created space where teachers and students could relate to each other, which ultimately enriched the teaching and learning process.[24] The community capital created ultimately led to interdependence and tolerance within the space.[25] In fact, researchers refer to the interaction between artist (first space) and viewer (second space) as the *third space*, a space where community is built as artists and observers seek to understand the meaning of the

---

21 William Cleveland, "Arts-based Community Development: Mapping the Terrain," *A Working Guide to the Landscape of Arts for Change* (New York: Americans for the Arts, 2011), 4.

22 Linda Frye Burnham, "Community Arts at Work across the U.S.," *A Working Guide to the Landscape of Arts for Change* (New York: Americans for the Arts, 2011), 4.

23 Lauren Stevenson and Richard J. Deasy, *Third Space: When Learning Matters* (Washington, DC: Arts Education Partnership, 2005), 17–36.

24 Ibid., 9–16.

25 Ibid.

piece of art.[26] In this third space, youth display their authenticity and what gives meaning to their lives. For those who work with youth, navigating this third space creates a prime opportunity to connect with youth at a deeper level.

CREATING SPACES FOR ART: AGENTS OF HOPE IN ACTION

An essential function of agents of hope in activating art as a pathway to courageous hope is to create spaces where youth can re-story their culture in constructive ways, and, with others, become coauthors of a new storyline for their future. In these ways, young people can experience the sheer delight of feeling affirmed and acknowledged for their capacity to be creative agents. The very act of "creating space" repositions agents of hope, in many ways, as artists. They are entrusted with the task of opening up both themselves and the location of encounter to authentic engagement with the heart of youth. In order to create these spaces, agents of hope must themselves be both critical and creative. Leaders need critical awareness of the societal and cultural realities that both young people and leaders bring into artistic endeavors. It may include experiences that are common and different for both them and youth. Awareness extends to leaders acknowledging personal feelings about their experiences, how their feelings have been processed, and attitudes they have about observations of young people's responses to difficult events. Moreover, it is important for leaders to get in touch with their own ways of processing personal feelings about their experiences and the impact of their own uses of artistic mediums on their personal embrace of and actions on courageous hope. Leaders become artists as they create and enter spaces where they, themselves, admit to grappling with the toughness of realities and yet are certain that hope that has its source in God does not disappoint, and art has a way of bringing forth new perceptions of a way forward.

The perspective we are setting forth on the role of agents of hope

---

26   Ibid.

is antithetical to the notion of a controlling space. Creating space is not the same as controlling space. While it may seem like a common-sense statement, it is an important distinction to draw. The temptation to control the space is strong for people who work with youth and feel threatened or distanced from what youth share. Before adults ever take delight in the presence of youth or extend a genuine welcome, they seek to set clear boundaries or rules, such as the expectation that youth show respect for others and exhibit helpfulness that contributes to positive group functioning. While boundaries are necessary for teens, the task for the agent of hope in artistic endeavors is to generate a hospitable space where young people's courageous, hopeful consciousness is built. Or, building on Zimbabwean educator Toby Moyana's view of revolutionary consciousness, the task is to create a hospitable space wherein youth may "create new artifacts or inform old ones with a new idiom of creative freedom" that reveals new ways of seeing and acting in the future.[27] This space is shown by the agent's seeing youth as valued creative beings, and seeing the creative power within them, in order that they might discover their own capacity for hope in action.

As the Great Artist, God places the gift of creativity in human beings. Agents of hope encourage youth to draw on that creativity. Exodus 31 marks the first instance where God displays God's endorsement of art as a legitimate form of spiritual work in the sight of God. According to Exodus 31:1-5, Bezalel the son of Uri was filled with "divine spirit, with ability, intelligence, and knowledge in every kind of craft, to devise artistic designs, to work in gold, silver, and bronze, in cutting stones for setting, and in carving wood, in every kind of craft." In other words, the work of the artist played a major role in honoring God. To connect Black youth who have been devalued and dismissed by larger society with their God-given role as creators—Black youth who partner with

---

27 Moyana writes about the demand of the educator to rehabilitate a previous, dysfunctional worldview by inserting a new revolutionary consciousness that leads to a new language, new values, and new meanings. These ideas appear in Toby Tafirenyika Moyana, *Education, Liberation and the Creative Art* (Harare, Zimbabwe: Zimbabwe Publishing House, 1988), 23.

God—activates hope in their identity as valued human beings. Further, the ability to actually affirm what youth create reinforces significance and merit in their capacity to produce something of value. In this sense, emphasizing art pedagogy as an invitational approach to ministry creates space for youth to move from naming their pain to envisioning life's possibility and a constructive future for themselves.

Lack of hospitality communicates a message of dominance and closed-off-ness. Rather than experiencing a sense of freedom and openness to be who they are, youth often feel limited, corrected, and judged. Furthermore, controlled spaces create suspicion in youth, where they feel more like they are being watched than engaged. To counter controlled space, agents of hope rely on one of the key pillars within invitational educational theory—place. The place of learning, wherever that may be, must "exude a positive, cared for and caring atmosphere, clean, sustainability conscious, welcoming and including."[28] The very art of caring limits fear and provides agents of hope with the courage necessary to act. It provides them with the courage to release control and trust youth's ability to be responsible, contributing participants.

INVITATION: CREATING SPACE FOR STORY INTERPRETATION

When we as leaders invite young people into arts activities, we are receiving them in a creative space of truth-telling that involves story sharing and interpretation in dialogue between them and adults. Within the first step of creative truth-telling, sometimes the message that youth seek to communicate can become misread or misinterpreted, which may sometimes lead to a dismissive response from adults who encounter the creative expression. This is especially the case when youth convey through artistic means the nature of pain inflicted on them in their specific contexts. In other words, the movements of dancing, or images used in spoken word poetry, acting, and rapping, may be devalued

---

28   Martin Haigh, "Invitational Education: Theory, Research and Practice," *Journal of Geography in Higher Education* 35, no. 2 (2011): 301.

because the communication methods are unfamiliar and sometimes difficult to interpret.

Invitation is about not simply calling for and encouraging youths' story sharing through arts media but being ready to receive what they share, as shown in the story of the teen who dramatized her story of being bullied. Those who work with youth are in a unique position to respond to creative truth-telling by listening to their stories in rap or spoken word, or being attentive to their dance or dramatization, affirming their voice or bodily movements, and even inviting youth to share more if they so choose, as was the case when the bullied teen was asked if she would say more about the meaning of her outstretched arms and pointing around the room that appeared as accusatory motions to individuals in the room. Recall that she responded by saying that it was meant to depict peers at her school who had not come to her defense. Listening, attentiveness, and affirmation are important invitational behaviors of leaders; they communicate to youth not to give into activated hopelessness. Central to the idea of creative truth-telling and sharing of personal and communal stories through art is the understanding that each youth has her or his own story to tell. Creating space requires an understanding of the value and worth of all insights. It also leaves the table open to grapple with fresh insights, even when those insights feel disruptive and hard, as in the case of a young male who, in the dramatization of his feelings of being racially profiled, took on the role of a boxer and began forcibly making punching jabs at the air that was followed shortly thereafter by loud shrieks, "Why? Why? It isn't fair! Punch them out! I wouldn't dare! [Expletive]!" The posture of agents of hope then is not to shut down expressiveness but to welcome expressiveness and subsequently guide youth through a process where they can fully share the source of what they have expressed. As a result, the way young people name their pain may require an intermediary act of story interpretation on their part that aims toward understanding their lives, affirming their creative agency, and promoting their formation of courageous hope.

Story Interpretation as Comprehension

When young people are invited to interpret the stories they have shared through artistic means, they in turn invite the receiver's comprehension of the story. Something of importance in the story is grasped. Something about the teen and the teen's life becomes more fully known. Within the context of art, it is the ability of youth to use their agency to share with adults the deeper meaning behind their creative expressions. As emphasized within invitational educational theory, the act of story interpretation promotes mutual respect and deliberative dialogue between youth and adults. It is an intentional act that requires cooperation from the interpreter and the one receiving the message. In the case of the earlier-mentioned story of the youth who had been profiled, the movement into story interpretation came through the invitation to him to share orally more fully from one of his encounters his feelings and actions during and after it happened. The result of his interpretation led to stories of episodes shared by many of the other youth, which signaled to the leaders the enormity of the issue in the lives of the teens. What followed was intense discussion around a range of nonviolent responses in the actual situation, rehearsing the mantra of the self as a valued creation of God, and venting on artist's canvas, in music, in prayer, or other artistic means, including artful, or real, boxing.

The assumption is that adolescents are the most effective interpreters of their own stories revealed in creative expressions; thus, it is essential for agents of hope to invite, encourage, and create space for youth to become interpreters of episodes in their life stories that matter most to them. Often, in the interpretive process, agents of hope experience a disruptive awareness that compels them to advocate on behalf of youth. This uncomfortable feeling jolts agents of hope from a place of complacency to a place where they recognize that the lived realities of youth are urgent and must be addressed in partnership with God and youth. For example, following the group's collective, narrative, interpretative process on racial profiling, the leaders invited a lawyer, police officer, and pastoral caregiver to engage the group in dialogue on their feelings and potential future responses.

Agents of hope recognize that youth have something to teach them, and thus, open up the space for youth to share, teach, and offer their creative expressions as a launching pad for deeper reflection. As part of the act of story interpretation, agents of hope become learners who observe, inquire about, and study the creative expressions of youth. They recognize that creative expressions are extensions of adolescence. As Freire notes, "To study is to uncover; it is to gain a more exact *comprehension* of an object; it is to realize its relationships to other objects. This implies a requirement for risk taking and venturing on the part of the student, the subject of learning, for without that they do not create or re-create."[29] In other words, as a student, agents of hope seek to fully comprehend adolescents by listening to what is said and not said through their creative expressions. For example, within YHBA, youth often share works of poetry during talent shows or in journaling activities in the class. These works of art contain meaning for the youth. Creating space for youth to openly share these meanings becomes an opportunity for youth to translate the ways in which what's on the page reflects what's on their hearts.

PRESENCE: CREATING SPACE AS BEARING WITNESS

As youth name experiences of pain and move toward visions of flourishing, agents of hope commit to the act of presence, which entails bearing witness. Art becomes a significant medium to invite agents of hope to place themselves in the shoes of the youth and, in a sense, see themselves in a youth's story. It is a kind of "crossing borders" that evokes an "inner understanding" of a young person's struggle and pain, which allows the agent of hope to subsequently help youth through times when they question the veracity of hope and their ability to act in life with courage. Regardless how disruptive youth's creative expressions may get, agents of hope refuse to be dismissive, and commit to critical engagement of the creative expressions produced by youth as well as critical engagement of the youth themselves. The presence of agents of hope bears witness to the pain, the movement from pain to hope, and the negotiations that take place when hope is in decline or stagnated. Through the varying places that agents of hope may find adolescents

---

29   Paulo Freire, *Teachers as Cultural Workers: Letters to Those Who Dare Teach*, The Edge, Critical Studies in Educational Theory (Boulder, CO: Westview Press, 1998), 40 (italics original).

within the categories of hope, they engage youth in active listening and offer guidance when youth seem open to the possibility. This sends a bold message to youth that says we see you, accept you, relate to you as part of us, and would like to actively involve you in our community by offering opportunities for you to lead.[30] The presence of agents of hope reminds adolescents that they are not alone in the world and that their creativity is valued in both the sight of caring adults and the sight of God. The faith-filled posture that agents of hope model through their presence in the lives of youth becomes a meme for youth to mirror in their own lives, ultimately pushing youth to deeper relationship with God.

GUIDANCE: CREATING SPACE TO MOVE THROUGH IMAGES OF PAIN TO VISIONS OF FLOURISHING

Agents of hope not only help youth name pain but also create space for them to announce possibility for new realities through the practice of art. While youth who face systemic oppression may boldly denounce their oppressive circumstance and find ways to resist that system, they may not always have the words to announce a vision of flourishing for their lives. As people who work with youth, one way to use art as a tool to form hope is to help youth move beyond simply denouncing oppression to a space of announcing possibility. This role of guidance gives attention to observation, experimentation, critical appraisal, and reauthoring.

Observation

Observation is the discipline of paying careful attention to subjects and objects. Within the context of art pedagogy, observation enables observers to "see" what might go unnoticed. To be clear, observation is not just about what we see with our eyes; it is about what we hear with our hearts. Intentional effort is given to learning, studying, and actively discerning. Observation is marked by mutuality. The work of observation

---

30 Anne E. Streaty Wimberly, "Worship in the Lives of Black Adolescents: Builder of Resilience and Hope," *Liturgy* 29, no. 1 (2014): 23–33 (26), http://dx.doi.org/10.1080/0458O 63X.2014.846742.

is, as mentioned above, for agents of hope who seek to learn from and about both the creative expression and the creator of that expression. Agents of hope also extend observation opportunities to artists. In a formal sense, this may be centered on youth perfecting their craft as artist. It may also be an invitation for youth and adults to reassess how they understand the world. In a figurative sense, observation is also about serving as a role model so that youth can first observe and then become actors in their own narratives and upon themselves. Observation takes on an invitational stance but often leads to the desire for youth's deeper engagement with pursuing possibilities for their own lives.

Experimentation

Agents of hope invite youth to explore their creativity by taking risks. Taking risks in the context of safe space prepares youth to take risks in other spaces. It builds confidence and provides a snapshot of the youth's true ability. For Black youth who recognize the world as hostile and untrustworthy, finding safe spaces to experiment is critical. Quite frankly, the very developmental tasks of adolescents to discover their identity require experimentation. If adolescents do not find these safe spaces, they create their own, some of which lead to pathways of despair and hardship.

Agents of hope, however, create spaces of experimentation so that adolescents can learn mastery and build a strong sense of self. Art can become a powerful medium for this learning. For example, agents of hope encourage youth to try new modes and mediums of creative expression. On a practical level, these new modes may be unfamiliar and a bit uncomfortable, yet these spaces of experimentation offer safety for adolescents to take risks and make mistakes without feeling judged or condemned.

Critical Appraisal

The task of critical appraisal is to raise questions and help facilitate critical reflection with adolescents on their present and future life. Art serves as a conversational piece, where "generative themes" emerge that agents of hope can explore deeper with adolescents.[31] Specific, critical appraisal takes seriously the student's experience as revealed through art. These experiences provide an analytic category for agents of hope to evaluate the forms of knowledge that shape the student's experience, while at the same time providing students an opportunity to examine the way these experiences were "produced, legitimated, or disconfirmed."[32] In other words, agents of hope spend time examining with adolescents why these experiences hold so much meaning for youth and how these experiences shape their understanding of self and the world.

Further, agents of hope not only help adolescents reflect on their experiences but also where God is in the midst of those experiences. As the centering story demonstrates, the ring shout honored the experiences of enslaved Black people in ways that moved youth toward open conversation with God. Open conversations with God enable youth to critically appraise how life and vocation intertwine with a larger world. Often, a youth's critical appraisal with an agent of hope leads directly into opportunities for youth to reframe negative experiences in light of God's call upon his or her life.

Reauthoring

Reauthoring is a practice often used by narrative-oriented pastoral caregivers to guide individuals in envisioning their life stories in more positive or constructive ways.[33] Agents of hope create spaces

---

31 Paulo Freire, *Pedagogy of the Oppressed*, A Continuum Book (New York: Seabury Press, 1970), 87–124.

32 Peter McLaren, *Life in Schools: Introduction to Critical Pedagogy in the Foundations of Education* (New York: Longman, 1989), 242.

33 In some psychotherapeutic or pastoral-care contexts, the process is called *reframing*. This process is aimed toward placing experiences in a new frame of mind or picture, as seen in Donald Capps, *Reframing: A New Method in Pastoral Care* (Minneapolis: Fortress Press, 1990), 9–26. However, the use of a story re-authoring process is meant to convey the understanding that particular incidents or events in an individual's life are part of the whole of the life story, which has a past, present, and future. It is more than a single "frame." In the process of story re-authoring, an incident or event is seen as being wholly part of and having an impact on the whole of life. A thorough discussion of the nature of story re-authoring appears in Michael White and Donald Epston, *Narrative Means to Therapeutic Ends* (New York: W.W. Norton, 1990).

where youth cannot simply see but move toward hope-filled possibilities. Adolescents do not always have the capacity to make the shift from hope declined or hope stagnated toward a more positive vision of life. Within the context of adolescents who dare to speak their truth about the grim realities they face, agents of hope help youth reauthor their stories in ways that reveal their embrace of hope-bearing attitudes, which leads to positive self-concept and purposeful action in the world. Art, because of its narrative character, can become a powerful vehicle in the reauthoring process, including envisioning new or alternative attitudes, behaviors, and directions in life. For example, in *Girl Time: Literacy, Justice, and the School-to-Prison Pipeline*, Maisha Winn shares about the ways theatre helps formerly incarcerated girls see themselves and their lives in new ways. Winn does not romanticize the role of arts in the lives of formerly incarcerated girls. In order for the many negative issues related to incarceration to improve, systematic changes have to accompany their release and manifest in their daily situations. Nevertheless, Winn recognizes that art is a seed of participation that can have multiple outcomes and open the door for change to take place.[34]

Agents of hope, then, use art as a medium to invite youth into conversations with themselves, others, and God that will encourage youth to act courageously in a hostile world. The centering story illustrated one way in which the intentional participation of youth in the ring shout helped facilitate a life-changing conversation with God that resulted in acceptance of a youth's place in the world as a minister. Ultimately, even when situations may be unchangeable, agents of hope guide youths' involvement in forms of art-making through which they see and claim their own worth and value in the world. This guidance serves as a trigger for story reauthoring. It opens the door for youth to embark on pathways of courageous hope rather than remain stuck in anger, frustration, or rage at the way the world is.

---

34 Maisha T. Winn, *Girl Time: Literacy, Justice, and the School-to-Prison Pipeline*, The Teaching for Social Justice Series (New York: Teachers College Press, 2011), 126–27.

A CONTINUUM OF ART-MAKING

Agents of hope need not be limited to one way of art. There are a variety of modes and mediums to express one's self. The centering story focused on artistic movement, but art takes on many forms, each with its own unique power to enact courageous hope. The artistic pedagogical practices embedded in YHBA, for example, rested on a continuum between unstructured and structured forms of art-making. As indicated in table 6.1, each point on the continuum offers a valuable opening for students to express, experiment, discover, and proclaim meaning and value in the world.

Unstructured Art-Making

Unstructured art-making consists of recreational forms of art that youth initiate themselves. These practices include krumping, freestyling, and other informal participation in art that youth engage. Some of these unstructured forms of art-making can also be seen as negative by larger society, such as graffiti. Nevertheless, all these unstructured forms of art-making are a direct expression of youth culture and contain rich lessons about what gives meaning to youth. Unstructured art-making is important for youth because it allows them to be the initiators of creative expression. Organically, they form their own community of creativity and choose to release a wide spectrum of emotions through their participation in creative expressions.

Within the context of YHBA, we encourage unstructured forms of art-making. This form of art usually emerges from the youth in response to some internal or external stimuli, outside of direct staff encouragement, that inspire them to express themselves through their bodies. It manifests in spontaneous dance, poems created and shared in mentoring sessions, and recreation with their peers. In incidents such as these, agents of courageous hope affirm the willingness of youth to openly share their creative expressions. Agents of hope create space rather than shut it down.

Semi-Structured Art-Making

Semi-structured art-making consists of events where youth are invited to share. Many times, the sharing takes place within the context of an audience. Examples of semi-structured art-making include journaling and talent shows. As Wimberly observes, especially in the context of worship, semi-structured art-making can also include Black sacred dance, mime, stepping, spoken word, the "word made flesh," singing, and rapping.[35] Many times, agents of hope initiate semi-structured art-making, yet this form of art-making leaves room for youth to express themselves as they wish. The opportunity for youth to share their art with adults is an invitation to connect with youth at a heart-level.

Structured Art-Making

Structured art-making consists of liturgical forms of art, whereby agents of hope provide structured environments for youth participation. These may include rehearsed performances or structured artistic activities. Unlike unstructured art-making that may be initiated by youth, structured art-making activities are planned and initiated by adults; youth are invited to participate. As indicated in the centering story, these more structured forms of art-making represent intentional acts by agents of hope to guide youth into experiences that will contribute to an enhanced sense of self. Through varied emphases, they attempt to provide youth with the courage to act on their best possible self while also acting courageously in the world.

A CONTINUUM OF ART-MAKING

Unstructured Art-Making (consists of recreational forms of art that often emerge from the creativity of the youth themselves)

Semi-Structured Forms of Art-Making (consists of events, where youth are invited to share as they choose within the context of an audience)

Structured Art-Making (consists of liturgical forms of art through worship or rehearsed performance where youth display their talents)

---

35   Wimberly, "Worship in the Lives of Black Adolescents," 27.

CONCLUSION: ART AND ADOLESCENT FLOURISHING

Art has a way of recruiting one's emotions into places that become inexpressible with words. Yet it also contains the capacity to invoke a disruptive awareness that calls agents of hope to act in ways that invite, guide, and provide adolescents with the presence necessary to hope. Overall, art contributes to: creative well-being by inviting youth to affirm their gifts, spiritual well-being by introducing youth to alternate ways of connecting with God, and relational well-being by fostering intergenerational and cross-generational connections.

Agents of hope use art to invite youth to name, vent, and publically share their pain through creative truth-telling, while moving youth toward envisioning and moving into pathways of courageous hope. The move toward pathways of hope sometimes creates external and internal conflicts that youth must face. An understanding of conflict transformation is crucial for both agents of hope and youth. The following chapter explores the role of a pedagogy of conflict transformation in creating a pathway of courageous hope for youth.

CHAPTER 7

TRANSFORMING CONFLICT: A PEACEMAKING PATHWAY

*The greatest single antidote to violence is conversa-
tion, speaking our fears, listening to the fears of others,
and in that sharing of vulnerabilities discovering a genesis of hope.*

—Jonathan Sacks

*Blessed are the peacemakers, for they will be called
children of God.*

—Matthew 5:9

[A CENTERING STORY]

The daily interaction of teens in a retreat setting is not always tension free. As time unfolds, cliques form that exclude some while welcoming others. During one particular extended retreat, it was not hard for staff members to see who had been excluded. We noticed the isolation from the group of a young man who was physically small in size, wore glasses, and was soft-spoken. His tendency to withdraw from interactions with the group signaled to the group that perhaps he wanted to be an outsider. Unfortunately, the young man's experience of exclusion by the group resulted in his acting out with verbal insults and noncooperative behavior during planned retreat activities. His behavior annoyed his peers and proved problematic for the staff and the overall residential environment. As a staff, we knew we had to address the situation. A series of conversations with the young man and other youth centered on both the actions of the young man and the impact of cliques on others. Further attention was given to teen reports and staff observations of other tensions within the larger group. We decided to culminate the discussions with a hand-washing ceremony.

Two of the adult leaders invited the entire group of youth and leaders into a designated room. After being guided to sit in the circular arrangement of chairs, one of the leaders indicated that we are invited into a time of being together as sisters and brothers in Christ, reflecting on that meaning, and entering into confessions of occasions in which we have fallen short of that meaning in our time together during the retreat. It was said that none of us is perfect, and during our time of living together, we are apt to say or do something that causes hard feelings or hurt in another person—in fact, that is part of being human. The other leader followed by saying that we will link the confessions with a hand-washing ceremony, which is a ritual of offering forgiveness and coming to a shared moment of reconciliation.

The leader read a scripture and indicated it was to show that forgiveness and reconciliation represent a biblical response to offense. In addition, the journey of confession, forgiveness, and reconciliation is an important one of making God's love and care in human relations concrete. The biblical text was the Lord's Prayer, during which we were asked to repeat in unison the words, "And forgive us our trespasses, as we forgive those who trespass against us." Then the story was told of Jacob's journey back to his brother Esau, who was a resentful rival. The leader highlighted God's appeal to Jacob to return. God also promised to be with Jacob to let him know that he would not be alone in the journey of confession, forgiveness, and reconciliation (see Gen. 32–33). In like manner, God will accompany each one of us as we go to someone in the circle with whom we have had disagreement, have created feelings of discomfort, or who has hurt us in some way. After moments of sharing, we were told that, after two individuals have shared with each other, we were to mutually invite each other to go to the bowl of water and gently pour water on each other's hands as a sign of forgiving the other, followed by drying each other's hands with the towels placed beside the bowl, as a symbol of reconciliation.

Moments of silence and an initial sense of apprehension were finally broken by a teen's walk across the circle to the young man who had been excluded. The quiet manner in which they shared prevented others from hearing their conversation. But all of us observed the two of them walking together to the bowl, washing, and taking the towel to dry each other's hands. Before they ended, several other youth surrounded the two with hugs and words of affirmation. Some of them asked the young man to join them in the hand-washing ceremony. The room became filled with youth in twos and even in small groups who entered fully into the ritual. We noted that, in some cases, young people went to staff members and staff members approached youth. Whether youth paired with peers or with staff, the interchanges, at times, evolved into deeper conversation about where the offense originated. Other times, two individuals would look at each other knowingly and nod with acknowledgment of the apology.

THE NECESSITY OF RESPONSE TO CONFLICT

As in many contexts with youth, those in the Youth Hope-Builders Academy faced conflict as they interacted with one another. Sometimes, it took place because someone failed to acknowledge another, leaving a peer feeling invisible. Often, conflict was unintentional but left bitter feelings for the ones offended. The appearance of conflict among a group of Christian teens in the context of a Christian retreat calls us to awareness that, whoever and wherever we are, as humans we are social beings. We have individual identities; we are willful and have perspectives, attitudes, goals, and interests that can come into conflict with others. As Douglass Lewis states, "Conflict is a natural, inevitable, and central part of human existence."[1] The experience of conflict, especially when the source of it is hostile attitudes, rejection, or other types of negative treatment directed toward others, can have destructive consequences in the lives of individuals and communities. It is necessary to respond to conflict in ways that restore peace and wholeness to all who are part

---

1   Douglass Lewis, "Conflict and Conflict Management," in Rodney J. Hunter, ed., *Dictionary of Pastoral Care and Counseling* (Nashville: Abingdon Press, 1990), 211.

of conflictual circumstances, while recognizing that it is not always easy and that it requires intentionality, ingenuity, and unswerving effort.

The importance of the Christian faith in addressing conflict cannot be overemphasized. Through it, leaders communicate to youth a distinctive way of living and acting, even in the midst of mayhem, which is meant to make God's love and valuing of God's creation concrete in their lives and that of others. Over the years of Academy retreats, we have persisted in sessions that engage young people in open and frank dialogue on issues of conflict, its impact, and ways of addressing it, such as the one alluded to in the centering story above. Moreover, we have often used Christian rituals and language, such as the hand-washing ceremony that was described in the centering story, to address tension and engage young people in a process of confession, forgiveness, and reconciliation. The hand-washing ceremony demonstrates an attempt to right wrongs. Often practiced as a purification ceremony in Jewish culture, hand washing represents the removal of guilt, shame, and unforgiveness. It also represents an intentional space of conflict transformation that enables teens to be vulnerable, take ownership of their offense, and offer forgiveness to others within the group. Engaging in this religious rite is also considered a time of incorporating young people into a way of living as God's people that includes creating the conditions for goodwill, justice, and peace. Of course, it must be understood that the context of a retreat is a particular kind of setting in which conflict arises among youth. Myriad forms of conflict occur in the daily lives of young people that require attention. This chapter turns attention to this reality in the lives of Black youth and the importance and nature of a pedagogy of conflict transformation.

SIGNIFICANCE OF CONFLICT-TRANSFORMATION PEDAGOGY IN THE LIVES OF BLACK YOUTH

In the twenty-first century, Black teens witnessed the election of the first Black president, Barack Obama, a feat that seemed impossible just thirty-five years prior to the onset of the third millennium. However, at the close of Obama's presidency, these young people and those entering adolescence gazed toward the future with intense awareness of great divides around race, class, gender, immigration, and orientation, in addition to a pervading lack of sensitivity to these concerns. Their experiences and observations of adverse treatment based on color and, for many, on both color *and* social class, confirmed the myth of the arrival of a post-racial society.[2] Black youth exist in a society that denigrates them in ways that evoke their anger and violent response. Indeed, the personal affronts to their dignity and welfare have continued to be plentiful, and pose threats to their hope for change. A complicating factor is that they also exist in a seductive culture of violence where people seem to be drawn to the spectacle of violence, begin to see violence as normal, and assign normalcy to the notion of life and the future as disposable.[3] The implicit message that North America communicates has been, and is even now, quite telling. What shall church leaders and other adults say about conflict transformation in such a time as this? How shall we urge Black youth to have courage and hope entwined enough "to be" in a society that still raises questions about the humanity of Black people?

Conflict-transformation pedagogy teaches youth how to transform conflict before it escalates to violence by being aware of their own triggers as well as understanding the significance of addressing people's needs as human beings. In a citywide survey conducted with more than four hundred Boston teens, which explored their knowledge, attitudes, and experiences with violence, results demonstrated that most teens' knowledge about violence comes from experience.[4] Data suggest that attention should be given to helping adolescents

---

2   The designation of post-racial America as a myth, and extensive description of prevailing circumstances that have led to and currently corroborate the myth, are presented in H. Roy Kaplan, *The Myth of Post-Racial America: Searching for Equality in the Age of Materialism* (Lanham, MD: Rowman & Littlefield Education, 2011). See pages 1–6, 129–98 for an overview of the challenges posed by race and class in white America, the prevalence of inequalities and social disparities, and particularly the myth of the prevailing American meritocratic system.

3   The presence of a seductive culture of violence is described in Henry Giroux and Brad Evans, *Disposable Futures: The Seduction of Violence in the Age of Spectacle* (San Francisco: City Lights Publishers, 2015).

4   Alice J. Hausman, Howard Spivak, and Deborah Prothrow-Smith, "Adolescents' Knowledge and Attitudes about and Experience with Violence," *Journal of Adolescent Health* 15, no. 5 (1994): 406.

understand the risks associated with violence and the value of enhancing their conflict-transformation skills.[5] Curricula directed toward heightening young people's critical awareness of risk factors and teaching them functional conflict-transformation skills can disrupt an unhealthy pattern of learning about violence through negative experiences with violence. In a study with middle- and high-school youth, research showed that typically the initiating act of violence was something perceived as minor that then escalated into violence.[6] Further, this study revealed that conflict was more likely to occur between youth who know one another, not because of the absence of values, but because violence was viewed as an acceptable way to handle conflict.[7] What this study ultimately reveals is that youth violence is a learned response to conflict, but it can also be unlearned with intentional efforts.

With the detention center or prison as a real threat to youth who participate in violence, we must present alternative pathways. We are increasingly aware of stereotypical views of youth as violent, which actually contribute to behavior leading to incarceration. These dynamics create a sense of urgency for agents of hope to provide hope-filled pathways and invigorate the courage of youth to choose those pathways. Violence prevention has traditionally been relegated to law enforcement and the criminal justice system. Yet a shift has taken place. Violence is now seen as a public health concern.[8] This current emphasis encourages nonprofits, schools, and faith-based organization partnerships to address violence in local communities. In addition, a helpful direction is to expand the focus on preventing violence to include conflict transformation. This course moves action toward preventing, intervening, and reconciling conflicting interests. Admittedly, the process is complex. Yet response to the need must happen.

---

5   Ibid.

6   Daniel P. Lockwood, "Violence among Middle School and High School Students: Analysis and Implications for Prevention," *Research in Brief* (October 1997): 1–12.

7   Ibid.

8   Etienne G. Krug, Linda L. Dahlberg, James A. Mercy, Anthony B. Zwi, and Rafael Lozano, *World Report on Violence and Health: Summary* (Geneva: World Health Organization, 2002), 3–4.

For a moment, let's consider both violence and conflict. We define *conflict* as a disagreement or divergence in views. *Violence*, however, is "the intentional use of physical force or power threatened or actual, against oneself, another person, or against a group or community, which either results in or has a high likelihood of resulting in injury, death, psychological harm, mal-development, or deprivation."[9] If conflict is not resolved in the early stage, it can easily lead to violence. Because conflict and violence sometimes are used interchangeably, making the distinction between the two is critical for the work of agents of hope with youth. Talking about violence and conflict as related is important and necessary for teaching youth to identify how and when it is simply a conflict that can be transformed and when it is violence that needs to be confronted and obliterated. We will limit our focus here by simply addressing the significance of conflict transformation in the lives of African American youth and ways agents of hope can use peacemaking to invite, be present with, and guide youth in the midst of conflict.

VIOLENCE AS MULTILEVEL

Adolescents live in a world rife with conflict and turmoil. The broadcast of these realities in the daily news sounds an urgent alarm for youth ministry leaders and people of faith to guide our youth in a way that enables them to navigate what is seen and, quite frankly, exists in real life. Youth are constantly negotiating among many forms of internal and external conflict simultaneously. They experience multilevel violence—or violence experienced at intrapersonal, interpersonal, communal, and structural levels—that shapes their understanding of the world. Adolescents also naturally find themselves in a context of conflict because they are in the process of resolving the crisis of identity versus identity confusion.[10] They are learning how to differentiate themselves from the world around them while at the same time clarifying where they fit into the world. Youth also face turmoil in their home lives, schools,

---

9   Ibid., 4.

10   Erik H. Erikson, "Identity and the Life Cycle: Selected Papers," *Psychological Issues*, 1959.

neighborhoods, and churches. These external and internal struggles shape who they are and who they are becoming.

Ecological models of violence attempt to describe the multifaceted nature of violence through four specific risk factors—biological, relational, community-based, and societal. Each factor uniquely contributes to the root causes of violence while also interacting with the others, making violence a complex phenomenon to describe.[11] In our understanding of multilevel violence, we mirror the ecological model but emphasize how violence functions rather than the risk factors that serve as root causes of violence. We propose that agents of hope must come to understand violence as multilevel—intrapersonal, interpersonal, communal, and structural.

Intrapersonal Violence

Intrapersonal violence is self-inflicted damage or harm. It could include suicidal attempts as well as negative thoughts. This kind of violence is internalized and targeted at the self and can result in shame, low self-esteem, and other forms of self-hate. Intrapersonal violence is compounded by stereotypes that circulate about and are internalized by Black youth, such as views of these persons as naturally violent or susceptible to criminal behavior.

Interpersonal Violence

Interpersonal violence consists of damage or harm that takes place within the context of close relationships. These relationships include familial, friendships, or intimate partners. The context of close relationship contributes both to one's experience of violence and one's participation in violence. For example, research indicates that familial environments can both increase the risk of violence as well as the protective factors necessary in preventing violence.[12] As a result, violence committed

---

11   Krug, et al., *World Report on Violence and Health: Summary*, 9.

12   Le'Roy E. Reese, Elizabeth M. Vera, Thomas R. Simon, and Robin M. Ikeda, "The Role of Families and Care Givers as Risk and Protective Factors in Preventing Youth Violence," *Clinical Child and Family Psychology Review* 3, no. 1 (March 2000): 61–77.

in the context of close relationships must be taken into account when thinking of adolescent violence.

Communal Violence

Communal violence is damage or harm that takes place within communities because of physical force or power that makes those living in the community vulnerable to harm. Communal violence can affect anyone living within a particular neighborhood or community. For example, even youth that come from stable homes may experience communal violence because of where they live. Furthermore, even when youth have not personally experienced violence, the fear of violence increases when they see or hear about it taking place in close proximity to them. Sociologist Elijah Anderson asserts how violence is part of the code of the streets in many inner-city communities.[13] Even for youth who come from families not prone to violence, familiarity and sometimes compliance with the "code" is real. In fact, violence may still be seen as the only option to maintain respect and avoid bullying.

Youth from all backgrounds navigate a peer "code of the street," particularly within school contexts. A perceived need to comply with the code, which may relate to dress, hairstyle, language, and walk, can be a daunting challenge for youth because of a legitimate need to be accepted by peers and maintain respect. Thus, conflict-transformation pedagogy prioritizes new codes and norms that center on the valued self that God created, how God sees them, and what it means to have courage to decide what or how much they are willing to sacrifice to affirm this valued self. Engagement in this process is needed in order to create a hope-forming pathway for young people's courageous living. Indeed, agents of hope are faced with the challenge of inspiring courage so that youth move from what they *learn about* conflict transformation to actually *enacting* conflict-transformation skills in the heat of conflict, in preparation to do so in adulthood.

---

13   Elijah Anderson, *Code of the Street: Decency, Violence, and the Moral Life of the Inner City* (New York: W.W Norton, 1999), 107–41.

Systemic Violence

Black youth are critically aware that they may be faced with not only peer violence or familial violence but also society-sanctioned and structural violence. Systemic violence consists of the ways structures of power contribute to harm individuals or particular groups of people. Systemic violence is often supported by systems, policies, or institutions that tend not to recognize diversity or marginalized groups but rather function in the interests of greater political and financial gain for those already in power. Examples exist in schools that make certain a school-to-prison pipeline for young girls and boys, limits to needed access to health resources that result in mental- and physical-health disparities, and the exacerbation of deaths by law enforcement. Conflict-transformation pedagogies engage young people's critical thinking so they might be more aware of the interlocking systems of oppression that perpetuate violence as well as develop understanding and skills to address human rights and behaviors for response.

Schrock-Shenk and Ressler make the point that "conflict equals differences plus tension."[14] Neither difference nor tension is negative, yet both can breed an awful lot of discomfort for persons in conflict. Nevertheless, we assert that conflict, while uncomfortable, is not bad or negative. How one responds to conflict can be negative and contribute to the escalation of conflict so that the consequences of conflict are also negative. What we advocate is conflict that is transformative. Conflict is a natural and necessary part of life.[15] Often, our inborn response to conflict is either fight or flight. We take up arms against conflict or try to completely avoid it. Transforming conflict encourages adolescents not to avoid or fight against conflict but to walk through conflict in a creative and transformative way. We assert that conflict can be transformed into an opportunity for growth and renewal.

---

14 Carolyn Schrock-Shenk and Lawrence Ressler, *Making Peace with Conflict: Practical Skills for Conflict Transformation* (Scottdale, PA: Herald Press, 1999), 23.

15 Thomas Porter, *The Spirit and Art of Conflict Transformation: Creating a Culture of Just Peace* (Nashville: Upper Room Books, 2010), 13.

It can be a "site for constructive change."[16] Conflict-transformation pedagogy is a process that links the *way* we teach with the content, or *what* we teach. The attitude of the leader toward the youth, and the safe and caring environment that is formed, are as important as the content and functional skills being taught. In this way, conflict-transformation pedagogy, whether responding to low-level conflict or high-level violence, becomes a way for young people to experience positive and peaceful human connections, transform attitudes and behavior, build resilience, and promote shalom.

PEDAGOGY OF CONFLICT TRANSFORMATION AS RESILIENCE-BUILDING

Adolescents can bounce back from conflict in two ways—either through their own internal resources or through encounters with people, organizations, and activities that contribute to the emergence of resilience.[17] Further, a key factor in building resilience is communicating a "resiliency attitude."[18] In other words, reinforcing an attitude that adolescents already have the capacity to bounce back contributes to adolescents' courage to do just that. The use of self-talk that was introduced in chapter 5 is appropriate here. Like a cheerleader, agents of hope affirm to adolescents, "You can do it! Don't give up! Transform conflict! Don't let it transform you!" Youth may then respond with the same affirmative "cheers" using their own names; or they may choose to draw on the mantra: "Black lives matter! I [insert your name] matters! We matter!" Despite the difficulty of the circumstance, this resilient attitude affirms adolescents' ability to choose a hope-filled pathway that leads to conflict transformation and flourishing.

Agents of hope build resilience in adolescents both by nurturing

---

16   Ellen Ott Marshall, "Introduction: Learning through Conflict, Working for Transformation," *Conflict Transformation and Religion Essays on Faith, Power, and Relationship*, ed. Ellen Ott Marshall (New York: Palgrave Macmillan, 2016), 1.

17   Nan Henderson, "Hard-Wired to Bounce Back," in *Resiliency in Action: Practical Ideas for Overcoming Risks and Building Strengths in Youth, Families, and Communities* (Ojai, CA: Resiliency in Action, Inc., 2007), 9.

18   Ibid.

internal resources they can draw on in the midst of conflict and by offering structural and relational resources that will contribute to the emergence of resilience. Much of the research on building resilience in school contexts recognizes the importance of conflict transformation in providing a protective environment for adolescents. For example, one research study suggests that building resilience in school encompasses developing social-emotional competency, maximizing meaningful student participation, and strengthening relationships, all of which function as byproducts of conflict-transformation pedagogy.[19] This example is, in fact, an important word to congregations to provide opportunities for youth involvement in every aspect of church life.

Additionally, conflict transformation is an effort toward adolescent flourishing that seeks to respond to adverse circumstances by building resilience in youth. Adversity during childhood is not uncommon for any person. Research shows that nearly two-thirds of Americans from all demographics have had at least one adverse childhood experience. This means that they have been exposed to a negative life experience such as abuse or other form of personally experienced or observed violence; absence or illnesss of a parent; or sickness, incarceration or substance abuse of a family household member. From one in five to a quarter of adults reported having three or more adverse events.[20] The higher the risk for and experience of adverse childhood experiences, the higher the potential for health concerns, counterproductive behaviors, and diminished life opportunities throughout an individual's life.[21] Conflict-transformation pedagogy contributes to a person's ability to

---

19   Jean E. Brooks, "Strengthening Resilience in Children and Youths: Maximizing Opportunities through the Schools," *Children & Schools* 28, no. 2 (April 1, 2006): 69–76.

20   Find information and study findings on ACEs on: Centers for Disease Control and Prevention, "About the CDC-Kaiser ACE Study," (Centers for Disease Control and Prevention, National Center for Injury Prevention and Control, Division of Violence Prevention), https://www.cdc.gov/violenceprevention/acestudy/about.html; Vanessa Sacks, David Murphy, Kristen Moore, "Adverse Childhood Experiences: National and State Level Prevalence," *ChildTrends*, https://www.childtrends.org/wp-content/uploads/2014/07/Brief-adverse-childhood-experiences_FINAL.pdf; and Monique J. Brown, Leroy R. Thacker, and Steven A. Cohen, "Association between Adverse Childhood Experiences and Diagnosis of Cancer," PLoS One, 2013; 8(6): e65524, www.ncbi.nim.nih.gov/pmc/articles/PMC3679131/, accessed August 17, 2016.

21   Ibid.

bounce back from wounds caused by emotional and relational trauma caused by ACEs by increasing self-awareness.

The story-sharing pedagogy in chapter 5 is helpful in this respect. For example, in its use, we focus on self-awareness by inviting a group of teens to tell a story of their early or middle childhood when they were angry with someone. We then ask them to share what they were thinking or saying to themselves at that time, or what they actually did and why. In the next step, we guide them in getting in touch with ways they handle situations now that are either similar to or different from the earlier one. We followed with the questions: "What was helpful about the way you handled your previous and present situations? Why? What wasn't helpful? Why?" Often, young people have told of anger-provoking circumstances evolving from being disallowed from doing something, going somewhere, or not getting something they desired. Others told of negative attitudes toward them at home, bullying in school, relocation, or disruption or fear from parents' divorce. Responses ranged from talking back, withdrawing, crying and, in some cases, entering into a physical fight. There was always agreement that a physical fight was least helpful and that other responses depended on the situation. In every case, they told us that this opportunity to tell a story, often never shared before, was most helpful. It also gave them an opening to become aware of themselves, their thoughts, their responses, and a pattern for doing the same in the future. Overall, by becoming more aware of the interior as well as external circumstances that cause one's interior to be disturbed, conflict transformation increases critical self-awareness. Self-awareness is a significant skill that helps young people navigate conflict and cope with adverse circumstances.

PEDAGOGY OF CONFLICT TRANSFORMATION AS HUMAN CONNECTEDNESS

Transforming conflict is not about being at peace with everyone. Rather, it is learning how to love, respect, and accept the humanity of others even when there is dissidence and difference. It seeks "to find healing in our relationships, to flourish in community, to *be well together*.[22] It thrives on the principle of *Ubuntu* by recognizing not only others as human beings but also the interconnectedness of all humans. The question was raised of survivors, after the massacre of nine Black people in prayer and Bible study at Emanuel African Methodist Episcopal Church in Charleston, South Carolina, "How could you forgive Dylann Roof?" The answers simply were: "Because God forgives." "We will not let hate win." "We are a family that love built. We have no room for hating." "We are to pray for his soul."[23] In chapter 2, the question was also raised about how two hope-builders were able to continue walking after being assaulted and called "niggers" by white teens and later expressing forgiveness by shaking hands with those same youth. The answer in this case and in the one in South Carolina lies in the courage of people to live the gospel at the center of courageous living.

Archbishop Desmond Tutu reminds us of another aspect by emphasizing the interdependence of humanity. He asserts that the humanity of each of us is inextricably bound with that of another. For him, this interconnectedness reflects the character of *Ubuntu*; and this "quality of Ubuntu gives people resilience, enabling them to survive and emerge still human despite all efforts to dehumanize them."[24] The use of the concept of interdependence in conflict-transformation pedagogy is critical for adolescents, who are in danger of adopting principles of individualism and flourishing, that are centered only on the self without regard for others. Conflict transformation challenges this view by shifting the focus to the humanity of those who are connected to us. This includes even those named "enemy." In other words, conflict transformation involves more than addressing a single conflict. Conflict transformation creates new ways of envisioning and living life in relation to others.[25] In short, conflict-transformation pedagogy emphasizes human connectedness

22 Porter, *The Spirit and Art of Conflict Transformation*, 131 (italics original).

23 See Meg Wagner, "As trial against Dylann Roof begins, families of Charleston church shooting victims still show mercy," *New York Daily News* (November 3, 2016), http://www.nydailynews.com/news/national/s-church-shooting-victims-families-forgive-dylann-roof-article-1.2855446.

24 Quotation taken from *Ubuntu Village*, http://ubuntuvillage.org/index.html.

25 Porter, *The Spirit and Art of Conflict Transformation*, 131.

rather than the human as an autonomous, disconnected being. This has relevance for young people's friendships as well. The strongest friendships, for instance, can often point to a moment of great conflict where two parties chose to value their relationship over their positions, thus seeking a way to reconcile their differences so they could restore their connection as friends. In other relationships as well as in friendships, conflict can be a basis for alienation and distance; but it can also be an opportunity to know God, self, others, and the world better. When we are honest about conflict, we realize how conflicts open us up to be known by others. Conflict makes us vulnerable before others. Overall, conflict-transformation pedagogy assumes that humans not only desire but need connection; thus, transforming conflict is an opportunity to bond humans together.

PEDAGOGY OF CONFLICT TRANSFORMATION AS SHALOM

Conflict-transformation pedagogy offers hope-forming pathways to Black youth by introducing them to modes of responding to multilevel forms of violence they encounter in everyday life. Conflict-transformation pedagogy spreads a message of shalom or peace with justice in all aspects of life—intrapersonal, interpersonal, community-based, and societal. As part of this pedagogical emphasis, we have invited young people to answer the question: "What are the most pressing problems in our neighborhood, society, and the world that cause conflict? About which ones are you most passionate?" We have also introduced them to biblical stories of conflict, such as those found in the life of David (1 Sam. 17:1-55) for purposes of drawing similarities between David's life and current personal, social, and political issues raised by youth. Further guidance has taken the form of engaging them in discussing meanings of Romans 12:17-19: "Do not repay anyone evil for evil, but take thought for what is noble in the sight of all. If it is possible, so far as it depends on you, live peaceably with all. Beloved, never avenge yourselves, but leave room for the wrath of God; for it is written, 'Vengeance is mine. I will repay,' says the Lord." The purpose is for young people to envision a faith-oriented attitudinal disposition for entering into peace with justice. In implementing the curriculum on conflict transformation written by Sarah, we follow up by involving youth in developing a "Justice Stance," which has resulted in their drafting plans that include, for example, letters to media producers assailing the excessive negative media coverage on Black life and seeking more positive images, developing T-shirts and posters that identify a school as "A NO BULLYING ZONE" joining a rally in peaceful protest of police violence and a prayer vigil for victims of violence, and boycotting corner grocery stores where owner attitudes are negative and food is both old and expensive. We also add to the suggestions of young people the idea from Mark Gornick's work in inner-city Baltimore that residents' continuing efforts in their neighborhoods to demand and support revitalization is an act of shalom.[26] The mere presence of a person of faith in a community tells a story of redemption and becomes a protective factor against social toxins that may lead to harm and maladaptation. Participating in shalom takes courage and requires the work of the village.

ROLE OF AGENTS OF HOPE IN CONFLICT TRANSFORMATION: THE PRACTICE OF PEACEMAKING

Peace is not just the goal of conflict transformation; it is a way of being that influences what one says and how one acts. Peacemaking is how people inhabit the world in which they live despite the threat of conflict and violence against them. Peacemaking is a way to transform conflict into something that deepens relationship, develops character, encourages intimacy with God, and reveals the inner motives and intents of the heart. In what theologians identify as one of the most powerful sermons Jesus gave, the Sermon on the Mount, Jesus makes a clear statement about conflict transformation and peace building. In Matthew 5:9, Jesus says, "Blessed are the peacemakers, for they will be called children of God." Peacemaking is more than a social or emotional exercise;

---

26   Mark R. Gornik, *To Live in Peace: Biblical Faith and the Changing Inner City* (Grand Rapids, MI: W.B. Eerdmans, 2002), 254.

it is a spiritual practice that identifies people with the character of God. To invite, guide, and be present with youth through conflict is to reveal Christ as the Prince of Peace, even in the midst of turmoil. In light of a politically divided and racially intense period in history, the charge to be a peacemaker calls forth the very resources of the heart and soul of Black people.

INVITATION: PEACEMAKING THROUGH ACTIVE LISTENING

Agents of hope encourage youth to engage in communication that deepens relationships. Communication plays a key role in conflict transformation. In fact, the inability to communicate with respect and awareness often is at the basis of conflict. Verbal and nonverbal communication can be exploitative and violent. Our communication can also be inviting and life-giving. Nonviolent communication resists defensiveness, withdrawal, attacks on others, and judgmental criticism, which is characteristic of people's response when they have been deeply hurt or offended. Instead, it is a relational approach to communication that focuses on the needs of people. Marshall B. Rosenberg calls it "the language of compassion" or a gift given to another from the heart; the exchange promotes joy and well-being in both the giver and receiver.[27] "Life-alienating communication," however, encompasses communication that centers on moralistic judgments, comparisons, and denial of responsibility, all of which lead to clouded judgments and classifications of people.[28] This communication, in turn, alienates people from transforming conflict into something positive. Alternatively, conflict-transformation pedagogy offers communication skills that promote active listening.

Peacemaking centers on the art of listening. Listening is not just about digesting the words of others; it's about paying close attention to the verbal and nonverbal cues that communicate human need. Agents of hope teach youth the art of listening by modeling active listening

---

27 Marshall B. Rosenberg, *Nonviolent Communication: A Language of Compassion* (Del Mar, CA: PuddleDancer Press, 1999), 4.

28 Ibid., 15–23.

while, at the same time, creating environments where youth can practice active listening. Active listening prepares youth for a process of conflict transformation by not only enabling them to hear and see others
with whom they disagree but also creating opportunities to discern the
appropriateness of conflict prevention, conflict intervention, and reconciliation. Conflict prevention recognizes that the easiest conflict to avoid
is the conflict that has not yet occurred. Hope agency seeks to prevent
conflict by showing genuine respect for and acknowledgment of the
needs of others, intervening in conflict by mediating the positions and
needs of two conflicting parties, and reconciling by offering forgiveness
where needed.

PRESENCE: PEACEMAKING BY ADDRESSING
THE HUMAN NEED TO BE ACKNOWLEDGED

Agents of hope serve as bridges that help youth pay attention to their
own needs to belong, participate, and be acknowledged; as well as
provide acknowledgment, belonging, and a sense of participation to
others. They cannot create these feelings in youth but they help mediate these feelings in youth by inviting them into spaces where they are
both heard and valued as human beings. As Thomas Porter, former
director of JustPeace Center for Mediation and Conflict Transformation
of The United Methodist Church, writes: "A peace builder is not a fixer
but a mediating presence, a person with the courage to bring people
with differences together, creating a space that encourages openness
to the Spirit and to one another's stories, so they can solve their own
problems and find healing together."[29] In fact, we often wonder if the
gap we see between youth and young adult's attendance in a church
is just another symptom of unaddressed conflict. Agents of hope engage the act of peacemaking simply through their presence in the
lives of adolescents. Their presence addresses the human need for
acknowledgment, belonging, and participation. When these human
needs are not met, it often becomes a basis for conflicts to emerge,

---

29 Porter, *The Spirit and Art of Conflict Transformation*, 6.

which can lead to violence. Agents of hope recognize youth who are vulnerable to one another and are willing to share their need to be acknowledged, to belong, and to participate, and also create space for others to do the same. In this sense, agents of hope model a mediating presence that youth can one day emulate in their interactions with others.

Greetings are rituals that point to the human need for acknowledgment. The importance of acknowledgment and respect often reveals itself in unspoken norms in society. After much thought, we realized this idea of "greeting" is sometimes absent within the African American context. We have been in far too many conversations on diversity where African American students share how unacknowledged they feel when they see their classmates or professors in the hall without any sign of recognition. These same codes apply to the streets. Even to this day, when we walk in the neighborhood and see random Black men or women standing on the corner, we gently nod our heads. The bystander nods back in recognition of our acknowledgment of their presence. The point is that greetings serve as a ritual of respect and symbol of acknowledgment. Greeting others acknowledges their presence, which communicates their value and worth in the community. The failure to greet someone or to give an appropriate welcome can create immediate conflict. Greetings are not empty rituals; greetings are rituals that carry meaning in the African context. They speak to the need for people to be acknowledged or made visible before another. In developing the *Transforming Conflict* curriculum, Sarah was asked by our hope-builders unit in Nigeria to include an opening session on greetings, since no activity begins there without it. Greetings are considered to be antidotes to the potential for violence.[30] In short, greetings meet the human need for acknowledgment while simultaneously helping to prevent any potential conflict that might emerge from a failure to offer that acknowledgment to another individual.

---

30 Sarah F. Farmer, "Transforming Conflict: A Curriculum on Conflict Resolution with Adolescents," Kenya ed. (Atlanta, GA: Youth Hope-Builders Academy at Interdenominational Center, 2016), 9–10.

GUIDANCE: PEACEMAKING WITH SELF, GOD, OTHERS, AND THE WORLD

Within conflict transformation pedagogy, agents of hope play a critical role in guiding adolescents through peacemaking with self, God, others, and the world. In particular, we propose that restoring peace with the self requires truth seeking and forgiveness that enables healing and connection. Reconciling relationships with others requires truth sharing that enables honest dialogue and genuine embrace of the other. Agents of hope help adolescents renew intimacy with God by inviting their honest expressions of sorrow and grief; this opens one toward God's movement rather than shuts down possibilities of God's divine presence in one's life. Agents of hope invite peacemaking with the world by introducing practices of shalom to adolescents. Overall, agents of hope guide youth into deeper connection with themselves, God, others, and the world through the practice of peacemaking.

Restoring Peace with the Self: Truth Seeking and Forgiveness

Truth seeking is an introspective examination of the root cause of one's own internal conflicts. It seeks to reveal the "why" behind offenses, wounds, and unforgiveness. Critical to truth-seeking work with adolescents is the opportunity to teach the biblical norm of forgiveness. Forgiveness contributes to not only peacemaking with others but internal peacemaking. Forgiveness never justifies wrongdoing; instead, it releases the hold of unforgiveness and unresolved conflict over a person's heart. Forgiveness enables relational connectedness wherein the one offering forgiveness actually offers a gift from the heart. It beckons toward restoration by recognizing and accepting that others, along with ourselves, are human beings who sometimes think, speak, and act in ways that alienates them from others.

By nature, forgiveness is an activity of critical awareness. Forgiveness challenges youth to engage in introspection in order to see the ways they have harmed others through their work and actions. Agents of hope assist in this process by helping youth clean the lenses through which they view life. Adults and adolescents alike must be intentional about addressing these past wounds, even as they face the current conflicts they encounter in the relationships with themselves, God, and others. Unresolved conflict and offenses muddy our perceptions about people. Earlier, we called attention to a way of inviting youth into re-calling past incidents of conflict followed by questions to illuminate their self-awareness and resilience. It is also a pathway to healing that comes from arriving at a place identified by Everett Worthington as "holding onto forgiveness."[31] In this step, he makes clear that, even when forgiveness is offered, persons may not forget what has been done to them. It is important to remember that forgiveness is a choice, and persons have a choice to release the memories every time they recur. John H. Powell adds to this understanding: "Healing is the often difficult process in which we come to peace with our own baggage and the baggage others bring."[32] Agents of hope remain a constant presence, guiding adolescents through strategies to extend and hold onto forgive-ness to people who may have hurt them.

Reconciling Relationships with Others through Truth Sharing

Pedagogy of conflict transformation takes intentional steps toward the character development of adolescents. It sees conflict as a learning opportunity to prepare youth to manage their social and emotional lives, which is their ability to manage aspects of their lives "in ways that enable them to learn, form relationships, solve everyday problems, and adapt to the complex demands of growing up."[33] In particular, it seeks to increase social and emotional competencies. Socioemotional

---

31   This is the final step in Worthington's five-step process of forgiveness that centers on the acronym REACH: **R**ecall of hurtful events, **E**xpect God to know and understand your hurt and be with you in the effort to forgive, **A**ltruistic gift acceptance of a time when you have been forgiven that evokes the desire for giving the same to another, **C**ommitting yourself to forgive publicly, and finally **H**olding onto forgiveness. The steps are found in Everett L. Worthington, *Forgiving and Reconciling: Bridges to Wholeness and Hope* (Downers Grove, IL: InterVarsity Press, 2003), 73–145.

32   John H. Powell, "Forgiveness and Healing Conflict," in *Making Peace with Conflict: Practical Skills for Conflict Transformation*, eds. Carolyn Schrock-Shenk and Lawrence Ressler (Scottdale, PA: Herald Press, 1999), 121.

33   Donna K. Crawford and Richard J. Bodine, "Conflict Resolution Education: Preparing Youth for the Future" *Juvenile Justice Journal* 8, no. 1 (June 2001): 28.

competency enhances adolescents' skills to view other human beings as emotional creatures who can be easily triggered and might respond in particular ways. It also contributes to youth's capacity to share honestly about how they feel and what they need. The question that conflict-transformation pedagogy helps adolescents answer is whether they will exclude or embrace persons with whom they disagree. It is easier to equate a person as the problem rather than understand the problem as the "position" a person holds. Conflict-transformation pedagogy seeks to get to the root of the problem by identifying the positions of conflicting parties. Often, these "positions" become "truths" that alienate and block the deepening of relationships. These held positions create conflict. Agents of hope encourage youth to become truth sharers so that their positions and needs are made known, in order to work toward agreement with others. In this sense, reconciliation actually embraces the ability to share truth among one another; truth enables embrace. As Miroslav Volf says, "Without the will to embrace the other there will be no truth *between people*, and without truth between people, there will be no peace."[34] Overall, the ability to share truths, even when those truths are conflicting, leads people toward reconciliation and human connectedness.

Renewing Intimacy with God through Lament

Within conflict transformation, human beings express internal conflict through lament. Lament is an expression of grief or sorrow. Agents of hope encourage lament as a practice of peacemaking because lament creates a greater intimacy between adolescents and God, provides space for wholesale acceptance of feelings, and helps them understand the suffering in the world. Nurturing these habits in youth increases their ability to engage in hope agency that facilitates transformation in the world. To move toward hope, agents of hope do not ignore the conflict youth may experience. Rather they encourage

---

34 Miroslav Volf, *Exclusion and Embrace: A Theological Exploration of Identity, Otherness, and Reconciliation* (Nashville: Abingdon Press, 1996), 258 (italics original).

peacemaking by encouraging lament. An activity of lament was presented at the end of chapter 5.

When adolescents experience personal or interpersonal conflict, they may also be experiencing spiritual conflict, whereby they are in a tense disagreement with God about the way things are. During these times of deep conflict with God youth may find their hope in crisis. The mere act of voicing anger, frustration, disappointment, and confusion with God and the world is an act of agency. This is particularly true in a culture that often sanitizes God so much that youth begin to feel they are doing something wrong when they have such strong emotions toward God and others. Agents of hope use conflict-transformation pedagogy as a way to remind youth that emotions are not wrong; instead, they remind us that we are human. The willingness and know-how to express these emotions is actually a first step toward any form of conflict transformation.

For example, when YHBA staff faced hard truths about youth who encountered abuse in their past, they had to walk youth through the interpersonal conflict that emerged as well as evidences of spiritual conflict. Youth began to ask big questions about God, including "How could you let this happen to me? How could a good God allow such evil?" Walking with youth as they struggle with answers to these questions becomes a prime opportunity for agents of hope to simply listen. At times, the only response may be "What happened must be deeply wounding. Sometimes, arriving at answers is hard and simply calls for courage to continue on in the heat of real pain." At other times, in response to the question of why, we have engaged youth in conversations focused on the free will of human beings given by God, and that this freedom of choice to act in life does result in an individual's harming another in ways that are contrary to God's desire. Furthermore, agents of hope assist youth in reframing their image of God so they understand God's love as unconditional, knowledge as omniscient, and grace as new every day. Instead of God being angry at adolescents for expressing their emotions, agents of hope remind youth that God invites their transparency in order to form a deeper and more authentic relationship with them. As Schrock-Shenk points out, the psalmist's lament to

God does not result in alienation from God. To the contrary, it creates a sense of intimacy and knowing between the psalmist and God.[35] The voice expressed in lament becomes an entryway into knowledge of pertinent concerns held by the psalmist. It also reveals harm done to the psalmist at the hands of others.

Agents of hope walk with and guide youth through their lamenting process. To guide youth through the naming of pain, agents of hope can share the biblical practice of lament with youth. Lament, often found in prayers or poetry, are expressions to God of rage, frustration, confusion, and despair. These expressions often emerge from deep pain. The biblical tradition of lament includes those prayers and expressions of complaint, anger, grief, despair, and protest. Old Testament scholar Kathleen O'Conner suggests lament are prayers that

> erupt from wounds, burst out of unbearable pain, and bring it to language. Laments complain, shout, and protest. They take anger and despair before God and community. They grieve. They argue. They find fault. . . . Although laments appear disruptive of God's world, they are acts of fidelity. In vulnerability and honesty, they cling to God and demand for God to see, hear, and act. . . . In the process of harsh complaint and resistance, they also express faith in God in the midst of chaos, doubt, and confusion.[36]

It is important to communicate to young people that complaining, crying, even shouting or screaming to God in lament is not blasphemy. Instead, it is an invitation for God to engage in conversation. It beckons God to respond to human conflict and pain. Edward Wimberly positions God as a receiver of the emotional frustration that the psalmist experiences.[37] Lament includes a call for the attention of God, honest complaint (sometimes even against God for God's perceived silence), a genuine plea for God's intervention, and an acknowledgment that God has heard the plea. In this sense, lament actually restores intimacy with

---

35 Carolyn Schrock-Shenk, "Introducing Conflict and Conflict Transformation," *Making Peace with Conflict*, 27.

36 Kathleen M. O'Connor, *Lamentations and the Tears of the World* (Maryknoll, NY: Orbis Books, 2002), 9.

37 Edward P. Wimberly, *Claiming God, Reclaiming Dignity: African American Pastoral Care* (Nashville: Abingdon Press, 2003), 114.

God rather than destroys it. It recognizes pain as a conflict that needs to be addressed and does so through lament.

It is also crucial that youth who have a stoic view in the face of trouble and hurt—especially young men who have internalized a macho male image—understand that lament is a refusal to deny pain. Those who deny their pain deny their voice. As Kathleen M. O'Connor notes, "To gain a voice means to come into the truth of one's history corporately and individually, to recover one's life, to acquire moral agency by naming one's world. The voice brings from the depths of silence the creative power, energy, and wholeness of a person or a people in the midst of its world."[38] It takes courage to be a sharer of one's own truth. This becomes even more difficult when that truth is grounded in conflict. In a world that would rather keep peace, avoid conflict, and pretend everything is okay; it is sometimes difficult to express one's pain. Denial, silence, and trying to figure it out become much easier. But these responses to conflict and pain can be dangerous for hope and the human spirit where hope resides. As O'Connor points out, "When denial becomes a hardened way of life, it inhibits flourishing, cuts off the spirit as its roots, silences voices, and blocks passion for justice. Whether practiced by society or individuals, denial constricts hope, depletes life, and aborts praise. Crushed spirits cannot worship unless that spirit speaks from the pain."[39] On the one hand, regardless of what hope category an adolescent may be in, the ability to share about internal and external conflicts with a caring adult pivots toward hope. On the other hand, not finding this space to share could be detrimental to the adolescent's soul, leading to an implosion within the self or an explosion of rage toward others.

Lament contributes to peacemaking by positioning one's self to understand the suffering in the world. Those who deny their own pain are more likely to deny the pain of others and the suffering at work in this world. Thus, lament is not only the practice of being transparent about one's own feelings; it is also a move toward hearing and

---

38 O'Connor, *Lamentations and the Tears of the World*, 83.
39 Ibid., 87.

responding to the concerns of others. Only through the ability to hear others' laments can one adequately take steps toward the practice of peacemaking.

Repairing the World through Justice Seeking

Within the practice of peacemaking, agents of hope inspire youth to take action in the world through justice seeking. In line with shalom, agents of hope resist denying the brokenness in the world revealed through violence. Rightly so, O'Connor describes violence as a social mechanism of denying pain. Instead of facing the rage and alienation we may feel, we scapegoat and displace our rage on others.[40] This can be seen on both interpersonal and structural levels. Inviting youth to repair the world and confront systems of domination, such as racism, actually contributes to what Evelyn Parker calls an "integrated spirituality," whereby religious belief and social practice are intertwined in the life of the adolescent.[41] In this sense, shalom is not a self-directed approach to transform the world but an approach to transforming the world in partnership with God and others. Agents of hope encourage adolescents to repair the world by creating spaces where they can engage in advocacy and public lament.

CREATING VIOLENCE-FREE PEDAGOGICAL SPACES

Conflict transformation is not something to simply talk or teach about; it must be emulated by agents of hope. As stated earlier, environments that support violence are most likely to result in youth using violence as their primary means of resolving conflict. Providing alternatives to violence through conflict-transformation skills asserts that fight or flight are not the only options. The role of agents of hope is to create violence-free pedagogical spaces where youth can seek and share truth and justice in the context of a loving community. Youth need a

---

40 Ibid., 92.

41 Evelyn L. Parker, *Trouble Don't Last Always: Emancipatory Hope among African American Adolescents* (Cleveland, OH: Pilgrim Press, 2003).

stable environment that provides a sense of constancy amidst a rapidly changing and inconsistent world. Creating a structured environment does not foreclose youth participation. Rather, structured environments offer space where youth can gain and practice the necessary skills to enact peace wherever they are. We have found that curricula are desirable when the content addresses the daily concerns of youth and engages young people in envisioning the nature of peacemaking as central to their courageous living.

Practice What You Preach

What we are after here is an understanding that conflict transformation is not just something that is learned about. It is something that is lived. Hope agency guides youth to transform conflict into situations that can be used for personal growth, rather than allowing conflict to escalate into something that negates the self or others. To this end, agents of hope not only invite youth to reflect on their Christian values but also guide youth to be agents of peace in their daily lives. Lessons learned in structured environments that teach conflict transformation need to be not only relevant to but operative in the lives of youth. In other words, youth should know that what they're learning are not pie-in-the sky skills that cannot be translated to the streets. Rather, the skills they learn are translatable and can be used to transform conflict in daily situations that youth might encounter. Students learn that the skills they acquire can be translated to their lives. The absence of this translation could result in a lack of the application of knowledge learned during the most critical times. As a mode of teaching, YHBA staff employed the conflict-transformation skills taught to the youth when necessary. In order to facilitate retention of these skills, and for them to become second nature, one concrete tool agents of hope can use is role-play. Role-play invites adolescents to rehearse how they might respond to conflict before conflict ever takes place. They can try on roles such as "bully," "victim," "instigator," and "peacemaker" to empathize with how it might feel to walk in someone else's shoes. In short, practicing what you preach compels teachers and adolescents alike to embody peacemaking by employing conflict transformation in their everyday interactions with people.

Ritualizing Conflict Transformation

Conflict often extends beyond verbal words; conflict is messy, encompassing the emotions, interactions, and thoughts of people. To get to the root of conflict, conflict transformation must also employ responses that reach beyond mere words. Rituals function as a response to conflict that integrates the body, words, and emotions while at the same time helping to form individuals in the way of peace. As Lisa Schirich notes in her book *Ritual and Symbol in Peacebuilding*, "In ritual, the impossible and unlikely can come true as people create a unique context where, if only temporarily, symbols, sensory cues, and the expression of emotion communicate what words alone cannot."[42] The use of ritual within conflict-transformation pedagogy reminds us of the importance of bodies in the teaching and learning process. We store memory within our bodies. As we participate in embodied expressions of conflict transformation, our bodies learn how to engage in nonverbal and verbal expressions of conflict transformation as if it is second nature. The hand-washing ceremony described in this chapter's centering story demonstrates a way of transitioning from a state of offense to a state of internal and external peace. Adolescents imagined within their hearts and felt with their bodies what it meant to offer peace and forgiveness to someone else. This kind of peacemaking ritual invites adolescents to make a public declaration of their intent to be "called children of God."

CONCLUSION

Conflict transformation has its basis in hope. The vision of conflict-transformation pedagogy centers on practices of peacemaking that build resilience, promote human connectedness, and practice shalom.

---

42 Lisa Schirch, *Ritual and Symbol in Peacebuilding* (Bloomfield, CT: Kumarian Press, 2005), 86.

By creating hope-filled pathways where adolescents can lament, offer forgiveness, engage in truth-telling and sharing, and repair the world, conflict-transformation pedagogy creates space for adolescents to embody courageous hope. Agents of hope demonstrate hope agency as they journey with, invite, and guide youth on pathways that sometimes feel less traveled.

QUEST FOR AWARENESS: A PATHWAY OF EXPOSURE

Never be limited by other people's limited imagination. If you adopt their attitudes, then the possibility won't exist because you'll have already shut it out. . . . You can hear other people's wisdom, but you've got to re-evaluate the world for yourself.

— Mae Jemison[1]

*Be strong and courageous. Do not be afraid or terrified because of them, for the L*ORD *your God goes with you; [God] will never leave you nor forsake you.*

— Deuteronomy 31:6 (NIV)

[A CENTERING STORY]

As one of the leaders, I, Sarah, felt the excitement that rose throughout the bus as we approached the exit and informed the youth that we were only a few blocks away from the church that would be our point of service in New Orleans. Many of the youth who were part of the Youth Hope-Builders Academy Post-Katrina Service Project had never been to New Orleans and were looking intently from the window. But all of us became riveted by the image of abandoned and dilapidated houses that continued block after block. Frankly, the view before us disrupted any idea that this was a nice little excursion to help others in need.

---

1   Quoted at the Annual Biomedical Research Conference for Minority Students, November 2009 and appears in: Nola Taylor Redd, "Mae Jemison: Astronaut Biography," August 17, 2012, https://www.space.com/17169-mae-jemison-biography.html.

Breaking the silence that had engulfed us, one youth asked, "Why are all of those numbers on the buildings? What do they mean?" I responded, "They represent the people who were left behind in houses during the flood." Again, a hush covered the bus as several other leaders gave further details about deaths that the numbers on the buildings represented. We had arrived on our service trip two years after Hurricane Katrina; and the symbols on the buildings that still stood screamed of the injustice that had been done to the citizens of New Orleans, especially those who could not afford to live in some of the more expensive areas of the city.

All of us gathered in the small, predominately African American United Methodist church situated at an intersection. The church had graciously agreed to host us for a total of five days. The congregation had been actively involved in hosting large groups who came from out of state to assist in rebuilding New Orleans after Hurricane Katrina. A large portion of the church had been converted into sleeping quarters so that volunteer groups would be afforded living space with little concern about funds for lodging. Our group was among a limited number of African American volunteers that had opportunity to offer support to the residents of New Orleans. Our intent was to emphasize to our young people the necessity of response in times of crisis and to enable them to connect across diverse lived realities.

Eager to receive instructions, the youth gathered quickly in the seats. The youth partitioned themselves off. YHBA youth sat in the front of the church; youth from New Orleans sat in the back. It was as if the devastation that took place in New Orleans created a chasm between the youth, where youth from YHBA were perceived as, and perceived themselves as, those who were coming to do service; and the youth from New Orleans were perceived as, and perceived themselves as, those in need of assistance. YHBA staff noticed the separation.

Instead of moving into a description of the service projects we would engage during our time in New Orleans, we opened our time with worship, an invitation for our hearts to be in one accord and to recognize the grace of God in spite of the devastation that so many of our brothers and sisters had experienced. As the music began to play and the group began to sing, a youth from YHBA got up from his seat, walked to the back of the sanctuary and grabbed the hand of one of the youth from New Orleans. That New Orleanian youth, followed by the other youth from New Orleans, repositioned themselves in the front with the YHBA youth. Together, the group of youth and YHBA staff sang in unison the familiar words of a song by Hezekiah Walker entitled "I Need You to Survive." These words affirmed the need for connection in God's body in order to survive.

ON THE FRONT LINES OF EXPOSURE

The entire nation watched from afar, wondering how New Orleans could be hit with such devastation. We watched in utter confusion about why efforts to help those still stuck in New Orleans did not take place sooner. Our confusion was met with apologies from the president about the inefficient response displayed by the federal, state, and local government. It was also met with the anxious protests and survival efforts of New Orleans' residents, which manifested in great courage as well as great violence. Many wondered whether the lack of response correlated with the fact that those left behind were among the poorest residents in the city.

Being in New Orleans turned the strangers on the television into the faces of youth who had walked through the reality of personal loss of their possessions, relatives, and livelihoods. Not only did we see the mobile homes that now housed many schools; youth from New Orleans exposed teen participants in the Youth Hope-Builders Academy (YHBA) to the emotional trauma of feeling displaced. As youth from New Orleans shared their stories with youth in YHBA, the Academy youth could touch, feel, and empathize. They began to recognize that, while they had never been through a flood, they wrestled in their own communities with some of the same emotions that their peers in New Orleans experienced. The stark picture of loss could not be missed. People lost everything, including the pictures that held memories of loved ones now gone. It is not surprising that such great loss could put hope in decline. Events like Hurricane Katrina often leave adults and youth alike in a state of questioning God, hope, and a future. After seeing the devastation, youth from our program raised the same questions: questions centered on God's presence in the midst of the hurricane. The mutual interaction that took place between the youth and staff represented a major feature of why youth exposure to different contexts and people is critical to their personal and spiritual development.

The story above emphasizes the important role of the church to provide space for adolescents across cultures and varied experiences to connect and serve one another. In particular, the youth had the opportunity to see firsthand the deeply embedded injustices within the US system, while also participating in worthy attempts to respond on the ground to the devastation in New Orleans. The thousands of abandoned homes concentrated in particular parts of the city reflect the tendency of natural disasters to impact most the poorest neighborhoods. Those who could not afford insurance before the hurricane often had the most limited options post-storm. The service project to New Orleans not only promoted youth coming together to serve their community; it also became grounds to establish a trusted relationship with others outside of their community. Establishing these networks among adolescents and faith-based organizations is an example of a pedagogy of exposure, which seeks to build networks that produce lasting change in the lives of adolescents. That the faith community has to step in to serve as an advocate and resource for devastated communities stems from a long history within African American history.

The inability to participate within human society hinders the economic, social, physical, and vocational well-being of all people, including adolescents. Emerging from the slave era and after the Civil War, the historic Black Church played a critical role in ensuring that African Americans had avenues to meet their physical needs and participate fully in society. Religious institutions saw their role as responding to not only the spiritual needs of the people but also the social and economic needs that Black people faced. As a result, political, financial, and educational institutions emerged within the African American community that promoted their full participation within society. A key way that Black churches responded to the lack of access to social and political resources was, and is, by either creating their own organizations or partnering with mutual aid societies that offered resources. In this sense, the church and other agents of hope possess great potential to serve as a bridge to multidimensional hope. One such way is to provide exposure pedagogies that uplift enrichment opportunities, invite strong relational bonds, and offer opportunities to serve in other communities. Through the practice of bridging, agents of hope provide the structural and relational support necessary to invite, guide, and be present with youth as they choose hope-forming pathways for their lives.

SIGNIFICANCE OF EXPOSURE PEDAGOGIES IN THE LIVES OF AFRICAN AMERICAN ADOLESCENTS

A pedagogy of exposure centers on cultural, social, relational, civic, spiritual, and immersion experiences that help shape one's view of life. These experiences contribute to a strong sense of identity and purpose in the world. The purpose of exposure pedagogy is to empower youth. Empowerment is an active and participatory process that enables persons to become agents in securing the resources needed to control their lives and accomplish their life dreams and goals.[2] A pedagogy of exposure ultimately expands the view of what's needed to build healthy and hope-filled communities by exposing youth to both the promise and the challenges associated with diverse lived realities. Pastoral care theologian Joyce Mercer notes her experience teaching exposure learning in a multicultural Asian class about the "Red Light District." She writes:

> Exposures consist of short-term experiential learning events through participation and immersion into a specific context, preceded and followed by a process of study and reflection. Exposure learning holds the potential to provide experiences of disorientation/reorientation that call into question existing paradigms held by students, opening the way for the construction of new and transformed ways of knowing.[3]

---

2   Kenneth I. Maton and Deborah A. Salem, "Organizational Characteristics of Empowering Community Settings: A Multiple Case Study Approach," *American Journal of Community Psychology* 23, no. 5 (October 1995): 631–56.

3   Joyce A. Mercer, "Red Light Means Stop! Teaching Theology through Exposure Learning in Manila's Red Light District," *Teaching Theology & Religion* 5 (April 2002): 90–100 (91).

In this context, similar to the one above, students are exposed to lived realities quite different from their own. Often, these diverse contexts evoke a sense of discomfort, which may lead to disorientation. At this point, youth may have more questions than answers. This immersion into diverse contexts is an entry point in encountering structural oppression, which helps challenge deeply held convictions or beliefs. For example, youth in the centering story were bothered by the devastation, empathetic to the loss of youth from New Orleans, and angered by the response of the government. Nevertheless, the worship experience and the conversation that ensued help provide a reorienting framework that students could use as they wrestled with the various questions that emerged. The process of disorientation and reorientation that takes place in exposure pedagogy helps students better understand, perceive, and see in order to enact justice in society.

Other exposure learning centers on connection and gaining access to experiences that help enhance a sense of self. For the purposes of this chapter, we focus mainly on exposure pedagogies that bridge youth to opportunity. Rather than focusing solely on financial capital, exposure pedagogy understands the role of building strong social, cultural, and spiritual networks among and between communities. It exposes youth to networks that create greater access to resources that contribute to personal and vocational growth. To this end, agents of hope invite, guide, and serve as a steady presence in the lives of youth that helps facilitate the type of connections that will contribute to a hope-forming pathway for them. Exposure pedagogies signify an intentional need of caring adults to facilitate and initiate the type of opportunities that will help adolescents flourish.

For African American youth, especially those from low-income communities, exposure to enrichment opportunities, service, and relational networks become especially critical to flourishing. Some scholars, for example, have identified what they call an "institutional constellation" or a "specific set of institutions operating in an individual's *lived* experience of/within their institutional constellation."[4] Those who are

---

4   These include the key institutions operating in a child's life, such as school, family, peers, and state government, and the youth's perception of these institutions. JoAnn S. Lee, "An Institutional Framework for the Study of the Transition to Adulthood," *Youth & Society* 46, no. 5 (June 18, 2012): 706–30 (711).

integrated in an institutional constellation situated within dominant norms have greater advantages in making a transition to adulthood. Further, the research highlighted the increased vulnerability and disadvantages that ethnic, female, or poor youth have during this transition because of their marginal relationship to or within particular institutions.[5] These same adolescents often do not have the luxury to explore different career possibilities before making a long-term commitment to institutions that will produce financial stability for them and their families; instead, they enter "accelerated adulthood."[6] Overall, while having access to particular institutions cannot guarantee success, it does contribute to the adoption of lifelong commitments that are fulfilling and set one on a positive life trajectory.[7] To this end, caring adults use pedagogies of exposure to introduce youth to new institutions that might contribute to their formation.

Faith communities are a distinct institution within the institutional constellation that can contribute to adolescents' transition to adulthood. Agents of hope can be found within the family, school, and state government; they can also be found in the church. Faith communities have a unique institutional role to fulfill and can enhance the basis of support during adolescence that should not be overlooked. A primary role for Black churches, and the agents of hope who reside in them, is to connect youth to a viable future by removing some of the barriers that inhibit achievement and bridging them to positive self-concept development and role models.[8] Research discovered, in particular, that the faith community plays three key roles in promoting social capital among their members. First, they provide spiritual support for their active congregational members. Second, they foster social and cultural capital among their participants, offering communal support to those who express specific social and instrumental needs. Last, they serve as a major source

---

5   Ibid., 706.

6   Ibid., 712.

7   Ibid., 715.

8   Janice Hale-Benson, "Psychosocial Experiences," in *Working with Black Youth: Opportunities for Christian Ministry*, eds. Charles R. Foster and Grant S. Shockley (Nashville: Abingdon Press, 1989), 49.

for structural social change.[9] Overall, effective participation in US society requires access to life pathways that lead to meaningful engagement through relationships, productive careers, and acts of service. Connecting to meaningful experiences facilitates a hopeful quality of life that sees possibilities as actually possible. Agents of hope, then, ultimately employ exposure pedagogies to invite, guide, and be present with youth in their exploration of academic, cultural, social, and spiritual opportunities.

EXPOSURE PEDAGOGIES AS ENRICHMENT OPPORTUNITIES

Enrichment opportunities represent a hallmark of exposure pedagogy. These opportunities sit on a continuum of academic, cultural, social, and spiritual enrichment that enables adolescents to physically engage in holistic growth. They are concrete activities that place adolescents in close proximity to opportunities to see, discover, and develop new skills. An enrichment activity might be something as simple as going to a museum or something as involved as participation in a residential program with other youth. Enrichment opportunities seek to build the interior and exterior selves of youth so they can be active participants in their churches, communities, and world.

Academic Enrichment

Academic enrichment opportunities form hope by extending adolescents' exposure. Some academic activities and experiences help them excel in academic or marketplace settings. While this may include life skills, these activities actually contribute to critical thinking, skills-based learning, and communication skills that enhance future educational success. Furthermore, academic enrichment programs supplement education by providing tutoring, SAT, and GRE preparation, offering resume writing workshops, and other specific academic-centered training that prepares Black youth to thrive in a highly competitive world. By

---

9   Jo Anne Schneider, *The Role of Social Capital in Building Healthy Communities* (Baltimore, MD: Annie E. Casey Foundation, 2004), 47.

providing college and career preparation, students gain courage to explore life pathways that otherwise may not be easily accessible to them. In this sense, hope is an outcome of the opportunity, because it provides youth with confidence about their skills; it also helps adolescents overcome some of the social barriers that limit access to higher education because of race and class.

Spiritual Enrichment

Spiritual enrichment supports the spiritual formation of adolescents by providing activities that seek to awaken one's soul and promote spiritual growth. Processes of discernment, youth-led worship, discipleship studies, labyrinths, Bible studies, retreats, and nature walks all align with spiritual enrichment. It is an invitation to flee spiritual emptiness and embrace deep friendship with God. Moreover, spiritual enrichment seeks to provide the spiritual foundation adolescents need to thrive even amidst adversity. These activities introduce youth to spiritual practices and habits that contribute to a flourishing life. Within YHBA retreat settings, for example, we integrated a time for morning worship where youth would work within their small mentoring groups, called heart-to-heart groups, to plan worship services. Not only did youth bring their passion and gifts to the space; youth also invited their peers to engage in spiritual practices that provided grounding for the challenges they faced outside the youth retreat. Worship opened the door for them to communicate with God authentically. Overall, spiritual enrichment helps to develop, sustain, or introduce youth to authentic relationship with God.

Cultural Enrichment

Cultural enrichment opportunities provide valuable life skills by enhancing youth's awareness of diverse cultural practices. These include increasing awareness of cultural, intellectual, social, and artistic achievements of one's own culture as well as other cultures. The cultural enrichment opportunities, for example, provide sites of reflection and information wherein youth can relate, gain awareness, and understand other cultures. A hallmark of cultural enrichment is the ability to welcome and respect diversity. For African American youth, it is especially important to expose them to Afrocentric cultural enrichment. For example, YHBA sought opportunities to close the gap between African American and African youth. Exposing African American youth to African culture through video-conferencing and mission trips between Black American and African youth, Ghanaian Sunday worship experiences, curriculum that integrates the wisdom of Black history, and taking youth to South Africa to connect with other YHBA units served as opportunities to expand cultural intelligence among the youth. In addition, adult African mentors have been part of the leadership team. These experiences have sought to expose and connect youth with a world that is relevant to their identity as Blacks in America.

EXPOSURE PEDAGOGIES AS SOCIAL ENRICHMENT: FORMING STRONG RELATIONAL BONDS

Enrichment extends beyond the curricula and cultural learning that takes place; it also includes opportunities to form relational bonds with those who are vastly different. In the twenty-first century, when youth spend more time on social media than in face-to-face interactions with people, isolation is a serious concern. This is especially true for adolescents who are disconnected from familial, institutional, and church-based support. In fact, some would go so far as to say that there is a systemic abandonment of social support for youth that actually contributes to the isolation youth feel.[10] Many times youth create their own worlds that are completely separate from adults; these worlds operate with their own rules and moral codes and may lack positive social norms.[11] Without hopeful adult relationship in their lives, youth are left to develop friendships that center on their peers, some that are positive and others that may be self-destructive. While many studies lament the isolation and loneliness youth experience now, agents of hope occupy a prime location to counter alienation

---

10   Chap Clark, *Hurt: Inside the World of Today's Teenagers*, Youth, Family, and Culture Series (Grand Rapids, MI: Baker Academic Books, 2004), 39–56.

11   Ibid., 59.

by relocating youth back in the center of the faith community. These relational bonds provide mentorship, social support, and spiritual guidance that pay close attention to both the interior of adolescents as well as prospects for their future.

EXPOSURE PEDAGOGIES AS CIVIC ENRICHMENT: OPPORTUNITIES TO SERVE OTHERS

Exposure pedagogies embrace civic enrichment as a key feature of forming strong adolescent leaders for today's and tomorrow's world. Society often sends the message that youth are not needed, nor are they welcome in the economic or civic tasks that help renew society.[12] Civic enrichment, on the other hand, affirms the need for youth by inviting them to use their intelligence and physical strength to help repair the world. The assumption is that youth who are exposed to the purpose, possibility, and know-how of civic opportunities will also be more likely to engage in civic participation. In order to do so, exposure pedagogies invite youth into structured activities that center on civic engagement. While there are numerous examples of civic enrichment activities that agents of hope can expose youth to, we have chosen to focus on service. Service represents a critical exposure for adolescents, especially when it requires adolescents to encounter contexts that are different from one's own. In other words, youth enact hope agency when they are encouraged to engage in acts of service and justice within and beyond their community. Service that empowers change, encounters others, and expands faith leads youth on a pathway to courageous hope.

Empowering Change

The trip to New Orleans described in the centering story reminded us of how critical service is to empowering youth to become change agents in their local communities. The projects we completed, such as the beautification of vacant lots and neighborhood homes, repositioned

---

12   James Youniss and Miranda Yates, *Community Service and Social Responsibility in Youth* (Chicago: University of Chicago Press, 1997), x–xi.

service as something in which youth can engage, even in their local neighborhoods. Projects both big and small create a sense of youth making a difference in their world, which contributes to a larger vision of their participation in the community. In research with middle-class Black youth in Washington DC, for example, James Youniss and Miranda Yates note that service helps develop an activist identity in adolescents, whereby adolescents develop a sense of agency and responsibility for social change, emerging from the understanding that they are part of a historical tradition with moral authority.[13] In other words, service not only bridges youth to opportunities that help shape the present world but also enhances their potential to shape the future. Their ability to shape the future is critical to their own prospect of hope in the world.

Encountering Difference

One of the hallmarks of acts of service is the possibility of encountering difference. That difference may manifest in context, circumstance, or personhood. The encounter of difference may disorient one's thinking about what it means to be human or what courage looks like in the midst of difficulty. It may also be a key indicator to youth of the fact that difference in context, circumstance, or personhood does not negate our common humanity; we all bleed red blood. The contact that takes place across difference holds meaning for the present moment and moments beyond. Acts of missional service, such as described in the centering story, for example, align with meaningful experiences that can shape the life choices of adolescents. Service in the midst of devastation reminds youth of the interconnectedness among individuals. When one suffers, we all suffer. When one bleeds, we all bleed. And, it is in the midst of providing relief for the wounds of another that we ourselves are healed.

Expanding Faith

Service is not only an attempt to encourage youth's development

---

13   Ibid., 110–14.

into civic agents; it is an attempt to center adolescent hearts in the message of love for one's neighbor found in the gospel. Loving one's neighbor, especially when that neighbor is different, takes courage. Service combats the tendency of youth developing an insular faith. It reminds youth that they are connected to a world beyond themselves. Instead, youth are challenged to know that both social and personal salvation remain key priorities in bringing about flourishing in the world.

ROLE OF THE AGENT OF HOPE IN EXPOSURE PEDAGOGY: THE PRACTICE OF BRIDGING

The primary way agents of hope enact exposure pedagogies is through the practice of bridging. Bridging creates a connecting link that opens possibilities for youth and their families to touch, see, feel, and experience aspects of life that seem out of reach because of their current social or geographic location. Bridging creates access points along an adolescent's journey so he or she feels supported. The Search Institute released a document that identifies forty assets that are important to the flourishing of adolescents. Several of these external and internal assets get at the heart of pedagogies of exposure. For example, the external asset of empowerment, which includes community valuing of youth, viewing youth as resources, youth's service to others, and safety, all provide principles of learning embraced by exposure pedagogies.[14] Overall, the invitation to participate in strong relational bonds and broaden one's vantage point, coupled with the guidance of enrichment opportunities that contribute to emotional, social, and spiritual intelligence, help bridge youth to hope-forming pathways that extend their future possibilities. In particular, bridging focuses on agents of hope inviting youth into structured opportunities, functioning as a mentoring presence in the lives of youth, and providing guidance through mentoring conversations.

---

14   Peter L. Benson, *Sparks: How Parents Can Ignite the Hidden Strengths of Teenagers* (San Francisco: Jossey-Bass, 2008), 181–98.

INVITATION: INVESTING CARE, RAISING HOPE THROUGH STRUCTURING OPPORTUNITIES

Before bridging ever takes place, leaders who take on the role of agents of hope must "see" youth. Invitation represents a posture where agents of hope purposely see them. One of the main ways visibility occurs is by structuring opportunities of mutual accompaniment. Agents of hope not only invite but also accompany youth into structured, meaningful experiences. This dual act of invitation and accompaniment provides a foundation of support that gives adolescents the confidence to discover and explore new possibilities.

Structuring Opportunities for Enrichment Spaces

Enrichment spaces represent the structured activities that agents of hope plan that enable concrete connection to cultural, spiritual, social, relational, civic, or academic enrichment. They include a wide range of intentional opportunities designed to enhance the internal and external development of adolescents that include, but are certainly not limited to, Black heritage tours; special arts events, including visits to museums, plays, and concerts; health fairs; college/vocational-tech tours; public library programs; mission trips; service in hospitals, nursing homes, shelters for homeless people, and soup kitchens; neighborhood clean-ups; and sporting events. Choices of enrichment spaces may vary depending on the particular group of youth. This means that attention should be placed on contextualized enrichment that is based on the lived experiences of the youth with whom adults work. The experiences, then, signify that agents of hope are in touch with the challenges Black youth face in the world and their need for widened, new, and different opportunities for learning, serving, and developing. Not only are they in touch with these challenges; but agents of hope seek active ways to respond to these challenges by exposing youth to alternative pathways that lead to a hopeful pathway rather than a counterproductive one. The agents are, in fact, cognizant of what can promote hope and courageous living.

Structuring Opportunities for Active Listening

Active listening is the process of communicating so that you hear and seek to understand what's being communicated. Active listening demonstrates a message of worth and value to youth. By providing adolescents with one's undivided attention, agents of hope remind youth that they are worth being heard and that what they say actually has value. Agents of hope ask questions that help clarify their understanding and use nonverbal cues to signal that they care about what they hear. In other words, active listening is invitational because, when adolescents feel heard, they know they are always welcome at the table for conversation.

Structuring Opportunities for Physical Affirmation

With the many threats to the physical safety of adolescents and the new policies that seek to maintain sexual integrity between adults and adolescents, physical affirmation is perhaps an exposure activity that remains undiscussed. Yet physical affirmation is critical, especially for youth who have experienced abuse and exposure to inappropriate physical touch. To this end, we want to draw attention to the physical posture of agents of hope. This posture has both figurative and literal elements to it that we hope invoke deep reflection for agents of hope. The "Let the children come" expression demonstrated through Jesus' verbal and physical posture toward children represents the invitational presence of agents of hope in the lives of youth. At a time when the disciples decided that Jesus was too busy to tend to the children, Jesus prioritized the children, demonstrating the importance of the bodily gestures that signify a bridge for youth. Open arms are the invitational bridge that connect youth into the arms of caring adults and remind them that they are in the hands of a loving God. The bodies of agents of hope provide texts that speak hope in the midst of a busy and unwelcoming world. Human touch that is nonsexual but communicates unconditional love ultimately provides a rubric that helps guide adolescents in their other relationships.

This is manifested in the interactions at YHBA. It did not take youth long to call the director of YHBA "Mom" or "Grandmom." I often wondered what warranted such familial language in such a short amount of time. The hope agency of an extended hand from the YHBA youth to the New Orleanian youth reminded me of the many times I witnessed the open-armed approach of the director of YHBA and other staff who demonstrated their support through not only verbal acts but also non-verbal forms such as hugs, pats on the back, thumbs-up, and high fives. The bodily affirmation of youth's presence within YHBA reinforced their value and place within the community. It communicated love and functioned as a bridge to share with caring adults some of their deepest yearnings. It solidified the emotional trust needed to form sustainable mentoring relationships.

PRESENCE: INVESTING CARE, RAISING HOPE THROUGH A MENTORING PRESENCE

In order to bridge youth to opportunities, agents of hope employ pedagogies of exposure that emphasize the presence of agents of hope as a central way to inform young people's understanding that they are loved and valued by their community and by God. Through investing time, money, and thoughtful consideration in the lives of youth, agents of hope provide a solid source of support that encourages youth to risk internal growth. Pastoral care psychologist Gregory Ellison describes this mentoring presence as a "Reliable Other."[15] Reliable others are agents of hope who sow seeds of life that help nurture and nourish possibilities within the lives of adolescents.

Mentoring Presence as a Supportive Agent

Agents of hope who invest care simultaneously raise hope. Their willingness to create communities of support for adolescents has both short- and long-term payoffs. Feelings of enhanced worth and dignity are part of the return on their investment. Through living in community we construct our understanding of what it means to be

---

15   Gregory C. Ellison, *Cut Dead but Still Alive: Caring for African American Young Men* (Nashville: Abingdon Press, 2013), 146.

valued and worthy.[16] When practiced, this means, for example, that agents of hope do not simply point to places where young people may go to be enriched; they become the enriching presence when a young person is ill, when crises arise, and during times of celebration. A cliché that we have heard many times in our work with youth is that "people want you to show how much you care before you show how much you know." Youth give more weight to agents of hope who model care for them. Youth are more likely to trust, listen to, and share with those who they perceive authentically care about their lives and futures.

Mentoring Presence as Institutional Agent

Bridging to social, relational, and cultural networks requires important guidance. In some instances, guidance would be given by what may be referred to as an institutional agent. In other spaces, agents of hope would be considered the institutional agent, while other spaces would deem that agent of hope an intermediary to an institutional agent. The term "institutional agent" refers to "an individual who occupies one or more hierarchal positions of relatively *high-status*, either within society or within an institution (an organization)."[17] The work of an institutional agent is "to directly transmit, or negotiate the transmission of, highly valued resources."[18] This active negotiation requires intentional investment in youth, whereby agents of hope are willing to use their authority or reputation to advocate for the future of youth. This is akin to the times the YHBA director and staff have nominated scholars, written letters of recommendation, and introduced youth to specific opportunities. The agents of hope provide a sense of credibility for the youth that bridges them to the opportunity.

---

16   Edward P. Wimberly, *Claiming God, Reclaiming Dignity: African American Pastoral Care* (Nashville: Abingdon Press, 2003), 15.

17   Ricardo D. Stanton-Salazar, "A Social Capital Framework for the Study of Institutional Agents and Their Role in the Empowerment of Low-Status Students and Youth," *Youth & Society* 43, no. 3 (September 1, 2011): 1075 (italics added).

18   Ibid., 1067.

Mentoring Presence as Protective Agent

Within exposure pedagogies, agents of hope become a mentoring presence through which they give care and provide guidance to adolescents. Mentorship signifies a relationship in which a caring adult or more experienced peer provides trusted advice and direction for someone who is younger or less experienced. As mentors, agents of hope become aware of destructive paths youth may enter. In response, they function as intercessors by calling youth's attention to what is observed or learned, engage youth in conversation about reasons for the path that was taken, and suggest points of exposure that are hope-bearing and consistent with courageous living. For example, in a discussion about safe friends with a group of teens, one of the young men told of being in the car with several friends when one raised the topic of stealing some cigarettes in a convenience store. The youth who was sharing the story indicated that he thought his friend was joking until he identified a store to carry out a definite plan. When the mentor asked how the story ended, the young man responded by saying, "I was the driver of the car, and I just kept on driving. We just rode around awhile, and I dropped my friend off at a corner he chose." The mentor affirmed the young man's choice of not complying with his friend's intent. But he also provided information on laws of culpability that pertain to the presence of a so-called friend when a crime is committed, even when the friend is not part of the criminal act and is unaware of it happening. In addition, the mentor fulfilled the role of protector by exposing the entire group to statutes of law and consequences.

The point here is that, while youth often are expected to participate in high-risk behaviors, research demonstrates that adolescents who have mentors are less likely to participate in risky behaviors (such as illicit drug use, overindulgence in cigarette smoking, entertaining multiple sexual partners, carrying a weapon, or other offenses) that lead to increased possibilities of incarceration or addiction.[19] Further, in

---

19 Sharon R. Beier, Walter D. Rosenfeld, Kenneth C. Spitalny, Shelley M. Zansky, and Alexandra N. Bontempo, "The Potential Role of an Adult Mentor in Influencing High-Risk Behaviors in Adolescents," *Archives of Pediatrics & Adolescent Medicine* 154, no. 4 (2000): 327–31.

research comparing the impact of mentored youth with nonmentored youth, studies associated mentorship with positive youth development that helped transition youth in the foster care system to adulthood. In this study, mentored youth were less likely to report suicidal thoughts or involvement with physical fights and more likely to participate in higher education.[20] A mentoring presence creates a protective space for adolescents. The "mentor becomes a protective shield against inhibiting factors, a filter to screen outside influences during the elusive process of emergence of creative ideas and skills, and a stabilizer while the protégé consolidates the delicate web of creative ideas."[21] Overall, mentoring occupies an important role in the lives of youth, especially youth facing significant life challenges.

The protective stance may also extend to guest speakers from numerous walks of life who share with the youth about prisons, gangs, drugs, and other generative topics. For guest speakers that hold official titles such as "police officer" or "judge," these connections actually counter the adversarial relationships that seem to be the norm, establishing new pathways and potential for dynamic mentoring relationships. Not only the content of their lectures but their very presence within these spaces provide ambassadors of alternative pathways to assist youth in avoiding the social toxins that pervade many neighborhoods and schools.

GUIDANCE: INVESTING CARE, RAISING HOPE THROUGH MENTORING CONVERSATIONS

Mentorship leads to mentoring conversations that help guide youth. We assume that mentoring conversations emerge when agents of hope are in authentic relationship with adolescents. Agents of hope employ intentional efforts to ensure that the voices of adolescents remain a

---

20 Kym R. Ahrens, David Lane DuBois, Laura P. Richardson, Ming-Yu Fan, and Paula Lozano, "Youth in Foster Care with Adult Mentors During Adolescence Have Improved Adult Outcomes," *Pediatrics* 12, no. 2 (2008): e246–52.

21 Patricia A. Haensly and James L. Parsons, "Creative, Intellectual, and Psychosocial Development through Mentorship: Relationships and Stages," *Youth & Society* 25, no. 2 (1993): 213.

central part of the conversations. They are not drowned out in an attempt to demonstrate the knowledge of the agent of hope; rather, mentoring conversations recognize the adolescents as critical to the shaping of their own history. Further, the mentoring relationship is seen as reciprocal; thus, the conversations that take place are also seen as reciprocal. Agents of hope both give and receive, just like the adolescents they mentor. Mentoring conversations usually function to affirm youth, challenge youth, or provide concrete advice to youth about life direction. Conversations may center on a variety of life themes, from those that are affirmative to ones tackling difficulty, to conversations that call attention to life skills, or a mixture of these themes. Whatever the theme, conversations are important for the opportunity they offer for guidance given by agents of hope that enhance the perspectives of youth so that they can see life from a broader perspective.

An example of a mentoring conversation is that of a youth who continued to be overtly rude to a female mentor. But the rudeness typically did not take place where others could clearly identify it. In fact, the youth gave every indication of being a model participant in the youth program. The female mentor shared what was happening with the mentor that was assigned to the youth, and a meeting was arranged with the two mentors and the youth. However, before the meeting was held, the youth's mentor happened to be in the hallway when he heard a derogatory and belligerent comment made by the youth to the female mentor. The meeting was called immediately. In the conversation, the youth's mentor began by affirming the positive impression he had of the youth and the model behavior he had witnessed prior to the incident he had just seen and overheard.

The youth's mentor then asked probing questions about why the youth would act in such a manner with the female mentor. What evolved from the conversation was the youth's confession that the female mentor was a reminder of the youth's mother in looks and demeanor, and life in the single-parent home was tough. One outcome of the meeting was that the youth's mentor provided clear ground rules for respectful behavior and the necessity of an apology, with the understanding that the female mentor was not his mom. A further invitation was for the youth to enter into his mother's role for a moment while the youth's mentor took his role based on a typical incident of parent/youth blowups around completing household chores. What evolved from the reversed role drama was the youth beginning to appreciate another dimension of relationships that heretofore had been hidden.

It is important for agents of hope to engage in mentoring conversations that bridge adolescents with opportunities to connect with God. God-centered, affirmative conversations place God's presence, which operates in the midst of difficulty, front and center, so that youth can see life through that lens rather than through a lens that limits future possibility. Wimberly states, "Conversation with God counters the commodification of human worth, because it engages the person with a partner, God, who conveys a sense of unlimited worth and value to the person" through God's grace and unlimited love; this "love heals, guides, sustains, and reconciles such that persons can then reach out unselfishly *to others.*"[22] In this regard, liturgy becomes an important part of youth programs and offers opportunity for agents of hope to expose young people to the range of spiritual disciplines that may include spoken word; sentence, extemporaneous, and read prayers; prepared and youth-written litanies, and the range of artistic expressions presented in chapter 6. Visits to congregations with differing forms of worship are also further exposure opportunities that offer new ways of connecting and affirming young people's relationships with God.

In addition, our work puts us in contact with adolescents who share about the impact that specific mentors had on their lives, many of whom continue to maintain contact. We can recall one young man who, every time a particular mentor sees him, he quotes the first three or four lines of the poem she shared openly about her life experience. While the poem was performed in front of the young man, the conversation that ensued after he heard the poem left him with a deep understanding of Christ's pursuit for him.

Person-centered and God-centered affirmative conversations, as well as other forms of conversation, all serve as bridging media that

---

22 Wimberly, *Claiming God, Reclaiming Dignity*, 37 (italics original).

guide youth from where they are to another level of personal, social, spiritual, or vocational development. They provide the multidimensional hope that reminds youth of their valued ethnic identity and their worth before God. Overall, the conversations honor youth's capacity to achieve their goals and experience a flourishing life by providing them with kernels of possibility that can grow within their hearts, minds, and souls as they navigate the tough stuff of life. They offer hope and possibilities for courageous living by providing youth with the courage needed to explore and eventually seek out opportunities that enrich the self and others.

CONCLUSION

Agents of hope use pedagogies of exposure to connect youth with enrichment opportunities. These opportunities are meant to create more culturally, socially, spiritually, academically, and civically aware adolescents who are confident and competent in a highly competitive world. Bridging refers to connecting young people to relational, cultural, and social networks early in their adolescent development. In so doing, agents of hope invite youth to explore hope-building paths that are meaningful to them in the context of relationships that matter to them. Overall, pedagogies of exposure contribute to a flourishing life through enrichment opportunities that build hope and courage within youth.

BIBLIOGRAPHY

African American Policy Forum and Columbia Law School's Center for Intersectionality and School Policy Studies. *Black Girls Matter: Pushed Out, Overpoliced and Underprotected.* 2015. http://www.atlanticphilanthropies.org/app/uploads/2015/09/BlackGirlsMatter_Report.pdf.

Ahrens, Kym R., David Lane DuBois, Laura P. Richardson, Ming Yu Fan, and Paula Lozano. "Youth in Foster Care with Adult Mentors During Adolescence Have Improved Adult Outcomes." *Pediatrics* 121, no. 2 (February 2008): e246–52. doi:10.1542/peds.2007-0508.

Alkire, Sabina. "Dimensions of Human Development." *World Development* 30, no.2 (2002): 181–205. https://www.unicef.org/socialpolicy/files/Dimensions_of_Human_Development.pdf.

American Civil Liberties Union. "Talking Points: The School-To-Prison-Pipeline." https://www.aclu.org/files/assets/stpp_talkingpoints.pdf.

American Psychological Association (APA) Task Force on Resilience and Strength in Black Children and Adolescence. "Resilience and Strength in Black Children: A Vision for Optimal Development." Washington, DC: American Psychological Association, 2008. https://www.apa.org/pi/families/resources/resiliencept.pdf.

Anderson, Elijah. *Code of the Street: Decency, Violence, and the Moral Life of the Inner City.* New York: W.W. Norton, 1999.

Barboza, Steven, ed. *The African American Book of Values: Classic Moral Stories.* New York: Doubleday, 1998.

Barna, George. *Transforming Children into Spiritual Champions.* Ventura, CA: Regal Books, 2003.

Barnes, Sandra L., and Anne E. Streaty Wimberly. *Empowering Black Youth of Promise: Education and Socialization in the Village-minded Black Church.* New York: Routledge, 2016.

Batiste, Stephanie L. "Affect-ive Moves: Space, Violence, and the Body in Rize's Krump Dancing." In *The Oxford Handbook of Dance and the Popular Screen,* edited by Borelli, Melissa Blanco. New York: Oxford University Press, 2014.

Beier, Sharon R., Walter D. Rosenfeld, Kenneth C. Spitalny, Shelley M. Zansky, and Alexandra N. Bontempo. "The Potential Role of an Adult Mentor in Influencing High-Risk Behaviors in Adolescents." *Archives of Pediatrics & Adolescent Medicine* 154, no. 4 (2000): 327–331. doi:10.1001/archpeds.151.4.327.

Benson, Peter L. *Sparks: How Parents Can Ignite the Hidden Strengths of Teenagers.* San Francisco: Jossey-Bass Publishers, 2008.

Berger, Peter L. *Facing Up to Modernity: Excursions in Society, Politics, and Religion.* New York: Basic Books, 1977.

Biandi, Martha. *To Stand and Fight: The Struggle for Civil Rights in Postwar New York City.* Cambridge: Harvard University Press, 2003.

Billingsley, Andrew. *Climbing Jacob's Ladder: The Enduring Legacy of African-American Families.* New York: A Touchstone Book, 1992.

———. *Mighty Like a River: The Black Church and Social Reform.* New York: Oxford University Press, 1999.

Black Demographics.com. "African American Income." http://blackdemographics.com/households/african-american-income/.

Black Youth Project Staff. "Black Youth Dissuaded from Asking Questions?" *Black Youth Project*, January 31, 2012. http://blackyouthproject.com/black-youth-dissuaded-from-asking-questions/.

Blagen, Mark, and Julia Yang. "A Tool of Facilitating Courage: Hope is a Choice." Paper based on a program presented at the American Counseling Association Annual Conference and Exhibition, Charlotte, NC, 2009. http://www.counseling.org/resources/library/vistas/2009-V-Online/Blagen-Yang.pdf.

Bloom, Harold. *The American Religion: The Emergence of the Post-Christian Nation.* New York: Simon & Schuster, 1992.

Boal, Augusto. *Theater of the Oppressed.* New York: Theater Communications Group, 1985.

Brizee, Robert. *The Gift of Listening.* St. Louis: Chalice Press, 1993.

Brooks, Jean E. "Strengthening Resilience in Children and Youths: Maximizing Opportunities through the Schools," *Children & Schools* 28, no. 2 (April 1, 2006): 69–76: doi:10.1093/cs/28.2.69.

Brown, Monique J., Leroy R. Thacker, and Steven A. Cohen. "Association between Adverse Childhood Experiences and Diagnosis of Cancer," PLoS One, 2013; 8(6): e65524, https://ncbi.nim.nih.gov/pmc/articles/PMC3679131/.

Burnham, Linda Frye. "Community Arts at Work across the U.S." *A Working Guide to the Landscape of Arts for Change,* 1–18. New York: Americans for the Arts, 2011. http://www.animatingdemocracy.org/sites/default/files/LBurnham%20Trend%20Paper_2.pdf.

Capps, Donald. *Agents of Hope: A Pastoral Psychology.* Minneapolis: Fortress Press, 1995.

———. *Reframing: A New Method in Pastoral Care.* Minneapolis: Fortress Press, 1990.

Centers for Disease Control and Prevention. "About the CDC-Kaiser Adverse Childhood Experiences (ACE) Study." Atlanta, GA: Centers for Disease Control and Prevention, National Center for Injury Prevention and Control, Division of Violence Prevention. Last modified 2016. http://www.cdc.gov/violence prevention/acestudy/about.html.

Cho, Nan. "TransAfrica Forum (1977–)." www.blackpast.org/aah/transafrica-1977.

Chretien, Jean-Louis. *Under the Gaze of the Bible*. Translated by John Marson Dunaway. New York: Fordham University Press, 2015.

Clark, Chap. *Hurt: Inside the World of Today's Teenagers,* Youth, Family, and Culture Series. Grand Rapids, MI: Baker Academic Books, 2004.

Cleveland, William. "Arts-based Community Development: Mapping the Terrain." *A Working Guide to the Landscape of Arts for Change,* 1–12. New York: Americans for the Arts, 2011. http://www.americansforthearts.org/sites /default/files/BCleveland%20Trend%20Paper.pdf.

Clinebell, Howard. *Anchoring Your Well-Being: A Guide for Congregational Leaders*. Nashville: Upper Room, 1997.

Cohen, Cathy J. *Democracy Remixed: Black Youth and the Future of American Politics*. New York: Oxford University Press, 2010.

Cone, James H. *The Spirituals and the Blues: An Interpretation*. Maryknoll, NY: Orbis Books, 1972.

Corrie, Elizabeth W. "Becoming Christ's Hands and Feet in the World: The Vocational Formation of Staff." In *How Youth Ministry Can Change Theological Education— If We Let It*, edited by Kenda Creasy Dean and Christy Lang Hearlson, 231–46. Grand Rapids, MI: William B. Eerdmans Publishing Company, 2016.

Costen, Melva Wilson. *African American Christian Worship*. Nashville: Abingdon Press, 1993.

Crawford, Donna K., and Richard J. Bodine. "Conflict Resolution Education: Preparing Youth for the Future." *Juvenile Justice Journal* 8, no. 1 (June 2001): 21–29. http://www.ncjrs.gov/html/ojjdp/jjjournal_2001_6/jj3.html.

Crawford, Frances, Julie Dickinson, and Sabina Leitman. "Mirroring Meaning Making: Narrative Ways of Reflecting on Practice for Action." *Qualitative Social Work* 1, no. 2 (2002): 170–90.

Dash, Michael I. N., Jonathan Jackson, and Stephen C. Rasor. *Hidden Wholeness: An African American Spirituality for Individuals and Communities*. Cleveland: United Church Press, 1997.

Dennis, Kimya N. "The Complexities of Black Youth Suicide." Scholars Strategy Network, Cambridge, MA, September 2015. http://www.scholarsstrategy network.org/brief/complexities-black-youth-suicide.

Donaldson, Stewart I., Maren Dollwet, and Meghana A. Rao, "Happiness, Excellence, and Optimal Human Functioning Revisited: Examining the Peer-reviewed Literature Linked to Positive Psychology." *The Journal of Positive Psychology: Dedicated to Furthering Research and Promoting Good Practice* 10, no. 3 (2015?): 185–95. doi:10.1080/17430760.2014.943801. http://dx.doi.org/10.1080/17439760.2014.943801.

Du Bois, W. E. B. *The Negro Church in America.* 1903. Reprint, Walnut Creek, CA: Altimira Press, 2003.

Dunston, Philip, and Anne E. Streaty Wimberly. "A Matter of Discovery," In *Keep It Real: Working With Today's Black Youth*, edited by Anne E. Streaty Wimberly, 21–40. Nashville: Abingdon Press, 2005.

Edelman, Marian Wright. "Lessons from Noah's Ark." The WIP (Women's International Perspective). Posted October 5, 2010. http://thewip.net/2010/10/05/marian-wright-edelmans-lessons-from-noahs-ark/.

Ellison II, Gregory C. *Cut Dead but Still Alive: Caring for African American Young Men.* Nashville: Abingdon Press, 2013.

Erikson, Erik H. "Human Strength and the Cycle of Generations." *Insight and Responsibility.* New York: W.W. Norton, 1964.

———. "Identity and the Life Cycle: Selected Papers." *Psychological Issues*, monograph 1. New York: International Universities Press, 1959.

Evans, Brad, and Henry A. Giroux. *Disposable Futures: The Seduction of Violence in the Age of Spectacle.* San Francisco: City Lights Publishers, 2015.

Fackre, Gabriel. "Presence, Ministry of." In *Dictionary of Pastoral Care and Counseling*, edited by Rodney J. Hunter, 950–51. Nashville: Abingdon Press, 1990.

Farmer, Sarah. "Criminality of Black Youth in Inner-city Schools: 'Moral Panic,' Moral Imagination, and Moral Formation." *Race, Ethnicity and Education* 13, no. 3 (September 2010): 367–81.

———. "Transforming Conflict: A Curriculum on Conflict Resolution with Adolescents," Kenya edition. Atlanta, GA: Youth Hope-Builders Academy, 2016.

Feagin, Joe R., and Melvin P. Sikes. *Living with Racism: The Black Middle-Class Experience.* Boston: Beacon Press, 1995.

Frankie, Jeffrey, and Peter R. Orszog, "Retrospective on American Economic Policy in the 1990s," *Brookings Report* (Friday, November 2, 2001). http://www.brookings.edu/research/retrospective-on-american-economic-policy-in-the-1990s/.

Frazier, E. Franklin. *The Negro Church in America.* New York: Schocken Books, 1964.

Freire, Paulo. *Teachers as Cultural Workers: Letters to Those Who Dare Teach*, The Edge, Critical Studies in Educational Theory. Boulder, CO: Westview Press, 1998.

Gallup, Charles G., Jr. *The Next American Spirituality*. Colorado Springs, CO: David C. Cook, 2002.

Genovese, Eugene D. *Roll, Jordan, Roll: The World the Slaves Made*. New York: Vintage Books, 1976.

Gillham, Jane E., Andrew J. Shatte, Karen J. Reivich, and Martin E. P. Seligman. "Optimism, Pessimism, and Explanatory Style." In *Optimism & Pessimism: Implications for Theory, Research, and Practice*, edited by Edward C. Chang, 53–75. Washington, DC: American Psychological Association, 2001.

Goldbard, Arlene. *New Creative Community: The Art of Cultural Development*. Oakland, CA: New Village Press, 2006.

Gomes, Peter J. "Introduction." In Paul Tillich, *The Courage to Be*, 2nd edition. New Haven, CT: Yale University Press, 2000. Originally published in 1952.

Goud, Nelson H. "Courage: Its Nature and Development," *Journal of Humanistic Counseling, Education and Development* 44 (Spring 2005): 102–16.

Gornik, Mark R. *To Live in Peace: Biblical Faith and the Changing Inner City*. Grand Rapids, MI: W.B. Eerdmans, 2002.

Grace, Bill. *The Spirituality of Leadership*. Seattle, WA: Center for Ethical Leadership, 1999.

Grant, Jacqueline. "A Theological Framework." In *Working with Black Youth: Opportunities for Christian Ministry*, edited by Charles R. Foster and Grant S. Shockley, 55–76. Nashville: Abingdon Press, 1989.

Haensly, Patricia A., and James L. Parsons. "Creative, Intellectual, and Psychosocial Development through Mentorship: Relationships and Stages," *Youth & Society* 25, no. 2 (December 1, 1993): 202–21.

Haigh, Martin. "Invitational Education: Theory, Research and Practice," *Journal of Geography in Higher Education* 35, no. 2 (2011).

Hale-Benson, Janice. "Psychosocial Experience." In *Working with Black Youth: Opportunities for Christian Ministry*, edited by Charles R. Foster and Grant S. Shockley, 30–54. Nashville: Abingdon Press, 1989.

Harley, Dana. "Perceptions of Hope and Hopelessness among Low-Income African-American Adolescents." PhD diss. Graduate School, The Ohio State University, 2011. http://etd.ohiolink.edu/rws_etd/document/get/osu1313009132/inline.

Harris, James Henry. *The Courage to Lead: Leadership in the African American Urban Church*. Lanham, MD: Rowman & Littlefield Publishers, Inc., 2002.

Harrison, Renee K. *Enslaved Women and the Art of Resistance in Antebellum America.* New York: Palgrave Macmillan, 2009.

Hausman, Alice J., Howard Spivak, and Deborah Prothrow-Stith. "Adolescents' Knowledge and Attitudes About and Experience with Violence," *Journal of Adolescent Health* 15, no. 5 (July 1994): 400–406.

Henderson, Nan. "Hard-Wired to Bounce Back." In *Resilience in Action: Practical Ideas for Overcoming Risks and Building Strengths in Youth, Families, and Communities,* edited by Nan Henderson, 9–14. Ojai, CA: Resiliency in Action, Inc., 2007.

Hillman, James. *Healing Fiction.* Barrytown, NY: Station Hill Press, 1983.

Howard University Center for Urban Progress for the Lutheran Hour Ministries. *Faith-Based Organizations and African American Youth Development: A Report.* Washington, DC: The Howard University Center for Urban Progress, 2003.

Hunter, Melanie, and Kenneth H. Smith. "Inviting School Success: Invitational Education and the Art Class." *Journal of Invitational Theory and Practice* 13 (2007): 8–15.

Johnson, James Weldon. "Lift Every Voice and Sing." *African American Heritage Hymnal.* Chicago: GIA Publications, Inc., #540.

Johnson, Paul. *Psychology of Pastoral Care: The Pastoral Ministry in Theory and Practice.* Nashville: Abingdon Press, 1953.

Joseph, Janice. *Black Youth, Delinquency, and Juvenile Justice.* Westport, CT: Praeger, 1995.

Kaplan, H. Roy. *The Myth of Post-Racial America: Searching for Equality in the Age of Materialism.* Lanham, MD: Rowman & Littlefield Education, 2011.

Kendall, Philip C. "Cognitive-Behavioral Therapies with Youth: Guiding Theory, Current Status, and Emerging Developments," *Journal of Counseling and Clinical Psychology* 61, no. 2 (1993): 235–47.

Kimbro, Dennis. *What Keeps Me Standing: Letters from Black Grandmothers on Peace, Hope, and Inspiration.* New York: Harlem Moon, Broadway Books, 2003.

King, Martin Luther, Jr. "Antidotes for Fear." In *A Testament of Hope: The Essential Writings and Speeches of Martin Luther King Jr.,* edited by James M. Washington, 509–517. Copyright by Coretta Scott King, Executrix of the Estate of Martin Luther King Jr., 1986. New York: HarperSanFrancisco, A division of HarperCollins Publishers, 1991.

———. "A Christmas Sermon on Peace." In *A Testament of Hope: The Essential Writings and Speeches of Martin Luther King Jr.*, edited by James M. Washington, 253–58. Copyright by Coretta Scott King, Executrix of the Estate of Martin Luther King Jr., 1986. New York: HarperSanFrancisco, a division of HarperCollins Publishers, 1991.

———. "Draft of Chapter VIII, The Death of Evil Upon the Seashore," July 1962–March 1963, Atlanta, GA. In *The Papers of Martin Luther King Jr.: Volume VI, Advocate of the Social Gospel, September 1948–March 1963*, edited by Clayborne Carson, 494–504. Berkeley, CA: University of California Press, 2007.

Kleinberg, Ethan. "Prologue" and "Presence in Absentia." In *Presence: Philosophy, History, and Cultural Theory for the Twenty-first Century*, edited by Ranjan Ghosh and Ethan Kleinberg, 1–7; 8–25. Ithaca, NY: Cornell University Press, 2013.

Kohut, Heinz. *How Does Analysis Cure?* Chicago: The University of Chicago Press, 1984.

Kross, Ethan, Emma Bruehlman-Senecal, Jiyoung Park, Aleah Burson, Adrienne Dougherty, Holly Shablesh, Ryan Brenner, Jason Moser, and Ozlem Ayduk. "Self-Talk as a Regulatory Mechanism: How You Do It Matters," *Journal of Personality and Social Psychology* 106, no. 2 (2014): 304–24.

Krug, Etienne G., Linda L. Dahlberg, James A. Mercy, Anthony B. Zwi, and Rafael Lozano. *World Report on Violence and Health: Summary.* Geneva: World Health Organization, 2002.

Lee, JoAnn S. "An Institutional Framework for the Study of the Transition to Adulthood," *Youth & Society* 46, no. 5 (June 18, 2012): 706–30.

Lewis, Douglass. "Conflict and Conflict Management." In *Dictionary of Pastoral Care and Counseling*, edited by Rodney J. Hunter, 211–13. Nashville: Abingdon Press, 2005.

Lacey, Karyn R. *Blue-Chip Black: Race, Class, and Status in the New Black Middle Class.* Berkeley: University of California Press, 2007.

Laurie, Anna, and Robert A. "African Americans in Bereavement: Grief as a Function of Ethnicity," *Omega* 57, no. 2 (2008): 173–93.

Lieberman, Robert C. "Race and the Limits of Solidarity: American Welfare State Development and Comparative Perspective." In *Race and the Politics of Welfare Reform*, edited by Sanford F. Schram, Joe Soss, and Richard C. Fording, 22–46. Ann Arbor, MI: The University of Michigan Press, 2003.

Lincoln, C. Eric, and Lawrence H. Mamiya. *The Black Church in the African American Experience.* Durham, NC: Duke University Press, 1990.

Lopez, Shane J., Sage Rose, Cecil Robinson, Susana C. Marques, and Jose Pais-Ribeiro. "Measuring and Promoting Hope in Schoolchildren." In *Handbook of Positive Psychology in Schools*, edited by Richard Gilman, E. Scott Huebner, and Michael J. Furlong, 37–50. New York: Routledge, 2000.

Lockwood, Daniel. "Violence Among Middle School and High School Students: Analysis and Implications for Prevention." *Research in Brief*. National Institute of Justice, US Department of Justice, Office of Justice (October 1997): 1–12.

Marshall, Ellen Ott. "Introduction: Learning Through Conflict, Working for Transformation," *Conflict Transformation and Religion Essays on Faith, Power, and Relationship*, edited by Ellen Ott Marshall, 1–12. New York: Palgrave Macmillan, 2016.

Maton, Kenneth I. and Deborah A. Salem. "Organizational Characteristics of Empowering Community Settings: A Multiple Case Study Approach," *American Journal of Community Psychology* 23, no. 5 (October 1995): 631–56.

Matthews, William, and Christa Black Gifford. "All My Hope Is in You." Bethel Music Publishing Company (ASCAP)/Christa Joy Music (BMI), 2010. Lyrics: www.songlyrics.com/bethel-church/hopes-anthem-Lyrics/.

May, Rollo. *The Courage to Create*. New York: W.W. Norton, 1975. Reprinted 1994.

Mays, Benjamin E., and Joseph W. Nicholson. *The Negro's Church*. New York: Institute of Social and Religious Research, 1933.

Mbiti, John. *African Religions and Philosophies*. New York: Doubleday and Company, 1970.

McDermott, Brain O., SJ. "Partnering with God: Ignatian Spirituality and Leadership in Groups." In *Spirit at Work: Discovering the Spirituality in Leadership*, edited by Jay Conger and Associates, 132–61. San Francisco: Jossey-Bass Publishers, 1994.

McKenzie, Vashti M. "But Some of Us Are Brave," *The African American Pulpit* 4, no. 3 (Summer 2001): 56–59.

McManus, Erwin Raphael. *The Artisan Soul: Crafting Your Life into a Work of Art*. New York: HarperOne, 2014.

McLaren, Peter. *Life in Schools: Introduction to Critical Pedagogy in the Foundations of Education*. New York: Longman, 1989.

Mercer, Joyce A. "Red Light Means Stop! Teaching Theology through Exposure Learning in Manila's Red Light District." *Teaching Theology and Religion* 5 (2002).

Meyerson, Collier. "The Women Behind Black Lives Matter," *Glamour*, December 2016): 218–19, 241.

Miller, Douglas. "My Soul Is Anchored in the Lord." Gospel song. http://www.lyriczz.com/lyrics/douglas-miller/21104-my-soul-has-been-anchored.

Miller, Rielle. "Moral Courage: Definition and Development." Ethics Review Center (March 2005). http://www.emotionalcompetency.com/papers/Moral_Courage _Definition_and_Development.pdf.

Mills, Kay. *This Little Light of Mine: The Life of Fannie Lou Hamer.* New York: Penguin Books, 1993.

Moltmann, Jürgen. *The Experiment Hope*, translated by M. Douglas Meeks. Philadelphia: Fortress Press, 1975.

Moyana, Toby Tafirenyika. *Education, Liberation and the Creative Act.* Harare, Zimbabwe: Zimbabwe Publishing House, 1988.

Nepo, Mark. *Finding Inner Courage.* Conari Press, 2011.

Nichols, Michael P. *The Lost Art of Listening: Learning to Listen Can Improve Relationships.* 2nd ed. New York: Guilford Press, 2007.

Nussbaum, M. C. *Women and Human Development: The Capabilities Approach.* Cambridge: Cambridge University Press, 2000.

O'Connor, Kathleen M. *Lamentations and the Tears of the World.* Maryknoll, NY: Orbis Books, 2002.

Ong, Anthony. "A Life Worth Living: The Science of Human Flourishing," *Outreach & Extension*, 1–2. Department of Human Development, Cornell University, n.d. http://human.cornell.edu/hd/outreach-extension/upload/ong.pdf.

Osswald, Silvia, Tobias Greitmeyer, Peter Fischer and Dieter Frey. "What is Moral Courage? Definitions, Explications, and Classification of a Complex Construct." In *The Psychology of Courage: Modern Research on An Ancient Virtue*, edited by Cynthia L. S. Pury and Shane J. Lopez, 149–64. Washington, DC: American Psychological Association, 2010.

Palmer, Parker J. *The Courage to Teach: Exploring the Inner Landscape of a Teacher's Life.* Tenth Anniversary Edition. San Francisco: John Wiley & Sons, 2007.

———. "Leading from Within," *Spirit at Work: Discovering the Spirituality in Leadership*, edited by Jay A. Conger and Associates, 19–40. San Francisco: Jossey-Bass Publishers, 1994.

Paris, Peter J. "When Feeling Like a Motherless Child." In *Lament: Reclaiming Practices in Pulpit, Pew, and Public Square*, edited by Sally A. Brown and Patrick D. Miller, 111–20. Louisville: Westminster John Knox Press, 2005.

Parker, Evelyn L. *Trouble Don't Last Always: Emancipatory Hope among African American Adolescents.* Cleveland, OH: Pilgrim Press, 2003.

Parks, Rosa. *My Story.* New York: Dial Books, 1992.

Patillo, Mary, and Annette Lareau. *Black Picket Fences: Privilege and Peril Among the Black Middle Class,* 2nd ed. Chicago: University of Chicago Press, 2013.

Patterson, Orlando, and Ethan Fosse. *The Cultural Matrix: Understanding Black Youth*, edited by Orlando Patterson. Cambridge, MA: Harvard University Press. Reprint edition, 2016.

Porter, Thomas. *The Spirit and Art of Conflict Transformation: Creating a Culture of Just Peace*. Nashville: Upper Room Books, 2010.

Poulsen, Richard C. *The Body as Text: In a Perpetual Age of Non-Reason*. New York: Peter Lang, 1996.

Poussaint, Alvin, and Atkinson, Carolyn. "Black Youth and Motivation." In *Black Psychology*, edited by Reginald L. Jones, 113–23. New York: Harper & Row, 1972.

Powe, F. Douglas, Jr., and Jasmine Rose Smothers. *Not Safe for Church: Ten Commandments for Reaching New Generations*. Nashville: Abingdon Press, 2015.

Powell, John H. "Forgiveness and Healing Conflict." In *Making Peace with Conflict: Practical Skills for Conflict Transformation*, edited by Carolyn Schrock-Shenk and Lawrence Ressler, 119–26. Scottdale, PA: Herald Press, 1999.

Price-Mitchell, "Disadvantages of Social Networking: Surprising Insights from Teens." http://www.rootsofaction.com/disadvantages-of-social-networking/.

Purkey, William Watson. "An Introduction to Invitational Theory," *Journal of Invitational Theory and Practice* 1, no. 1 (1992): 5–15.

Purkey, William Watson, and John N. Novak. *Inviting School Success: A Self-Concept Approach to Teaching and Learning*, 3rd ed. Belmont, CA: Wadsworth, 1996.

Rate, Christopher. "Defining the Features of Courage: A Search for Meaning." In *The Psychology of Courage: Modern Research on an Ancient Virtue*, edited by Cynthia L. S. Pury and Shane J. Lopez, 47–66. Washington, DC: American Psychological Association, 2010.

Redd, Nola Taylor. "Mae Jemison: Astronaut Biography," August 17, 2012, https://www.space.com/17169-mae-jemison-biography.html.

Reese, Le'Roy E., Elizabeth M. Vera, Thomas R. Simon, and Robin M. Ikeda. "The Role of Families and Care Givers as Risk and Protective Factors in Preventing Youth Violence." *Clinical Child and Family Psychology Review* 3, no. 1 (March 2000): 61–77. http://dx.doi.org/10.1023/a:1009519503260.

Reverby, Susan M. *Examining Tuskegee: The Infamous Syphilis Study and Its Legacy*. John Hope Franklin Series in African American History and Culture. Chapel Hill, NC: The University of North Carolina Press, 2013.

Rogers, Carl. "Empathic: An Unappreciated Way of Being," *Counseling Psychologist* 5 (1975): 2–10.

———. "A Theory of Therapy, Personality and Interpersonal Relationships, Developed in the Client-Centered Framework." *Psychology: A Study of Science*, vol. 3, edited by Sigmund Koch. New York: McGraw-Hill, 1959.

Rosenbaum, Art. *Shout Because You're Free: The African American Ring Shout Tradition in Coastal Georgia.* Athens: The University of Georgia Press, 2013.

Rosenberg, Marshall B. *Nonviolent Communication: A Language of Compassion.* Del Mar, CA: Puddle Dancer Press, 1999.

Rosenzweig, Roy, and David Thelen. *The Presence of the Past: Popular Uses of History in American Life.* New York: Columbia University Press, 1998.

Ruggiero, Vincent. *Beyond Feelings: A Guide to Critical Thinking,* 9th ed. New York: McGraw-Hill Education, 2011.

Ryff, Carol D., and Corey Lee M. Keyes. "The Structure of Psychological Well-Being Revisited." *Journal of Personality and Social Psychology* 69, no. 4 (1995): 719–27. http://midus.wisc.edu/findings/pdfs/830.pdf.

Sacks, Jonathan. *The Dignity of Difference: How to Avoid the Clash of Civilization,* Revised edition. New York: Continuum, 2003.

Sacks, Vanessa, David Murphey, and Kristan Moore. "Adverse Childhood Experiences: National and State Level Prevalence," *ChildTrends,* https://www.childtrends.org/wp-content/uploads/2014/07/Brief-adverse-childhood-experiences_FINAL.pdf.

Schneider, Jo Anne. *The Role of Social Capital in Building Healthy Communities.* Baltimore: Annie E. Casey Foundation, 2004.

Schmidt, John J. "Diversity and Invitational Theology and Practice." *Journal of Invitational Theory and Practice* 10 (2004): 27–46.

Seligman, Martin E. P., and Mihaly Csikszentmihalyi. "Positive Psychology: An Introduction." *American Psychologist* (January 2000): 1–14.

Shaw, Daniel E., Betty L. Siegel, and Allyson Schoenlein. "The Basic Tenets of Invitational Theory and Practice: An Invitational Glossary." *Journal of Invitational Theory and Practice* 19 (2013): 342.

Shelby, Tommie. "Foundations of Black Solidarity: Collective Identity or Common Oppression." *Ethics, An International Journal of Social, Political, and Legal Philosophy* (January 2002): 231. http://www.tommieshelby.com/uploads/4/5/1/0/45107805/foundations.pdf.

Shervington, Walter W. "We Can No Longer Ignore the Rising Rate of African-American Suicide," President's Column. *Journal of the National Medical Association* 92, no. 4 (February 2000): 53–54.

Schirch, Lisa. *Ritual and Symbol in Peacebuilding.* Bloomfield, CT: Kumarian Press, 2005.

Schrock-Shenk, Carolyn and Lawrence Ressler. *Making Peace with Conflict: Practical Skills for Conflict Transformation*. Scottdale, PA: Herald Press, 1999.

Sinha, Jill W., Ram A. Cnaan, Richard W. Gelles, "Adolescent Risk Behaviors and Religion: Findings from a National Study," *Journal of Adolescence* 30, no. 2 (April 2007): 231–49. http://repository.upenn.edu/cgi/viewcontent.cgi?article =1056&context=spp_papers.

Smith, Christian. "Theorizing Religious Effects among American Adolescents." *Journal for the Scientific Study of Religion* 42, no. 1 (2003): 17–30. http://csrs .nd.edu/assets/50016/theorizing_religious_effects_among_american _adolescents.pdf.

Smith, Gregory, Primary Researcher. "America's Changing Religious Landscape." Pew Research Center Report (May 12, 2015). www.pewforum.org/2015/05 /12/americas-changing-religious-landscape/.

Snyder, C. Richard. "Hope Theory: Rainbows in the Mind." *Psychological Inquiry* 13, no. 4 (2002): 249–75.

———. "Hypothesis: There Is Hope." *Handbook of Hope: Theory, Measures, and Applications*, edited by C. Richard Snyder, 3–19. New York: Academic Press, 2000.

Snyder, C. Richard, Susie C. Sympson, Scott T. Michael, and Jen Cheavens. "Optimism and Hope Constructs: Variants on a Positive Expectancy Theme." In *Optimism & Pessimism: Implications for Theory, Research, and Practice*, edited by Edward C. Chang, 101–26. Washington, DC: American Psychological Association, 2001.

Stanton-Salazar, Ricardo D. "A Social Capital Framework for the Study of Institutional Agents and Their Role in the Empowerment of Low-Status Students and Youth." *Youth & Society* 43, no. 3 (October 11, 2010): 1066–1109.

Stevenson, Lauren, and Richard J. Deasy. *Third Space: When Learning Matters*. Washington, DC: Arts Education Partnership, 2005.

Thomas, Anita Jones, Devin Carey, Kia-Rai Prewitt, Edna Romero, Marysa Richards, and Katrina Dyonne Thompson. *Ring Shout, Wheel About: The Racial Politics of Music and Dance in North American Slavery*. Urbana, IL: University of Illinois Press, 2014.

Thurman, Howard. *Deep Is the Hunger: Meditations for Apostles of Sensitiveness*. Richmond, IN: Friends United Press; New York: Harper & Row, Reprint, 1951.

———. "Introduction." In *Footprints of a Dream: The Story of the Church for the Fellowship of All Peoples*. Eugene, OR: Wipf & Stock, 2009.

———. *The Inward Journey: Meditations on the Spiritual Quest*. Richmond, IN: Friends United Press, 1977.

———. *Jesus and the Disinherited*. Richmond, IN: Friends United Press, 1981.

————. *The Luminous Darkness: A Personal Interpretation of the Anatomy of Segregation and the Ground of Hope.* New York: Harper & Row, 1965.

Tillich, Paul. *The Courage to Be,* 2nd ed. New Haven, CT: Yale University Press, 2000.

Topos Partnership with consultants Janet Dewart Bell and Elani Delimpaltadki Janis. "Social Science Literature Review: Media Representations and Impact on the Lives of Black Men and Boys." *The Opportunity Agenda.* A Project of Tide Center, October 2011. https://opportunityagenda.org/literature_review_media _representations_and_impact_lives_black_men_and_boys.

Townes, Emilie M. "Teaching and the Imagination," *Religious Education* 111, no. 4 (July–September, 2016): 366–79.

Trier-Bienek, Adrienne, ed. *The Beyoncé Effect: Essays on Sexuality, Race and Feminism.* Jefferson, NC: McFarland & Company, Inc., 2016.

Tutu, Desmond, and Mpho Tutu. *Made for Goodness: And Why This Makes All the Difference,* edited by Douglas C. Abrams. London: Rider, 2010.

Velsor-Friedrich, Barbara. "African-American Youth and Exposure to Community Violence: Supporting Change from the Inside." *Journal of Social Action in Counseling and Psychology* 4, no. 1 (Spring 2012): 54–68. http://www.psysr.org /jsacp/Thomas-v4n1-12_54-68.

Volf, Miroslav. "The Crown of the Good Life: An Hypothesis." *Joy and Human Flourishing: Essays on Theology, Culture, and the Good Life,* edited by Miroslav Volf and Justin E. Crisp, 127–36. Minneapolis, MN: Fortress Press, 2015.

————. *Exclusion and Embrace: A Theological Exploration of Identity, Otherness, and Reconciliation.* Nashville: Abingdon Press, 1996.

Wagner, Meg. "As trial against Dylann Roof begins, families of Charleston church shooting victims still show mercy." *New York Daily News.* Thursday, November 3, 2016. http://www.nydailynews.com/news/national/s-church-shooting -victims-families-forgive-dylann-roof-article-1.2855446.

Walker, Alice. *In Search of Our Mothers' Garden: Womanist Prose.* 1967. New York: A Harvest Book, Harcourt, Inc., 1983.

Walston, Sandra Ford. "Courage in the Workplace." *Chief Learning Officer.* (December 2011): 22–25. http://www.clomedia.com/2011/12/08/courage-in-the -workplace/.

Warner, Tara D., and Raymond R. Swisher. "Adolescent Survival Expectations: Variations by Race, Ethnicity, and Nativity." *Journal of Health and Social Behavior* 56, no. 4 (November 2015): 478–94. http://www.asanet.org/journals /JHSB/DEC15JHSBFeature.pdf.

Weinger, Susan. "Children Living in Poverty: Their Perception of Career Opportunities," Paper 5. In *Social Work Faculty Publications,* 324–25. Western Michigan University, 1998. http://scholarworks.wmich.edu/socialwork_pubs/5/.

Welch, Gabriela, and Ken Smith. "From Theory to Praxis: Applying Invitational Education Beyond Schools." *Journal of Invitational Theory and Practice* 20 (2014): 5–10.

West, Traci C. *Disruptive Christian Ethics: When Racism and Women's Lives Matter.* Louisville, KY: Westminster John Knox Press, 2006.

White, Michael, and Donald Epston. *Narrative Means to Therapeutic Ends.* New York: W.W. Norton, 1990.

White, Richelle B. *Repertory with Roots: Black Youth, Black History, Black Culture, Black Music, and the Bible.* Xulon Press, n.d. http://www.aymeducators.org /wp-content/uploads/Repertory-with-Roots-White.pdf.

———. "'Whitewashing' in Mass Media: Exploring Colorism and the Damaging Effects of Beauty Hierarchies," *Race and Technology: Exploring Race and Community in the Digital World.* (December 10, 2014). http://www.raceand technology.wordpress.com/2014/12/10/whitewashing-in-mass-media -exploring-colorism-and-the-damaging-effects-of-beauty-hierarchies/.

Wilson, Emily Herring. *Hope and Dignity: Older Black Women of the South.* Philadelphia: Temple University Press, 1983.

Winn, Maisha T. *Girl Time: Literacy, Justice, and the School-to-Prison Pipeline.* The Teaching for Social Justice Series. New York: Teachers College Press, 2011.

Wimberly, Anne Streaty, "Give Me Mentors: Pedagogies of Spiritual Accompaniment." In *How Youth Ministry Can Change Theological Education— If We Let It*, edited by Kenda Creasy Dean and Christy Lang Hearlson, 79–99. Grand Rapids, MI: William B. Eerdmans Publishing Company, 2016.

———, ed. *Honoring African American Elders: A Ministry in the Soul Community.* San Francisco: Jossey-Bass Publishers, 1997.

———. *Nurturing Faith & Hope: Black Worship as a Model for Christian Education.* Cleveland: Pilgrim Press, 2004.

———. "What Honoring Elders Means." In *Honoring African American Elders: A Ministry in the Soul Community*, edited by Anne Streaty Wimberly, 3–11. San Francisco: Jossey-Bass Publishers, 1997.

Wimberly, Anne E. Streaty, "A Black Christian Pedagogy of Hope: Religious Education in Black Perspective." *Forging a Better Religious Education in the Third Millennium*, edited by James Michael Lee, 158–77. Birmingham, AL: Religious Education Press, 2000.

———. "Congregational Care in the Lives of Black Older Adults." In *Aging, Spirituality, and Religion*, vol. 2, edited by Melvin A. Kimble and Susan H. McFadden, 101–20. Minneapolis: Fortress Press, 2003.

———, ed. *Keep It Real: Working with Today's Black Youth.* Nashville: Abingdon Press, 2005.

———. "Preparing for a Vocation of Hope," A Message from the Director. *The Hope Messenger* 7, no. 2 (Summer 2009): 1.

———. *Soul Stories: African American Christian Education*, Revised edition. Nashville: Abingdon Press, 2005.

———. "Worship in the Lives of Black Adolescents: Builder of Resilience and Hope." *Liturgy* 29, no. 1 (2014): 23–33. http://dx.doi.org/10.1080/045863X.2014.846742.

Wimberly, Anne E. Streaty, Sandra L. Barnes, and Karma D. Johnson. *Youth Ministry in the Black Church: Centered in Hope*. Valley Forge, PA: Judson Press, 2014.

Wimberly, Edward P. *Claiming God, Reclaiming Dignity: African American Pastoral Care*. Nashville: Abingdon Press, 2003.

Wolf, Dennis Palmer. "The Art of Questioning." *Academic Connections* (Winter 1987): 1–7. https://www.exploratorium.edu/sites/default/files/pdfs/ifi/Raising_Questions.pdf.

Woodson, Carter G. *The Mis-Education of the Negro*. Washington, DC: The Associated Publishers, 1921 [1945]; New York: Tribeca Books, 1969.

Worthington, Everett L. *Forgiving and Reconciling: Bridges to Wholeness and Hope*. Downers Grove, IL: InterVarsity Press, 2003.

Youniss, James, and Miranda Yates. *Community Service and Social Responsibility in Youth*. Chicago: University of Chicago Press, 1997.

Zipes, Jack. "The Cultural Evolution of Storytelling and Fairy Tales: Human Communication and Memetics." http://press.princeton.edu/chapters/s9676.pdf.

INDEX

CPSIA information can be obtained
at www.ICGtesting.com
Printed in the USA
LVHW050111080921
697192LV00007B/862